The Early F.A. Cup Finals

and the Southern Amateurs

Keith Warsop

A *SoccerData* publication

Published in Great Britain by Tony Brown,
4 Adrian Close, Beeston, Nottingham NG9 6FL.
Telephone 0115 973 6086.   E-mail soccer@innotts.co.uk
www.soccerdata.com

First published 2004

© Keith Warsop 2004

All rights reserved. No part of this publication may be reproduced, stored in a retrieval system, or transmitted in any form, or by any means, electronic, mechanical, photocopying, recording or otherwise without the prior permission in writing of the Copyright holders, nor be otherwise circulated in any form or binding or cover other than in which it is published and without a similar condition including this condition being imposed on the subsequent publisher.

Keith Warsop was born in Nottingham in a Notts County relegation year, 1935. He first saw the Magpies play just before the Lawton era dawned. He also started to support Nottinghamshire cricket in the heyday of Joe Hardstaff and Reg Simpson. His interest in football and cricket history and statistics began at this time; he became an active member of the Association of Football Statisticians and the Association of Cricket Statisticians and Historians. As a journalist, he worked on provincial evening and morning papers in Derby, Nottingham, Birmingham and Leeds. On retirement he moved back to Nottingham. He has had works on both sports in print; for football, books include his 1984 history of Notts County *The Magpies* and the recent *British and Irish Special and Intermediate Internationals*.

Front cover illustrations: the Old Carthusians of 1881 are surrounded by (clockwise, from top right) The Hon. A. Lyttelton, H. Whitfeld, E.G. Wynyard, S.W. Scott, H.W. Bainbridge, P.J. de Paravicini.

SoccerData is a specialist publisher of books and computer databases on association football. Please write to the publisher or visit the website for a catalogue.

Printed and bound by the Cromwell Press, Trowbridge, Wiltshire

ISBN 1 899468 78 1

CONTENTS

Introduction	*Page 5*
The Social Background	*Page 7*
Formation and Tactics	*Page 9*
The Referee and Umpires	*Page 17*
The Clubs	*Page 20*
The Grounds	*Page 26*
Match Facts 1871-72 to 1882-83	*Page 29*
Who's Who	*Page 55*
Bibliography	*Page 141*

FOREWORD

This book is concerned solely with the six southern amateur clubs who contested the early F.A. Cup finals from the first in 1871-72 to 1882-83 when the victory of Blackburn Olympic over the Old Etonians signalled the end of an epoch in football history. Blackburn Rovers, the beaten finalists in 1881-82, and Blackburn Olympic are not dealt with in these pages for reasons explained later.

The core of the book is a Who's Who of the 158 players who appeared for the Wanderers, Royal Engineers, Oxford University, Old Etonians, Clapham Rovers and Old Carthusians in the twelve finals plus two replays of the period. In order to place the players in context, match facts give basic information for each of the 14 games and there is an introductory section covering their social and cultural world along with a look at various facets of the game as it was played and developed throughout those years.

The intention has been to make the Who's Who as comprehensive as possible so that it might become a helpful contribution to the early history of association football. Because some of the players led interesting and varied lives while others did not and because the amount of biographical material about them varies in volume, no attempt has been made to provide entries of equal proportions, thus violating one of the cardinal rules of most Who's Who compilations. The justification for flouting this is that most of these details are unlikely to be researched again except by anyone focusing on a particular player or club so that it becomes essential to put as much information as possible into the public domain for the benefit of future sports historians.

It is necessary to point out that in view of the number of books on the history of football that have carried detailed accounts of the origins and introduction of the F.A. Challenge Cup competition, there is no attempt here to go over this ground again. Books which cover this information are listed in the bibliography.

Naturally, in a work of reference and research such as this there are bound to be errors and gaps so that, while perfection is always the objective, its achievement is never completely possible. The hope is that such failings have been kept to a minimum. Any mistakes must be blamed on the author who takes this opportunity to thank the many people and organisations which have provided information or clues in the most pleasant and helpful way. Many of the private individuals, librarians, archivists and registrars have themselves been enthused by the somewhat esoteric nature of the research and have often responded well beyond the call of duty. I would like especially to pay tribute to the help given by Philip Thorn with much of the biographical research and to Kit Bartlett for his tireless work on my behalf at the British Newspaper Library at Colindale as well as at the Family Records Centre.

Keith Warsop,
Gedling, Nottingham, 2004

INTRODUCTION

WHY a book on the early F.A. Cup finalists? The simple answer: 'because they are there' demands some expansion. The original motivation for this project arose from a request for help in discovering the Christian names of the early finalists. During the search for these it became clear that comprehensive material about the players of this period was available. Because of their social status, most of them attended public school and went on to Oxford or Cambridge University before entering one of the major professions such as the Army, the church or the law. This in turn meant that many archives were accessible, a substantial number of which had been published so that a detailed who's who would not be an insurmountable task with the use of, among others, many public school 'old boy' registers, volumes of Oxford and Cambridge alumni, the annual *Army List, Crockford's Clerical Directory, Men at the Bar, The Medical Directory, Who Was Who* from 1897 to 1953 plus obituaries in *The Times* and *Wisden's Cricketers' Almanack*.

The next stage was to define exactly what comprised 'the early Cup finals'. Obviously, the finals from the first one in 1871-72 to 1880-81, the last season in which two southern amateur teams met, would be included. However, in 1881-82 Blackburn Rovers were beaten by the Old Etonians and the following season the Etonians lost to Blackburn Olympic. As most of the players in these Etonian teams had appeared in earlier finals, it made sense to include their 1881-82 and 1882-83 sides in the project but the decision was taken to exclude the Blackburn clubs on the grounds that rather different research methods would have to be followed and that they also included professionals even though the F.A. had not yet made them legal. *Bell's Life* of 1st April 1882 quite clearly stated:

> 'No winning team has ever met with the enthusiastic reception which greeted the Old Etonians on Saturday last. The causes of this satisfaction are not difficult to find. It was practically a contest between an eleven of amateurs, in the strictest sense of the word, and a team mostly composed of professionals, some of them according to the ordinary acceptation, of the most pronounced type.'

From these games a list of players then had to be compiled. As details given in modern reference publications did not look completely reliable and threw up a number of questions, it was necessary to return to the match reports in the leading sporting newspapers of the day, in particular *The Sportsman, Bell's Life in London, The Field* and *The Sporting Life*.

These clarified a number of issues; that there were two A.H. Tod(d)s, one with a second 'd' and one without; that Quintin Hogg did not take part in the 1875 replay, instead Francis Heathcote Wilson replaced him in goal; that 'A. Boyle' and 'M. Faner' in modern publications were actually Adam Bogle and Matthew George Farrer whose names have been misprinted in the list of finalists given in Geoffrey Green's 1953 F.A. history and copied inaccurately into later books such as Rothmans Yearbook.

There was also confusion caused by changes of name. For instance, in February 1873 Frederick Patey Chappell changed his name to Frederick Brunning Maddison; then the brothers Albert Childers and Charles Maude Thompson hyphenated their surname as Meysey-Thompson in 1874 so that in the 1875-76 final Albert played as 'Meysey-Thompson' and Charles as 'Meysey', a complication which caused problems for reporters at the time which, even in today's record books, have not always been sorted out. In later years Henry Edward Drummond Moray became H.E. Stirling-Home-Drummond when he succeeded to the Blair Drummond estate in 1884 and Frederick Crofton Heath became Heath-Caldwell in 1913. The original 'prince of dribblers', Robert Walpole Sealy Vidal became R.W. Sealy from 1892 because that had been the family name and his father had adopted Vidal only on inheriting some Vidal property.

Eventually, though, the definitive list of players was completed and it totalled 158. The research into these has produced the dates of birth for all except Edward Albert Ram (Clapham Rovers 1879-80) and the dates of death for all except William Dallas Ochterlony Greig (Wanderers 1875-76).

Oxford University 1877-78. Back: HS Otter; Standing: EH Parry, AF Hills, JT Twist*; Seated: EH Alington, JH Savory, OR Dunell, WR Page, PJM Rogers*; Front: E Waddington, RT Heygate (* did not play in final).

THE SOCIAL BACKGROUND

During the first ten seasons of the F.A. Cup, only six clubs played in the final of the competition and each of them won the trophy at least once. Wanderers had five wins and never finished on the losing side in a final; Old Carthusians were victors in their only appearance in the final; both Oxford University and Royal Engineers won one and lost three of their four finals; Clapham Rovers had one victory and one defeat in their two finals; while Old Etonians, counting in their 1881-82 and 1882-83 finals, were successful twice and featured as losers four times. These six clubs typified the southern 'old boy' amateur ethos, for the Wanderers recruited mainly from ex-public schoolboys and university men, Royal Engineers fielded teams made up exclusively of officers and Clapham Rovers comprised public school old boys who were mostly in business in the city with strong Stock Exchange connections.

Indeed, from its formation in 1863 the F.A. was often seen as a clique of metropolitan 'upper-crust' clubs; for instance, in 1867 they were described as 'a band of antagonistic brethren who met together in London and attempted a compromise, but from whose efforts not much good has hitherto sprung.' This attitude persisted for some time after our chosen period and it was not just a matter of social class either; the 'north-south divide' also made an appearance. The Sheffield amateur J.C. Clegg (later Sir Charles), who played for England in the first official international in Scotland in 1872, claimed that none of the southern amateurs in the team spoke to him; when Sheffield's Willie Mosforth criticised the Hon. Alfred Lyttelton for trying to dribble through by himself during England's match against Scotland in 1877 he was told 'I play for my own pleasure.'

As late as 1886, Dr E.S. Morley, of Blackburn Rovers, sent a telegram to the President of the F.A., Major Francis Marindin, complaining on behalf of his northern colleagues: 'We protest against the studied discourtesies and lack of consideration shown towards the northern members of the Committee and decline to assist in the selection of the England team.'

The patrician attitude of the southern amateurs seems to have extended to the sporting journalists too. At the end of its report of the 1880-81 final, *The Sportsman* felt it necessary to chide the captain of the victorious Old Carthusians, Edward Hagarty Parry: 'Allowance must at all times be made for "giddy youth" when intoxicated with sudden success. However, we cannot but call attention to the reticence with which the captain of the winning team acted in regard to the press. We would remind him that in giving our representative the necessary information he would have been only discharging a moral obligation.'

We have to accept that these players were men of their class and period during which the Amateur Athletic Club, at the time of the first F.A. Cup final in 1872, could issue the following 'definition of a gentleman amateur': 'Any gentleman who has never competed in any open competition, or for public money, or for admission money, or with professionals for a prize, public money, or admission money; and who has never taught, pursued or assisted in the pursuit of athletic exercises as a means of livelihood, nor is a mechanic, artisan or labourer. The committee reserve the right of requiring a reference or of refusing an entry.' The main objection to mechanics, artisans or labourers was a financial and ethical one. It was felt that their financial need would leave them open to corruption by gamblers who could offer inducements for them to throw games or 'fix' the result. Only gentlemen amateurs, because of their own wealth, could be above this sort of temptation.

The social and cultural world of these southern amateur footballers is exemplified by Robert Henry Benson. He was the senior partner in a firm of merchant bankers, a Trustee of the National Gallery, a Council Member of the Royal College of Music and he owned a collection of early Italian paintings, early Chinese porcelain and other objects of art. But these interests did not prevent him from appearing in two Cup finals and also winning the amateur athletic championship mile race in 1870.

The general social background to which the bulk of the 158 players belonged can be seen from some of their professions: they included 38 Army officers, 25 barristers, 16 clergymen, 16 schoolmasters and tutors, 15 solicitors, nine in the brewing and wine business, nine in the financial services sector, seven bankers, six civil servants, six merchants, five farmers, ranchers or planters, five publishers, authors, editors or journalists, four engineers, two medical men, two politicians, two professors and one architect. These add up to more than 158 because some of them switched professions; for instance a number of clergymen were also schoolmasters. A few could afford to live off their income and were accordingly shown as 'gentleman' or 'esquire' in the archives.

The great proportion of these players also received their education at one of the major public schools. As many as 48 went to Eton, 15 to Charterhouse, 12 to Winchester, 11 to Harrow, 11 also to Westminster, seven to Cheltenham, five to Lancing and three each to Malvern, Marlborough and Wellington. In addition there were two each at Brentwood, Brighton, Forest, Highgate, Mill Hill, Repton, Rugby and Shrewsbury. Those Royal Engineers who did not attend public school were in the main educated at a military academy, most often at the Royal Military Academy, Woolwich.

The wide sporting range of these 158 players is also typical of men from their social background. As many as 46 played first-class or minor counties cricket with another ten appearing at public school or major club level. Charles James Longman was archery champion of England in 1883 and wrote the guide to the sport for the Badminton Library; Edward George Wynyard not only played Test cricket for England and hockey for Hampshire but was also toboggan champion of Europe in 1894; Harold Baily Dixon made exploring climbs in the Canadian Rockies; Matthew George Farrer rowed for Oxford in the Boat Race and was a champion oarsman at Henley Regatta; Colonel James Henry Cowan was a Bisley crack shot; Arthur John Stanley twice reached the men's doubles finals at Wimbledon; Reginald Halsey Birkett won selection for England at football and rugby; Henry Waugh Renny-Tailyour repeated this feat but for Scotland; and William Francis Howard Stafford played rugby for England.

FORMATION AND TACTICS

The period from 1871-72 to 1882-83 produced many important developments, both in the Laws of the game and in changes in tactics and playing style. At the time of the first final, the F.A. Laws did not include modern-style corner kicks (the Sheffield F.A. had them in their own independent code), throw-ins were one-handed (Scotland had already pioneered the two-handed throw) and ends were changed each time a goal was scored. The notion of switching ends at half-time applied only if the match was 0-0 after 45 minutes and, even then, ends continued to be changed after later goals.

The modern form of the corner kick was incorporated in the Laws in 1873 and the first one in a final was awarded to Oxford University in 1873-74, a matter of some significance as it led to their first goal. It was not until 1927 that the Law was amended to allow a goal to be scored direct from a corner kick yet, if the newspaper reports of the day are accepted, that is exactly what Alexander George Bonsor did in the final of 1874-75. *The Sporting Life* confirms that Bonsor took the corner: 'After thirty minutes play, from an excellent corner-kick by Bonsor, a goal was scored.' *The Sportsman* tells us more including the fact that the wind carried the ball into the goal: 'For half an hour the game remained without decisive issue, but here a corner kick fell to the Etonians, and the ball was so skilfully handled by Bonsor, with the proper allowance for the wind, that it went between the posts before Major Merriman could divert its course.' In this context, 'handled' means 'managed' or 'dealt with', as we shall see. *Bell's Life* says: 'Matters went on in this way for half an hour, when a corner kick for the Old Etonians was entrusted to Bonsor, and, helped by the wind, the ball bounded under the line.' Finally, *The Field* makes it clear that goalkeeper Merriman did not help the ball on its way: 'For half an hour the Engineers faced the wind without loss, but here a corner kick fell to the Etonians, and a gust catching the ball well aimed by Bonsor carried it between the Engineers' posts just out of the reach of the goalkeeper.' Perhaps no one was aware that a goal could not be scored direct from a corner kick; after all it was only the second season of this particular Law and such direct scores have never been very frequent. Presumably, once the goal had been appealed for and allowed, that was that.

John Bailey has explained in simple terms the pre-1873 position of the corner kick in the F.A. Laws as follows: 'When the ball went behind the goal-line (but not over the tape or bar), a corner accrued to whichever side did not put the ball over the line. When the ball cleared the goal, a goal-kick resulted, regardless of which team sent the ball out.' Thus, a defending side might gain a corner kick at their own end though, of course, the ball would then be booted upfield as with a goal-kick.

The abolition of switching ends after each goal and the institution of the change-over at half-time whatever the score came in 1875 and a strong influence on the alteration came from this very final of 1874-75 in which, as we have seen above, the wind played a crucial part. The game was actually played in a howling gale and though the Royal Engineers were by far the superior side, they had to kick into the gale and could make no progress. When Bonsor scored from the corner after 30 minutes, ends were changed and the Engineers went straight down to equalise. Ends were changed again and then extra time was added but the match ended 1-1 with the Engineers having played for 100 minutes out of the 120 into the teeth of the gale, a situation which was felt to be unfair. Incidentally, justice was done as the Engineers went on to win the replay 2-0 in convincing style. It was also in 1875 that the use of a wooden crossbar replaced the tape that F.A. Laws had laid down previously though the crossbar had been optional before and continued to be so in lesser matches until 6th December 1882. However, reporters continued to refer to 'the tape' for some time afterwards as old habits die hard. Finally, the two-handed throw-in was incorporated in the Laws in 1882.

Goal nets were totally unknown during the years of these early finals; they were first tested in the North v South match at Nottingham Forest's Town Ground on 12th January 1891, and used for the first time in an F.A. Cup final that season when Blackburn Rovers met Notts County at Kennington Oval on 21st March as can be seen in a frequently reproduced illustration. Geoffrey Green, in his official F.A. history, is incorrect in stating that they were first used in the 1892 final. The F.A. Council meeting on 11th March 1891, decided that 'nets be provided for the goals at the final match', and so brought into being that modern journalistic standby 'the ball hit the back of the net' to describe a goal being scored. During our period, the cliché was 'struck the ball between the posts'.

In the first final the Wanderers lined up with a goalkeeper, a full-back, a half-back and eight forwards whereas the Royal Engineers made do with seven forwards and had a second full-back. Sometimes reporters mention a threequarter-back but this is really a full-back; the concept of a title for that particular position had not yet been clarified and a goalkeeper was, perhaps logically, occasionally thought to be 'full back'.

In 1872-73 both sides adopted the single full-back and eight forwards formation. However, some ten minutes after Oxford University fell behind to the Wanderers on the half-hour, they added their goalkeeper to the attack and left the goal unguarded, a tactic that was blamed for the concession of a second goal in the 80th minute. For 1873-74 Oxford University introduced an extra half-back, with one full-back, two half-backs and seven forwards, though the Royal Engineers made do with one full-back, one half-back and eight forwards.

The next season, 1874-75 both teams lined up with one full-back, two half-backs and seven forwards but while the Etonians retained this format in 1875-76, the Wanderers introduced a significant development by fielding two backs, two half-backs and six forwards, which remained the standard line-up for the southern amateur teams in all subsequent finals. The mould was only broken by the conquerors of the Old Etonians in 1882-83, when Blackburn Olympic switched to what became the classic 2-3-5 combination which remained the fashion for decades.

The position of goalkeeper was then of considerably lesser importance than it subsequently became. When Wanderers goalkeeper James Kirkpatrick broke an arm in a scrimmage during the 1877-78 final, *Bell's Life* tells us: 'Though he must have been in considerable pain he saved the goal, and pluckily stuck to his post to the end.' In later years, but before the introduction of substitutes, he would have been replaced in goal by an outfield player and have become a 'passenger on the wing' as the football writers used to phrase it. In the 1870s, though, it was the practice for injured players to move **INTO** goal! This happened with the Old Etonian captain, the Hon. Arthur Kinnaird, in the drawn first final of 1875-76 when 'keeper Quintin Hogg moved to half-back to allow his lame skipper to 'retire into goal'.

We have already seen above that in the latter part of the 1872-73 final, Oxford University did without a goalkeeper at all as they added him to their attack. Here are some other examples which show how little emphasis was put on the position as a specialist one: in the drawn final of 1874-75 Charles Edward Farmer was in goal for the Old Etonians but in the replay he was one of the centre-forwards; Francis Heathcote Wilson, who was at half-back in this replay, kept goal for the Etonians in the following season's replay; in the 1875-76 drawn final and the replay Wanderers had William Dallas Ochterlony Greig in goal but he had figured at half-back for them in some earlier non-Cup games; in the 1876-77 final Kinnaird kept goal for the Wanderers for the first half but early in the second half Wollaston was injured and took over that position. It was the only time in his nine finals plus two replays that Kinnaird was ever selected to start the match as goalkeeper.

However, there were players who specialised in goalkeeping such as Capt. (later Major) William Merriman, referred to in *The Royal Engineers Journal* as 'an uncommonly good goal-keeper, a fact not infrequently mentioned in the records of matches'; such as, for instance, *The Sportsman*'s report of the first final in 1871-72 when the Wanderers won by the only goal of the match: 'More than one would doubtless have been successful but for the extremely efficient goal-keeping of Capt. Merriman.' *The Field* was equally enthusiastic about his performance in this final: 'So resolute was the front offered by Capt. Merriman, the goal keeper of the Sappers, and so judicious his defence, that further reverses were averted for his side.' Summing up, the same report said: 'Capt. Merriman's goalkeeping was perfect, and to him alone was due the preservation of the military fortress from further surrenders.'

On a lighter note, the *Forest School Magazine* for Lent Term 1876 explained the choice of their first XI goalkeeper: 'We have chosen him because he would fill up the space between the posts better than anyone else. If he goes on increasing latitudinally he ought to be a splendid *stop-gap* next year', though it goes on: 'He has acquitted himself with honour in more than one emergency and has proved himself equal to the position he holds – the most responsible position on the field.' This is one of the few accounts of the period which stresses the importance of the goalkeeper.

The goalkeeper's armoury was less plentiful than it became later. He relied to a great extent on kicking the ball away backed up by catching it and throwing it out. Montague Shearman, in the 1888 Badminton Library volume *Athletics and Football*, says: 'In days gone by goal-keepers used to kick far more than they do at present; they "dropped" and "punted" often, and it was not unusual to see a Rugby Union back player set to defend the goal in the Association game. One player, indeed, R.H. Birkett, of the Clapham Rovers, achieved the distinction of earning his International colours in both games, playing back in several years for the Rugby Unionists and in goal for the Association eleven.' Early reports mention occasions when the goalkeeper was forced to use his hands, rather as if this was an infrequent practice, though as the 1870s progressed the novelty of this feat wore off and reporters did not make so much of it. Punching or fisting the ball away was unknown until the advent around 1880 of Harry Albemarle Swepstone (born 18 January 1859; died 7 May 1907) of Pilgrims, Swifts and England. So unused were reporters to this tactic that they had not yet developed the vocabulary to describe it: 'Has a peculiar aptitude for striking the ball away with his arm' was one attempt. Swepstone's 1907 obituary in *The Sportsman*, however, makes it clear that he fisted or punched the ball: 'The first to introduce to a wonderstruck public the goalkeeper's fistic art.' The obituary goes on to mention blows which carried the ball some hundred yards upfield with the fist doing duty for the foot.

The use of only a single full-back in the earliest finals was a tactic designed to catch probing forwards offside, according to Shearman in his Badminton Library volume. But the development of the passing or combination game meant that the single back could easily be evaded and so it became necessary to introduce a second back. We quote more from Shearman as his comments are valid for our period. He puts the development of the game to 1888 mainly in forward play and says 'the tactics and tricks of back play have always been the same', later adding 'both in the old and new games back, half-back and goal-keeping play has varied but little.'

Shearman specifies accurate and powerful kicking, even though being charged or making a charge oneself, as the main requisite for good backs. He goes on to explain how the two must work as a partnership: 'When one advances to charge the forward the other must drop back to receive the ball if the kick and charge of his companion are ineffective. Often it is the business of one back to hamper or harass an opponent while his fellow kicks the ball ... It is, however, the combination play of the two backs with each other which makes the defence really effective.' Specialist backs were there from the first Cup final and those with the most powerful and longest kicks achieved the most fame, such as Charles James Stuart King of Oxford University who was reputed to kick enormous distances.

Robust charging was, of course, all part of the game but even though there was vigorous physical play, the charge from behind was outlawed, even then. Shearman explains that the defender 'must follow back and hamper and hustle the forward whom he is catching up, never attempting to charge him from behind, but trying to shoulder him round and send him staggering off the ball when the leg which is nearest is off the ground and his weight is thus balanced to lean away from the back who is hampering him.' He goes on to warn: 'A back should not dribble; once or twice, perhaps, in a match when a forward is charging him he may dodge for an instant with the ball to get a freer kick, but his main aim is to send the ball hard back without the slightest loss of time.' Shearman's claim that 'the tactics and tricks of back play have always been the same' is proved accurate by advice given to full-backs some 18 years earlier in *The Harrovian* in 1870 which differs hardly at all from Shearman in 1888 when it states that backs 'must remember that it is not their office to dribble. They must remember that there is nothing between them and their base [i.e. their goal]. If once the ball is past them, there is small chance of their preventing a base being got. Why then risk all this simply from a desire to dribble? The backs are not chosen for their dribbling but for their kicking powers.'

The *Forest School Magazine* for Lent Term 1876 follows this principle too: 'C.J. Fox. Played last term as half-back but was not so successful in that place as in the one he now occupies (back). As half-back, though he frequently showed brilliant play, he kicked far too strongly and without sufficient judgment, he was also too fond of dribbling instead of leaving that for the forwards to do. We are sorry to say this is still a fault of his, we think it is the one fault which mars his play. He should take all pains to correct it.'

One practice which developed during the 1870s was heading the ball and its introduction in the south can probably be credited to a full-back. Many modern football historians suggest that this feature was introduced by northern teams around 1880 and was shunned by southern amateurs as somehow 'not the done thing' but evidence proves otherwise. Royal Engineers back George Hamilton Sim was the southern pioneer of this skill according to his team-mate Richard Mathews Ruck, writing in *The Royal Engineers Journal* in 1928. Ruck says that Sim, who appeared on the scene in 1873, was 'the first player who made a practice of heading the ball.' Sim was a member of the Royal Engineers team who played matches in Sheffield, Derbyshire and Nottingham at Christmas 1873 and he might have come across the practice then. That it was not new to Sheffield is shown in *The Field*'s report of the inaugural Sheffield-Glasgow match played at Bramall Lane on 14th March 1874. Glasgow's first goal is described as follows: 'W. McKinnon took the ball right up to into the Sheffield lines, and H. McNeill, heading it on to F. Anderson, the latter headed it between the English posts, a piece of play so congenial to Sheffield as to produce hearty cheering from all parts of the ground.' This new skill spread quickly and by 1879, *The Carthusian*, for example, could say of Charterhouse School first XI half-back Joseph Vintcent: 'Nearly as good with his head as his legs.'

It should not be thought that the game in the 1870s was all attack with the back or backs being left to deal alone with opposition forwards. An illustration in Charles William Alcock's 1874 book *Football: Our Winter Game* shows all eleven players back behind the ball defending their goal as three forwards close in. This tactic may well have been an innovation around that time for a Sheffield newspaper report of the Royal Engineers' match there during their 1873 Northern tour says: 'Their defence of the Citadel was remarkable, and in one case of more than ordinary danger the whole eleven were discovered in the mouth of the goal, much to the amusement of the spectators. The ball was no sooner out of danger than out went the skirmishers to return again if need be.' The Sheffield public, at any rate, appear to have found it a novelty. It was also in the 1873-74 University match that Oxford's R.W.S. Vidal recalled: 'We found that try as we would we could not get through their defence. Their whole eleven was back on their goal line and we were bombarding them ceaselessly with no result.' A final point about the early defenders; they were expected to keep to their position on the field and they did not race forward to bolster an attack despite the modern belief that in those days, as one current author suggests, 'it would have resembled a game between schoolboys in a playground with everyone chasing the ball and virtually no passing or recognisable defenders on show.' Only one of the backs in the early Cup finals, in fact, got onto the scoresheet. The idea that all of the players chased the ball in a pack may have applied in the 1860s but by the time of the institution of the F.A.Cup in 1871 the game was becoming a little more sophisticated, especially in forward play as we shall see.

By the time of the third Cup final in 1873-74 both sides fielded two half-backs in order to cope with the increasing use of the width of the pitch by opposing forwards. Otherwise, their tactical role was similar to that which later devolved on the three half-backs up until the time of the 'stopper' centre-half or 'third back' in the mid-1920s. Their job was mainly to feed the forwards and support attacks or drop back to help the full-backs and they were especially expected to be good at tackling in midfield. Shearman makes the point that the half-back must be adept at throw-ins as this duty generally fell to him. Half-backs are so closely linked to the forwards, says Shearman, that they must be able to dribble and be steady kickers and chargers. Half-backs seem to have survived for the longest careers among our early Cup finalists; Kinnaird, for instance, retired around 1890 and Norman Coles Bailey played until the late 1880s.

It was in attack that the greatest developments took place, so much so that Shearman was able to speak of 'two ages of Association play, the dribbling and the passing.' He describes the dribbling period as follows: 'Each forward then strove to distinguish himself by making sensational dribbles, getting the ball in front of him and piloting it by clever dodging and twisting clean through the gaps in the opposing ranks, and combination play was thought to consist in backing up the dribbling forward, so as to carry on the ball as soon as he was deprived of it by an opponent.' C.W. Alcock recalled, in his 1890 book *Football: the Association Game*: 'To be a good dribbler was the Alpha and Omega of the forward's creed in the early days of Association football. At the same time it must not be understood that he was unprovided with support in case of any obstruction in the course of a run. There was the provision, of course, of backing-up, i.e. of a player who followed the ball ready either to receive the ball if it were passed to him, or to hustle or ward off any interference by the opposing forwards or backs.' In his 1881 edition of *The Football Annual*, Alcock records the change which took place during the 1870s: 'Dribbling was everything but the frequent changes in the game of late have placed dribblers a little in the shade, and players advancing with the times have had to go in for the more effective and less showy practice of passing on. "Passing on" is different to "backing up" and it was only the conversion to pass on at the proper time that suggested the necessity of more general passing on, and placed dribblers, comparatively, at a discount.'

Alcock at work in his office

Shearman, in 1888, suggests that it was from 1875 or 1876 that 'the game began to be played substantially in its present form; and "passing on" completely superseded dribbling about the same time that the great provincial centres suddenly came to the front, about 1878 or 1879.' Alcock, in his 1881 article, claims that the combination of the passing and dribbling game was a feature of the finest teams of that time.

In fact, contemporary evidence shows that Shearman's 'dribbling period' was already being transformed through a greater degree of teamwork by the time the F.A. Cup competition was instituted. In its preview of the first final, between the Wanderers and Royal Engineers in 1871-72, *The Morning Post* said: 'The habit of working together and understanding each other's play materially will help the Engineers. The leading club will doubtless show more exceptional brilliant form than the Engineers can be expected to do, but if we mistake not, there will be an amount of cohesion, co-operation and almost of discipline among the soldiers that will at all events go far to place them on a par with their, so to speak, more loosely organized but highly-skilled rivals.' And R.M. Ruck, stated in his 1928 article: 'The keynote of the R.E. was combination, not individuality, and that was the great advantage which the R.E. possessed over their opponents; the *esprit de corps* which was so marked in their professional capacity permeated their games; individually, as most of us knew, we were sometimes up against better players than ourselves, but, collectively, we felt equal to any club. In fact, Lord Kinnaird, than whom it would have been difficult to have found a better judge, was heard to remark that "the Sappers have discovered a new development of the game due to their greater combination."'

Star dribblers, though, did not go quietly. George Borlase Childs, who played for Oxford University in the 1879-80 Cup final and was noted for his dribbling skills, when captain of the Forest School XI wrote in the school magazine for Lent Term 1875: 'The system of *passing*, which has lately come much into fashion in the association game, is thoroughly carried out by our Eleven. There is in fact too much "passing" done, and fellows are apt to "pass" when dribbling would be of more service. In a match, sometimes we see one boy pass the ball to another who is in a more suitable place for taking on the ball, but he, instead of doing so, passes it back whence it came, and so the opportunity is lost. This mistake is sometimes made, but not often; and, as a rule, passing is executed with skill and judgment.' So by 1875 passing had already percolated through to the public schools, those bastions of the dribbling game.

A year later in his 1876 review, Childs has become a convert to the passing game. Of one player, he says: 'The latter we advise to put no faith in dribbling but to use his weight and pass when he gets the opportunity', while of another we are told: 'At the beginning of the season was too fond of keeping the ball to himself, and found great difficulty in passing it but has since greatly improved in that respect.'

The idea of a horde of forwards chasing after the ball rather like a swarm of bees also does not stand up to scrutiny. The wings were already being used, hence the eventual need for more backs and half-backs, and the technique of centring the ball (then called 'middling') had been developed. *The Sportsman* was highly critical of Oxford University in the 1872-73 final, commenting: 'Oxford had more than one chance but, instead of middling the ball through from the side of the ground, they seemed anxious to force it through the goal and in this they were unsuccessful.' Certainly, dribbling was still an important factor in the first few finals but the role of the supporting forwards was being planned in more detail. For instance, the disposition of the attack when seven forwards were fielded did not resemble that of the classic five-man line of later years with the two additional centre-forwards squashed in. Instead, the three centre-forwards lined up rather like the inside-right, centre-forward and inside-left of subsequent times. The wingers then acted as a pair on each side of the pitch. In fact they were described as right side and left side so the wheel has turned full circle; in the 2000s we again have right-sided and left-sided players just as in the 1870s! This was an ideal opportunity for the often mentioned 'backing up' practice to come in. The 'back-up' winger would be slightly behind his partner, ready to collect the ball when necessary if his colleague lost possession but also ready to hamper opponents closing in on the dribbler.

One final point on tactics involves the kick-off. This was treated as a place kick and was booted as hard and as far as possible upfield. The kick was usually taken by a half-back or the side's captain and the first time a centre-forward is recorded as kicking-off in a final is 1877-78 when Robert Shafto Hedley of the Royal Engineers undertook the task. As he was also the team captain, we cannot be sure whether or not the tactical change happened then. The same consideration applies to 1879-80 when Oxford University captain and winger Reginald Thomas Heygate kicked off. What we can say with certainty is that the first centre-forward to kick-off who was not the captain was Reginald Heber Macaulay for the Old Etonians in 1880-81. Presumably, the earlier choice of a non-attacker to kick off was in order to leave all of the forwards free to surge into the opponents' half after the ball. Kicking off with a gentle pass to a fellow-forward was an idea that does not seem to have struck anyone for some years, perhaps not until the adoption and more widespread use of the passing game. Certainly, in the 1881-82 final, *The Field* thought it worth reporting that when Blackburn Rovers lost the toss they had to start the game 'which was done by a short pass from Brown to Strachan'.

Blackburn Rovers also astonished *The Sporting Life* sartorially: 'The visitors were closely scanned as they came into the field, all attired alike in narrow blue and white striped jerseys; whilst, as a peculiarity, nearly every one of them wore shin-guards on their right legs – some on both; a peculiarity the more noticeable from the fact that many played minus long stockings.' The only other match reports which have been found to refer to the teams' colours are those on the 1874-75 games which state: 'The Engineers' colours were scarlet and blue; those of the Old Etonians light blue and white.'

F.A. Cup winner's medals from 1876 (left) and 1877

THE REFEREE AND UMPIRES

The very first rules laid down for F.A. Cup games in 1871 specified that: 'The Committee shall appoint two umpires and a referee to act at each of the matches in the Final Ties. Neither the umpires nor the referee shall be members of either of the contending Clubs and the decision of the umpires shall be final except in the case of the umpires disagreeing when an appeal shall be made to the referee, whose decision shall be final.' These three officials were already a feature of football, especially in the most important games, though many ordinary club matches made do with just the two umpires, who were usually members of the contending clubs, a proceeding which was prohibited in the above F.A. Cup rule. Maurice Golesworthy has made the point that: 'The wording of this rule shows just how much the increased competition was already beginning to change the attitude of the players. The days of the gentlemen players, who were proud of the manner in which rival teams generally conducted themselves, and settled any disputes, were beginning to fade. The time had come not only to specify the appointment of both umpires and referees but to insist upon these men being **NEUTRAL**.'

The division of labour between the two umpires was that each of them looked after one half of the field. However, it is a mistake to suppose that their 'half' was that of the side they represented. In this context 'one half of the field' means dividing it by an imaginary line drawn between goal and goal; in other words the umpires operated like modern linesmen (now, of course, referees' assistants) with the exception that they were inside the field of play rather than restricted to running the touchline. Also faulty is the supposition that, until the abolition of umpires in 1891, the referee stood on the touchline waiting to be called upon by them to adjudicate. In fact, there is pictorial evidence from the 1870s and 1880s that shows the referee inside the pitch and keeping up with the play.

A game in progress in the 1880s. The referee is in the foreground

Shearman explains how the system worked: 'Each side has its own umpire, who is armed with a stick or flag; the referee carries a whistle. When a claim for infringement of rules is made, if both umpires are agreed, each holds up his stick, and the referee calls the game to a halt by sounding his whistle. If one umpire allows the claim, and the referee agree with him, he calls a halt as before; if the other umpire and the referee agree that the claim be disallowed, the whistle is not sounded. Two of the three officials must therefore agree in allowing the claim or the whistle is silent, and players continue the game until the whistle calls them off. Both umpires and referee, therefore, must lose no time in arriving at a decision, or so much play is wasted.'

Mention here of the referee's whistle raises the question of when this was introduced. Modern references to its first use in 1878 in a match between Nottingham Forest and Sheffield Norfolk must clearly be wrong for the two clubs did not meet in that year. In fact their last encounter was on 17th January 1874 and reports of that game or earlier ones between the two clubs make no mention of a whistle though that is not necessarily proof that it was not used. However, the referee's whistle and Forest have been linked from at least 1891 when a booklet was issued in connection with a fund-raising bazaar in Nottingham in which it is stated: 'The referee's whistle was introduced by the Forest Club, and was used for the first time on the Forest Cricket Ground in the year 1878, when Sheffield Norfolk were trying conclusions with the Reds.'

Therefore, one would expect to find some connection, even if not in 1878, and so it proves. In 1868 Walter Roe Lymbery became secretary-treasurer of Forest and his first account book survived into modern times in the possession of members of his family. In December 1872 he records spending fivepence 'for an umpire's whistle.' No doubt in matches where a referee was also involved that official took over the whistle. So we can now take the use of a whistle by a football official back to December 1872, some six years before the generally accepted date. This is pretty well confirmed by R.M. Ruck's 1928 article in which he recalls his time in the Royal Engineers team in the early 1870s: 'It was considered the correct thing that, when the ball touched a player's hand or arm, and "hand" was challenged, he at once threw up his hand and acknowledged it without waiting for the umpire's whistle.' Of course, it is probable that the use of the whistle took some time to spread throughout the game and at first, no doubt, the whistle was used to stop play, then the referee called time. Match reports into the early 1880s still use the phrase 'time was called' to note the end of the game.

Incidentally, in February 1886 the Bangor Club wrote to the Football Association to ask 'whether it is correct for umpires to have whistles' and the F.A. Committee answered in the negative.

Ruck's mention of claiming 'hands' is a reminder of the fact that until 1891 everything had to be appealed for. As late as March 1891, just months before the abolition of umpires, the F.A. Council affirmed that an umpire had no right to give a decision until an appeal had been made by a player. Appealing quickly grew more prevalent during the 1870s and the sportsmanlike play which characterised the game in much of the pre-F.A. Cup era was soon diluted by the keenness of teams seeking to win the trophy. *The Sportsman* was severe on both finalists in 1875-76, those paragons of the sporting virtues, the Wanderers and the Old Etonians: 'Several times "hands" were called by either side on the most frivolous pretexts but no advantage accrued therefrom.' The replay brought further criticism: 'Free kicks abounded through the same vexatious and unmeaning calls of "hands" which had been so frequent during the last match.' Nevertheless, sportsmanship was not dead; in 1879-80 the same newspaper praised Clapham Rovers and Oxford University: 'There was not one appeal in the game', though there must have been one for Clapham's goal.

That a determination to win the F.A. Cup tempted clubs to go a little bit further than they would in ordinary matches is shown by the Royal Engineers in 1873-74. It has been stated frequently that Blackburn Olympic in 1882-83 were the first team to go away for special pre-final training and while that remains strictly true in the geographical sense, the Engineers went into special training nearly ten years before. Their secretary records: 'Determined to leave no stone unturned in order to secure the victory and if possible bring back the cup in triumph, for the last fortnight before the match we had gone into a regular course of training at least as far as was sufficient to get us into thorough good condition.'

The 1891 final between Notts County (stripes) and Blackburn Rovers at the Oval. Admittedly outside of the period discussed in this book, but an illustration of the first use of a net behind the goal in a Cup final.

THE CLUBS

The Wanderers
They were formed in 1864 and developed from the Forest Club, founded in 1859 by a group of Old Harrovians. Forest played on a part of Epping Forest close to the Merchant Seaman's Orphan Asylum at Snaresbrook but when local recruitment diminished they were disbanded and re-formed as The Wanderers. The new club used Kennington Oval as their home ground from 1870 whenever possible; earlier they claimed no permanent home venue but played a number of 'home' fixtures at Battersea Park. Their colours were originally orange, violet and black but in 1870 became purple, yellow and black. They competed in the F.A. Cup from the first season of 1871-72 until 1879-80 inclusive and also entered in the two following seasons but scratched without playing a match. Their total F.A. Cup record was P.30, W.21, D.5, L.4, F.96, A.22. The Cup became their absolute property after they won it for the third successive season in 1877-78 but they handed it back to the F.A. with the stipulation that it could never be won outright again. As an active club, they were defunct by 1882 but do not appear to have been formally disbanded.

Royal Engineers
R.E. football on Chatham Lines dates back to 1842 and the club joined the Football Association in December 1863 though according to *The Football Annual* they were formed in 1867. Perhaps that is when they adopted F.A. Laws in full. They continued to play at the Great Lines and their colours were scarlet and dark blue horizontal stripes. In the four seasons 1871-72 to 1874-75 they played 86 matches, lost only three, scored 240 goals and conceded just 20! They competed in the F.A. Cup from 1871-72 to 1888-89 inclusive, finishing with a record of P.58, W.34, D.7, L.17, F.144, A.72 (plus one 3-0 victory later declared void on appeal). They entered the first F.A. Amateur Cup competition in 1893-94 but lost in the second qualifying round. That was the final fling for the 'gentlemen officers' team. From that point different battalion teams were formed, mainly from 'other ranks' and it was the Depot Battalion Royal Engineers who won the Amateur Cup in 1907-08. The Service Battalion and the Training Battalion also took part in the Amateur Cup. These teams also competed in the Army Cup, the Kent Amateur Cup and the Kent League.

Oxford University
The association football club dates from 9th November 1871, played in The Parks until 1899 and their colours were and remain dark blue. They first entered the F.A. Cup in 1872-73 when they agreed to adopt the F.A. Law on offside, but their appearance in the 1879-80 final was their last game in the competition as they decided not to enter in the future. Their Cup record was P.41, W.27, D.7, L.7, F.99, A.33. Their ground since 1899 has been Iffley Road and the annual match against Cambridge University which was first played in 1873-74 still continues.

Old Etonians
Various old Etonians formed clubs in the 1860s such as the Eton Cambridge Club but the present Old Etonian club claims to date from 1871 though Alcock's *Football Annual* gave 1865; perhaps 1871 was when they adopted the F.A. Laws. Their colours were and remain light blue and white and in their great years of the 1870s and 1880s they staged their home games at Kennington Oval when possible though they now play at Dutchman's, Eton College. The club competed in the F.A. Cup from 1873-74 to 1876-77 at which stage they became almost moribund but thanks especially to Major F.A. Marindin as captain and R.D. Anderson as secretary, they were revived in October 1878 and competed again from 1878-79 to 1892-93. Their Cup record was P.69, W.44, D.10, L.15, F.198, A.107. They switched to the F.A. Amateur Cup on the institution of that competition in 1893-94 and took part for the last time in 1901-02. Then they joined most of the other old boy teams in the new Arthur Dunn Cup which was instituted in 1902 in memory of the Old Etonian, England international and Cup finalist, who had died earlier that year. The Etonians, though, have yet to win it, their closest attempts being in 1951-52 and 1991-92 when they were beaten finalists. The club were among those involved in the breakaway Amateur Football Association of 1907. The Old Etonians are still in what is now the Amateur Football Alliance, have been members of the Arthurian League since its formation in 1962-63 and were the league champions in 1992-93. To celebrate the centenary of their Cup final against Blackburn Rovers, the two clubs held a joint banquet in 1982.

Clapham Rovers
They were formed on 10th August 1869, played originally on Clapham Common before moving to Tooting Bec Common in 1873 and finally switched to Wandsworth Common in 1878. Their colours were cerise (cherry red) and French (light) grey. They competed in the F.A. Cup from 1871-72 to 1886-87 inclusive to finish with a record of P.44, W.26, D.4, L.14, F.149, A.56. Rovers competed in the first F.A. Amateur Cup in 1893-94 and reached the first round proper where they scratched to Bishop Auckland. Earlier, they received a walkover in the third qualifying round against Tottenham Hotspur, who were suspended at the time. An unusual feature of Clapham Rovers was that they ran football and rugby union sections. In addition they ran a cricket team and a lawn tennis section during the summer. They continued as members of the F.A. until 1907 when they were among the breakaway Amateur Football Association clubs. They closed during the 1914-18 war and never restarted.

Old Carthusians
The old boys opposed the Charterhouse School team in an annual match from 1864, originally as 'Old v Present' but from 1866-67 as the school v Old Carthusians. However, these games were under school rules and were played in the cloisters until the school's move from central London to Godalming in 1872. On 17th March 1875 the school played its first game under strict Football Association Laws (a house match) and the current Old Carthusians trace their foundation to their match against the school on 25th November 1876. Their colours were brown, black and orange which were changed in 1880 to dark blue, cerise and pink which remains the case though now in stripes instead of the original quarters. They competed in the F.A. Cup from 1879-80 to 1891-92 with a final record of P.44, W.31, D.1, L.12, F.152, A.63. They then added to

their 1880-81 F.A. Cup success by becoming the first holders of the F.A. Amateur Cup in 1893-94, were runners up the following season and won it again in 1896-97. During this period they also won the London Senior Cup in 1894-95, 1895-96, 1896-97 and 1898-99 as well as the London Charity Cup in 1895-96 and 1897-98. The Carthusians remained for many years the only club to have won both F.A. cups before their record was equalled by Wimbledon in 1988. To mark this event the two clubs met on 2nd November 1988 at Charterhouse when Wimbledon, who fielded mainly youth team players, won 5-1. From 1902-03 the Carthusians, along with most other old boy clubs, shunned the Amateur Cup in favour of the Arthur Dunn Cup which they have won 19 times as follows: 1902-03 (joint), 1903-04, 1904-05, 1905-06, 1907-08, 1909-10, 1920-21, 1921-22, 1922-23, 1935-36, 1938-39, 1946-47, 1948-49, 1950-51, 1953-54, 1961-62, 1976-77, 1981-82 and 2000-01. They were also runners-up six times, 1910-11, 1928-29, 1949-50, 1983-84, 1990-91 and the centenary competition of 2002-03. As with the Old Etonians they joined the breakaway Amateur Football Association in 1907 and are currently members of what is now the Amateur Football Alliance. In 1907-08 they won both the A.F.A. Senior Cup and the Surrey A.F.A. Senior Cup, capturing the former trophy again in 1911-12. Since 1970 the Old Carthusians' home ground has been at Charterhouse School, Godalming, and they compete in the Arthurian League whose championship they won in 1978-79, 1981-82 and 1987-88.

The Royal Engineers 1871-72. Back: Merriman, Ord*, Marindin, Addison, Mitchell. Front: Hoskyns*, Renny-Tailyour, Creswell, Goodwyn, Barker*, Rich (* did not play in final)

The Royal Engineers team that toured the North at Christmas 1873. Back (from left): GT Jones*, HW Renny-Tailyour, HD Olivier (behind), Major FA Marindin (captain), Capt. W Merriman, CF Ellis*. Seated: JE Blackburn, HE Rawson, T Digby, CK Wood. On floor: PG von Donop, GH Sim, AG Goodwyn (* did not play in final)

Royal Engineers 1874-75
Back (from left): Lieut. HL Mulholland*, Lieut. GCP Onslow, Lieut. WFH Stafford, Lieut. HE Rawson, Lieut. AL Mein, Lieut. CV Wingfield-Stratford. Centre: Lieut. RM Ruck, Major W Merriman (captain), Lieut. HW Renny-Tailyour, Lieut. PG von Donop. Front: Lieut. GH Sim, Lieut. GT Jones* (* did not play in final)

Oxford University, Cup winners 1873-74. Standing (from left): RWS Vidal, FT Green, CC Mackarness, AH Johnson, RH Benson, FH Birley, CEB Nepean. Seated: CJ Ottaway, FJ Patton, FB Maddison, WS Rawson

Oxford University 1877. Back: RT Thornton*, HS Otter, TEB Guy*, J Bain, CHT Metcalf*, JH Savory, PH Fernandez. Front: TAC Hampson*, WS Rawson, EH Parry (*did not play in final)

Old Carthusians 1881. Standing (from left): LM Richards, WH Norris, EG Colvin, LF Gillet, WE Hansell. Seated: EG Wynyard, AH Tod, JFM Prinsep, WR Page, EH Parry, J Vintcent. Front: unknown.

THE GROUNDS

Kennington Oval

Cricket at the Oval in the 1890s

The ground was originally a market garden leased from the Duchy of Cornwall. It was opened for cricket in 1845; the turf was laid in March and the first match was on 13th May. Surrey County Cricket Club was formed on 18th October 1845. Football was first played at The Oval in 1849 following the formation of the Surrey Football Club as an offshoot of the county cricket club on 3rd October that year, though 'football' in this case was more like rugby. The Oval was used for all F.A. Cup finals from 1871-72 to 1891-92 with the exception of 1872-73 which was at Lillie Bridge, West Brompton, and the replayed final of 1885-86 which was staged at Derby County's then ground, the Racecourse. The football pitch at the Oval was at the Vauxhall end of the ground and had one goal at the Harleyford Road end and the other at the Gasometer end. Because of the growing attendances, for the 1888-89 final the playing area was moved nearer to the pavilion so that it covered the cricket square and it was Surrey's worries over the state of the cricket surface that led them eventually to end football at the Oval. The F.A. Council meeting of 25th January 1893 was informed that 'the Committee of Surrey County C.C. had resolved not to allow any Football to be played upon the middle of the ground. This would affect the venue of the final tie of the Cup Competition.' Altogether 22 F.A. Cup finals, including two replays, took place at the Oval. The fact that Surrey's secretary during this period was also F.A. secretary C.W. Alcock no doubt helped to smooth the path for the use of the Oval. Many other important football matches were also staged at the ground including ten full internationals. The first of these was England's 4-2 win against Scotland on 8th March 1873 and the last a 3-2 win by Scotland over England on 13th April 1889. Altogether England met Scotland in seven matches (won 2, drawn 2, lost 3) and Wales three times (all won). The last international of all was when England beat Canada 6-1 on 19th December 1891, a match which has since been ranked 'unofficial' but for which England international caps were awarded. There were also five 'pre-official' internationals between England and 'Scotland', games arranged by the F.A. in which the loosely-qualified Scottish players were London-based (England won 3, drawn 2). The first of these was on 5th March 1870. Major matches outside the international arena included many South v North, London v Sheffield and London v Glasgow contests. More than 60 years after Surrey ended football at the Oval they relented to allow the Corinthian-Casuals to use the ground in the 1950s though the football pitch was on its original site at the Vauxhall end, thus avoiding the cricket square. By the way, the footballers of the 1870s and 1880s would have seen a less substantial Oval pavilion than the present one which was not opened until 1897.

The Oval pavilion in the 1880s

Lillie Bridge

This ground in West Brompton was opened by Mr J.G. Chambers in 1867-68 as the headquarters of the Amateur Athletic Club, the forerunners of the Amateur Athletic Association. It was mainly used for athletics and cycling though cricket and football matches were also staged there. In 1870 it was rented by Middlesex County Cricket Club but because of the unsatisfactory state of the turf, they were unable to play there until 1871 when they met Surrey in their only match at the ground. They then moved elsewhere for 1872. The use of Lillie Bridge for the F.A. Cup final in 1872-73 came about because of the competition's original challenge rule. As holders, the Wanderers were exempt until the 'challenge round' (otherwise the final) and they also had choice of venue. This challenge rule was dropped after only the one season of operation. However, the selection by the Wanderers of this ground may have been influenced by the fact that the only available date for the final coincided with Boat Race day. In order for the players, officials and supporters to watch the Boat Race, they may have chosen a ground not too far from good viewing points and for the same reason the match also kicked off at 11.30 a.m. The Oxford-Cambridge athletics match took place at Lillie Bridge from 1869-1887. The ground was partially destroyed by fire on the evening of Monday 19th September 1887 when a disappointed mob ran riot after a professional athletics challenge race had been cancelled and they failed to get their gate money refunded. The pavilion, changing rooms, refreshment room, seating and fencing were all badly damaged, one man died from a heart attack, while a number of policemen and firemen were injured when the mob attacked them. The derelict site was later taken over by the railway. The Lillie Bridge ground was across the road from the present-day Earls Court Exhibition Centre. A car park and open market just off Seagrave Road across the railway line from West Brompton cemetery cover the site today. From the shape of the ground it seems certain that one goal would have been at the Lillie Road end with the other at the southern end, though match reports do not identify any ends. Seagrave Road ran the full length of the western side of the playing area and the railway line formed the eastern boundary.

> Wanderers v. Royal Engineers. On Saturday last the final tie in the competition for the silver challenge cup, recently presented by the committee of the Football Association, took place at Kennington Oval. The possession of the trophy for the first year thus rested between the two most powerful of all the Association clubs, and the interest felt on all sides in the chances of the contest was forcibly displayed, becoming steadily intensified as the day approached for the settlement of the question. It must be conceded that popular sympathy was certainly with the Engineers in some measure, owing to the fact that the forces from which they can derive an eleven are much more limited than those of their opponents, while the general feeling, too, seemed to be in favour of a victory for the Sappers, on the ground that they were likely to outstay their adversaries, as well as to outmatch them by the superiority of their general play. Both parties succeeded in mustering their full strength;. and indeed everything augured well for an exciting struggle, as the ground was in the very best condition, and the weather was so propitious in every way, that the assemblage of spectators was much above the average, despite the counter attraction of the University crews, and an increase in the rate normally charged for admission into the ground. Within a few minutes of three o'clock the ball was kicked off on behalf of the Engineers, the ill-success of their captain in the toss for choice of positions causing them at first to labour under a double disadvantage, in having both wind and sun in their faces. The game was at once commenced with remarkable vigour; the Wanderers, with the evident determination of making full use of their weight forward, attacking with an amount of energy that was well sustained throughout. Thus at the outset the Engineers were closely pressed, and only a quarter of an hour had elapsed when R.W.S. Vidal, after a good run, middled the ball so cleverly to A.H. Chequer that the latter was able to effect the reduction of the military goal with but little difficulty. Ends were then changed, but despite that they now enjoyed the advantages previously held by the Wanderers, the Engineers were not only unable to make any advance, but they were far from successful in keeping their opponents at bay. Indeed, although they worked hard and well, the general play of the Wanderers was so effective, and the kicking of their backs Thompson and Lubbock so admirable, that all the efforts of the Sappers were of little avail, being in most cases repulsed before they approached so far as to place the enemy's lines in peril. On the other hand, the Wanderers continued to press on without the least cessation of energy, and until the end they maintained a decided advantage, preserving their goal entirely free from danger, with the exception of one occasion, when a fine run by Lieut. Muirhead brought the ball within a few yards of the centre of their posts. Soon after the first achievement, the Wanderers secured what appeared to be a second goal from a kick by C.W. Alcock, but a previous infringement of the handling rule by C.H. Wollaston negatived this second success, and play was resumed. During the rest of the game several opportunities were offered to the Wanderers of increasing their score; but so resolute was the front offered by Capt. Merriman, the goal keeper of the Sappers, and so judicious his defence, that further reverses were averted for his side. So time was called soon after half-past four o'clock. and the Wanderers thus remained entitled to act as custodians of the cup for the term of one year, having gained this privilege after the fastest and hardest match that has ever been seen at the Oval, and by some of the best play on their part, individually and collectively, that has ever been shown in an Association game. The Engineers, it is only just to state, displayed all their accustomed energy and excellence of organisation; but their back play was by no means equal to that of the victors, and indeed it may safely be said that Wanderers could hardly have enjoyed the supremacy so decisively during the game had it not been for the absolutely faultless kicking of their two backs, E. Lubbock and A.C. Thompson. Each was in brilliant form, but the admirable manner in which they worked together was the great feature of the match, Thompson displaying especial energy throughout. On the side of the Engineers Capt. Merriman's goalkeeping was perfect, and to him alone was due the preservation of the military fortress from further surrenders. As an instance of the determination of the Sappers, it may be noticed that Lieut. Cresswell had his collar bone broken in a charge ten minutes after the commencement of play, and continued until the close of the contest. The cup will be presented to the victors at the annual dinner of the Wanderers' Football Club, to be held on the 11th April. Each member of the victorious eleven will be presented with a silken badge commemorative of the event by the committee of the Football Association, and in addition a gold medal with a suitable inscription by the committee of the Wanderers' Football Club.

An account of the first final, from The Field of March 23, 1872

MATCH FACTS

A note on the text
This section begins with extracts from contemporary reports on all of the goals scored. Then, for each final the following information is given, when available:

The date; the venue; the attendance; the winners of the toss and which end they chose to defend; starting time and the player kicking off; the youngest and oldest player in the match; the average age of each team plus the average age of the combined teams; the result with the half-time score; extra time details where applicable; the goalscorers with goal times; the players in their starting positions with †indicating the captain; the referee and umpires; a note of injuries and any positional changes these necessitated; other comments of interest such as, for example, brothers in the same match as well as significant points in the play; the paths to the final; and for the 1874-75 and 1875-76 replays, a note on team changes from the first match. The following points should be noted:

Attendances
All reports of the early finals give estimated attendances in round figures of so many thousand. These vary considerably in different sources so the ones given here are those which appear in current football reference books. If anything, they are marginally larger than those in the contemporary newspaper reports and so can be relied on as showing the upper limit of the possible attendance.

Average ages
Blackburn Rovers in 1881-82 and Blackburn Olympic in 1882-83 are not included in this compilation so that, for these seasons, only the average age of the Old Etonians is given. The exact date of the birth of E.A. Ram in the Clapham Rovers team of 1879-80 has not been discovered; in this case a date midway in the six-month period in which he is known to have been born has been assumed in working out his team's figure.

The Cup rules
The Match Facts for the finals of 1871-72 (Wanderers and Crystal Palace both included in the draw for the next round), 1872-73 (Wanderers exempt until the final) and 1877-78 (Wanderers won the Cup outright) mention three of the Cup rules. These are:

RULE 8: In the case of a drawn match, the Clubs shall be drawn in the next ties or shall compete again, at the discretion of the Committee.

RULE 9: The holder of the Cup shall be liable to play only the winner of the trial matches.

RULE 10: The holders of the Challenge Cup shall hand it over to the Secretary of The Football Association on or before 1st February in each year, unless the holders shall have won the Cup three years in succession, when the Cup shall become the absolute property of the Club so winning it. In addition to the Cup, the Committee will present to the winners of the Final Tie, eleven medals or badges of trifling value.

Goal times
The times given in this section are approximate ones and have been worked out from studying the various match reports.

Half-time scores
These are shown only from 1875-76 when the practice was introduced. Before this, the system was to change ends every time a goal was scored though a switch after 45 minutes did take place if the match was scoreless at that point. Even so, ends continued to be changed after any goals scored in the second period of 45 minutes.

THE GOALSCORERS

Reports in 19th century newspapers are sometimes hazy about the identity of the goalscorers; phrases such as 'rushed through' or 'scrimmaged in' are not uncommon and prove frustrating for modern researchers. One has to have sympathy for the hard-pressed reporters of the time. Players were not numbered, changes to the match cards were either not announced or else paraded round the ground before kick-off, chalked on a board and, especially in bad weather, were easily overlooked. In addition, press facilities were often meagre or non-existent and there was also the lack of help from the contending clubs; see above for *The Sportsman*'s complaint about their treatment in the final of 1880-81.

In the case of the F.A. Cup finals in general, though, we have to thank the importance of the occasion for the fact that the reporters in most cases did name the scorers; also, the huge amount of research carried out on these games over the years has helped to provide supporting evidence. Despite this, it is not possible to identify every one of the scorers of the 30 goals in the 14 finals to 1882-83 (including both first drawn game and replay in 1874-75 and 1875-76). Three goals are in doubt though we have unconfirmed names from modern researchers for two of them.

In this section, descriptions of the goals are given from *The Sportsman* and *The Field* with the addition of a selection of other reports, especially where they offer important extra information or differ substantially. In a few cases they name a scorer whom *The Sportsman* or *The Field* have failed to identify.

16th March 1872: Wanderers 1 Royal Engineers 0
1-0 (15 mins.): *The Sportsman*. The Wanderers set to work with the greatest determination, and at the outset their play forward displayed more co-operation than is their custom, the backing-up being vastly superior to anything they have shown during the present season. By this means, and with the aid of faultless kicking on the part of their backs, they were able during the first quarter of an hour to besiege the Sappers closely, to the surprise of many of the spectators. Thus consistently they maintained the attack, till at length, after some judicious 'middling' by R.W.S. Vidal, the goal of the Engineers fell to a well-directed kick by **A.H. CHEQUER** (this was the pseudonym used by **M.P. BETTS**).
The Field. Only a quarter of an hour had elapsed when R.W.S. Vidal, after a good run, middled the ball so cleverly to **A.H. CHEQUER** that the latter was able to effect the reduction of the military goal with but little difficulty.
NOTE: Although there is no contemporary dispute about Betts being the scorer of this goal, *The Times* of 24 September 1938, in its obituary of T.C. Hooman, stated: 'Mr. Thomas Charles Hooman, who died at Hythe on Thursday at the age of 87, scored the only goal in the first F.A. Cup final. That was at Kennington Oval in the 1871-72 season, and Mr. Hooman's goal enabled the Old Wanderers to beat the Royal Engineers to become the first holders of the cup.' Presumably this claim came from Hooman himself because the obituary quoted other comments on the game made by Hooman 'some time ago'. However, those 'comments' display a faulty memory in which he stated that the match took place without a referee or umpires, with the captains settling all disputes. Hooman is almost certainly confusing this match with others in which he played at this period.

29th March 1873: Wanderers 2 Oxford University 0

1-0 (27 mins.): *The Sportsman*. For twenty minutes the game thus proceeded with a visible superiority to Oxford, the whole eleven working well together and with great energy. Gradually, though, the Wanderers aroused, and almost half an hour had passed when **KINNAIRD** took advantage of a favourable opportunity, and by a splendid run outpacing the opposite backs, he placed a very well obtained goal to the credit of the Wanderers, to the intense delight of their eleven.

The Field. When about twenty-five minutes had expired, **A.F. KINNAIRD**, getting hold of the ball, passed all the Oxford backs, and finally landed a very fine goal for the Wanderers by the best piece of play shown during the match.

2-0 (80 mins.): *The Sportsman*. The Oxonians now tried every plan to retrieve their ground, and in the hopes of strengthening their attack, with questionable judgment determined on the removal of their goal-keeper. For a short time no disaster followed this *ruse*, but at length **C.H. WOLLASTON**, after a speedy run, reduced the Oxford goal by means of a neat kick with the left foot, thus placing the second goal to the credit of the Wanderers, entirely owing to the absence of the man between the post.

The Field. Oxford now attempted the expedient of playing without a goal-keeper, and this move proved fatal to their hopes, as about ten minutes before time, after a short run down the left side of the ground, **C.H. WOLLASTON**, by a clever kick with the left foot, secured a goal that would have been easily prevented with a goal-keeper in charge.

14th March 1874: Oxford University 2 Royal Engineers 0

1-0 (10 mins.): *The Sportsman*. The Engineers sent the ball behind their own line, and as a consequence a corner kick was allowed to the Oxonians, which resulted in a loose scrimmage directly in the jaws of the R.E. fortress, and it was not long before the ball was well kicked through the post by **MACKARNESS**, who thus was credited with the first goal for his university.

The Field. After some ten minutes indecisive play, the Oxford forwards again got away with the ball, and, bringing it into close proximity to the Sappers' goal, it was ultimately kicked behind by one of their own side, the advantage of a corner kick thus accruing to the Oxonians. From this kick a loose scrimmage ensued in front of the military goal, and **MACKARNESS**, who was in waiting behind, getting hold of the ball, kicked it sharply over the heads of the bully through the posts, the goal keeper being apparently unaware of its presence until it had passed him.

Royal Engineers secretary's manuscript report. After a slight scrimmage the ball was kicked behind by one of the Engineer backs. In kicking from the corner the ball was landed just in front of **MACKARNESS** who was playing half back, and he by a very good kick sent it through the Sappers' goal: it was rather disgusting losing a goal like this for anyone almost could have stopped, but naturally enough each thought it safer to leave it to the goal-keeper who could use his hands to it; unfortunately however owing to the crowd he did not see it and thus the ball went quietly through the posts.

2-0 (20 mins.): *The Sportsman*. The game became more than ever spirited, the Engineers, seemingly aroused to fresh efforts, strongly attacking the Oxford goal, and almost overthrowing the same. The 'Varsity men, however, were much elated with their primary success, and determined not to let slip a chance, they – chiefly by the aid of Ottaway, Maddison, and Vidal – again overcame all opposition, and rapidly carried the ball back into the Engineers quarters, and finally **PATTON** shot it between the posts, and thus obtained the second goal for the University.

The Field. Ere long a combined attack of the University forwards enabled **F.J. PATTON** to shoot the ball under the tape and thus score the second goal for the University.

Royal Engineers secretary's report. The next most conspicuous feature was a good run down the ground by Ottaway and Maddison, who failed to elude the Sappers' goal keeper who this time determined to die hard, his efforts were to no purpose for **PATTON** coming to the rescue, shot the ball through the posts – this was a really fine goal and Oxford deserved it.

13th March 1875: Royal Engineers 1 Old Etonians 1 (after extra time)
0-1 (30 mins.): *The Sportsman.* For half an hour the game remained without decisive issue, but here a corner kick fell to the Etonians, and the ball was so skilfully handled by **Bonsor**, with the proper allowance for the wind, that it went between the posts before Major Merriman could divert its course.
The Field. For half an hour the Engineers faced the wind without loss, but here a corner kick fell to the Etonians, and a gust catching the ball well aimed by **Bonsor** carried it between the Engineers' posts just out of reach of their goalkeeper.
The Sporting Life. After thirty minutes play, from an excellent corner-kick by **Bonsor**, a goal was secured.
Bell's Life in London. [Eton had] an exceedingly strong and cold north easterly wind at their backs. With such advantages they soon returned the ball to the Engineers' quarters, and made repeated attacks upon their fortress, which had many hairbreadth escapes, corner kicks and free kicks for Eton frequently occurring. Matters went on in this way for half an hour, when a corner kick for the Old Etonians was entrusted to **Bonsor**, and, helped by the wind, the ball bounded under the line.
1-1 (35 mins.): *The Sportsman.* Ends were changed, but the Engineers soon retorted, as the forwards, bearing down in a body, charged the Eton backs before they could get their kick, and the goal-keeper was unable to prevent them forcing their way between his posts.
The Field. Ends were changed, but the Etonians soon had their success neutralised, as within five minutes their backs were charged in the act of kicking by the Sapper forwards, and in the scrimmage the ball was taken safely into the Etonians' goal.
The Sporting Life. Ten minutes after change of ends, however, Von Donop made a fine run, and out of a bully in front of goal, the ball glanced off **Renny-Tailyour's** knee through the posts, thus matters were equalised.
Bell's Life in London. With the change of ends, the Engineers soon showed their superiority, and five minutes had scarcely elapsed before Von Donop ran the ball a short distance along the right side, planting it well in front of the Old Etonians' goal, and **Renny-Tailyour**, who was in waiting, had little difficulty in scoring the goal.

16th March 1875 (replay): Royal Engineers 2 Old Etonians 0
1-0 (15 mins.): *The Sportsman.* Some time elapsed before either side made any decided move. At length one of the Eton forwards handled the ball in the very front of his goal, and with the free kick that followed the Engineers rushed the ball through the Etonian goal.
The Field. At last an unfortunate piece of handling by T. Hamond close to the Etonian posts gave a free kick to the Engineers, and, with a vigorous dash, they carried the ball between the Eton posts.
The Sporting Life. After about fifteen minutes Patton unfortunately handled the ball right in front of the Eton goal, when it was carried through. An appeal on the ground of off-side, however, being made, the goal was disallowed, and the ball replaced in its old position, but the Engineers, after a sharp bully, forced it through the posts again, thus gaining the first goal.
Bell's Life in London. After about a quarter of an hour the Engineers began to show a little superiority, one of the Old Etonians handling the ball close in front of their goal, which gave the Engineers a free kick, and they managed to force the ball under the tape. An appeal of off-side was then made by the Etonians, and the ball had to be replaced, but the downfall of the Eton fortress was inevitable, as it collapsed immediately afterwards.
Note: None of the newspaper reports identify the scorer of this first goal but it can be credited to **Renny-Tailyour**. The following appeared in *The Royal Engineers Journal* for February, 1922: The Officer who wrote the Memoir on the late Colonel H.W. Renny-Tailyour which appeared in the *R.E. Journal* of September, 1920, has asked that an omission which was made in that Memoir may be made good. Colonel Renny-Tailyour not only played in the final Association Cup Match of 1875, but he kicked both goals scored in that Match by the victorious R.E. Team.

2-0 (75 mins.): *The Sportsman* The ball again found its way between the Eton posts, though a previous infringement of the off-side rule nullified this success. Not long afterwards, though, another onslaught was made, and this time **RENNY-TAILYOUR** safely secured the second goal for the Engineers.
The Field. The game continued until within a quarter of an hour of time, when a general rush of the Engineers' forwards enabled **RENNY-TAILYOUR** to secure the second goal for his side.
The Sporting Life. Fine back play, however, on each side prevented any serious results until with a quarter of an hour of time, when the Engineers completely penned their opponents, and after several spirited bullies in front of goal, forced it through.
Bell's Life in London. Each goal in turn was seriously menaced, but the back play of both teams was so well sustained that the ball was soon carried out of danger. In this way play continued until within 15 minutes of the call of time, when the Engineers had all the best of it, and penned their opponents several times, **RENNY-TAILYOUR** at last securing a second goal for the 'Sappers'.

11th March 1876: Wanderers 1 Old Etonians 1

1-0 (35 mins.): *The Sportsman.* For nearly half an hour the Etonians kept their opponents at bay, but at last Wollaston getting the ball cleverly past Thompson, took it into the centre, and thence Hawley **EDWARDS**, by a cleverly directed kick, shot it just under the bar of the Eton goal.
The Field. It was left for Wollaston and **EDWARDS** to compass the downfall of the Eton goal, the latter securing this result by a well-aimed kick just under the ball [probably a misprint for 'bar'; see the description in *The Sportsman* report] after the ball had been well brought to him by Wollaston.
The Sporting Life. A general advance on the part of the Wanderers enabled Wollaston and Hawley **EDWARDS** to obtain the first goal in the match after about thirty-five minutes play.
Bell's Life in London. The game was carried on with great spirit by both sides without much advantage to either for thirty-five minutes, when some capital play on the part of the Wanderers enabled them to score a goal, kicked by Hawley **EDWARDS**.
1-1 (50 mins.): *The Sportsman.* After the change of ends the Etonians set to work to make the best use of their opportunities, and they soon began to menace the Wanderers' positions. In a few minutes a corner kick fell to Eton, and neatly directed by Meysey Thompson, the result was a scrimmage, in which the Eton forwards scored a goal though the posts had been overturned in the rush.
The Field. The change of positions of course transferred both wind and sun to the Etonians and at first the Wanderers were a little abroad. Before long a corner kick fell to Eton, and after a good shot by Thompson the ball was carried between the Wanderers' posts which had been torn up in the scrimmage, by the forwards.
The Sporting Life. Ends had to be changed. Not many minutes then had elapsed before a general attack was made upon the Wanderers' goal, which fell in more senses than one, as owing to the wind and its defenders being forced back upon the posts, they were knocked down, and ball, Wanderers, and Etonians in a body went through the space between them which the tape should have covered. Thus both sides were equal.
Bell's Life in London. After half time the Old Etonians had the advantage of the wind, and they were not long in equalising matters, the ball going between the Wanderers' posts out of a loose scrimmage.
NOTE: Modern publications credit **BONSOR** with this goal but no sources are given and he cannot be confirmed from contemporary reports.

18th March 1876 (replay): Wanderers 3 Old Etonians 0
1-0 (30 mins.): *The Sportsman.* The Wanderers were steadily getting into form, and as time progressed their forwards improved visibly in their style of playing together. Half an hour elapsed without noteworthy incident, but here H. Heron and Wollaston took the ball down the side, and a general attack of the forwards carried the Eton goal, **WOLLASTON** administering the successful kick.
The Field. For half an hour the Eton backs resisted the onslaught of the opposite forwards; but at length **WOLLASTON** eluded the half backs, and, after some tough play in front of the posts, landed a goal for the Wanderers amidst some little excitement.
The Sporting Life. For about half an hour the play was of a very even character, whilst 'free' kicks abounded through the same vexatious and unmeaning calls of 'hands' which had been so frequent during the last match. A general charge on the part of the Wanderers then enabled them to score a goal, **WOLLASTON** being the player credited with the final kick, and this was almost directly afterwards followed by a second.
2-0 (33 mins.): *The Sportsman.* The ball was kicked off again without delay, and the Wanderers, taking advantage of a momentary abatement of energy on the side of the Etonians, took the ball in a body to the Eton goal, and **HUGHES** amidst great applause planted the ball for the second time between the Eton posts.
The Field. Not content with this one success, the Wanderer forwards made a desperate rush immediately the ball had been kicked off, and again carrying it in a body into the Eton lines, secured their second goal through the aid of a well-timed kick from the foot of **T.B. HUGHES**.
The Sporting Life. [The first goal] was almost directly afterwards followed by a second, kicked by **HUGHES**.
3-0 (50 mins.): *The Sportsman.* The Wanderers got to work immediately the ball was started again, and some well-concerted play by Kenrick and Hughes on the lower side, with Edwards and Heron in the centre, removed the fight again into the Eton defence, and **HUGHES** added to his other success another well-earned goal.
The Field. Within a few minutes after the kick off some fine play by Edwards, F. Heron, Kenrick and Hughes resulted in another goal, **HUGHES** again administering the final kick.
The Sporting Life. Still the Wanderers held their own, and pressing down on their antagonists quickly added a third to their previous successes.

24th March 1877: Wanderers 2 Oxford University 1 (after extra time)
0-1 (15 mins.): *The Sportsman.* The Wanderers, as usual, were by no means well together at the outset, and the Oxford forwards tried hard to profit by their opponents' want of energy. Bain and Fernandez made some excellent runs along the upper touchline, and Todd and Otter also worked hard. For a few minutes nothing fell to them, though at length a long kick by Waddington drove the ball sharply into the centre of the posts, and **KINNAIRD** inadvertantly stepped back between the posts with the ball in his hands. An immediate appeal was made to the umpires, and after some consultation the verdict was given in favour of Oxford – a decision that seemed to be quite correct, and fully confirmed by the spectators in the immediate vicinity of the Wanderers' goal.
The Field. For a quarter of an hour no score was obtained by either side; but at this point **KINNAIRD**, after stopping a long shot from Waddington, stepped back, ball in hand, between his posts, and a goal was rightly given to the University.
The Sporting Life. A corner kick, claimed by Oxford, was entrusted to Waddington, who dropped the ball into **KINNAIRD'S** hands, who staggering back, carried it through the posts just fifteen minutes after the commencement of the game.
Bell's Life in London. Some most determined play ensued for about 15 minutes, when a goal was made by the Oxonians, resulting from a corner kick, the goal-keeper on the Wanderers' side falling through the goal with the ball in his hands.

NOTE: *The Sporting Life* report on the opening goal makes it clear that Waddington's 'long kick' mentioned by *The Sportsman* was in fact a corner and therefore Kinnaird must be debited with an own goal. This was the famous 'missing goal' which has been reinstated in Cup records by the Football Association in modern times following research by Morley Farror some 20 years ago. Previously, all lists of Cup final results published from 1877 onwards recorded the score as 2-0 after extra time. It appears that the F.A. Committee, who met shortly after the final, accepted Kinnaird's assurance that he had not stepped back over the line and deleted the goal though, to be logical, the result should in that case have been amended to 1-0 and the extra time details expunged. All of the above newspaper reports confirm that the goal was a valid one.

1-1 (86 mins.): *The Sportsman.* When only a few minutes remained of time the Oxford score had not been reduced, but here a fine run by Heron along the upper side, followed by a good kick, placed the ball neatly to **KENRICK**, and the latter got it securely through the Oxford posts.

The Field. It seemed as if time must come with the one goal of Oxford undisturbed. Just before the close, however, a splendid run by Hubert Heron took the ball well down the side, and a fine middle enabled **KENRICK** to secure a goal.

The Sporting Life. **KENRICK** now made a good run and being well backed up, avoided Alington, and kicked a goal.

Bell's Life in London. This looked like being a most unfortunate piece of business for the Wanderers, for, despite their most energetic play, they were unable to equalise matters until very nearly the call of time, when **KENRICK** was successful.

2-1 (97 mins.): *The Sportsman.* The captains tossed for choice of ends for the extra half hour that had been agreed upon in the event of a drawn game. The Wanderers winning, retained their positions at the Harleyford road end, and before long a corner kick fell to them. **LINDSAY** planted the ball well in the centre, and when it was headed out by Oxford he had a second kick, again directing it into the centre of the Oxford posts, this time so cleverly that the goal keeper could not save his charge.

The Field. Soon after the kick off [in extra time] a corner kick fell to the Wanderers, and after the ball had been put into the middle by **LINDSAY** it came back to him, and he sent the leather this time just under the Oxford tape, and out of reach of the goal keeper.

The Sporting Life. A fierce attack by the Wanderers led to a desperate bully in front of the Oxonians' goal-posts, through which **LINDSAY** passed the ball.

Bell's Life in London. For the first quarter of an hour the play was carried on with the greatest spirit, but after this the ball was nearly always in the Oxford territory, and the Wanderers eventually won by two goals to one.

23rd March 1878: Wanderers 3 Royal Engineers 1

1-0 (5 mins.): *The Sportsman.* The Wanderers were quickly at work, and Kinnaird had an unsuccessful shot at the opposite goal. Immediately afterwards Wace at the end of a short run crossed the ball, and **KENRICK** directed it safely into the centre of the Engineers' posts, this first score being obtained within five minutes of the start.

The Sporting Life. During the first portion of the game the Wanderers secured two goals (the first kicked by **KENRICK**, and the second resulting from a free kick by Kinnaird), the ball being forced through out of a bully in front of the posts.

Bell's Life in London. At length the superior tactics of the Wanderers began to tell, and principally through the instrumentality of Wace and **KENRICK** the Engineers' colours were lowered.

The Field. The Wanderers were warm favourites, and within a very few minutes they were able to score, **KENRICK** securing the downfall of the Sappers' goal after a neat run by Wace.

1-1 (20 mins.): *The Sportsman.* The Sapper forwards gave the Wanderers little chance of rallying, and at last a good throw in by Morris enabled them to carry the Wanderers' goal with a determined rush.

The Field. After the kick off the Engineers set to work with energy, and for a time their policy of hustling the opposite backs was effective. The ball was chiefly in Wanderers' territory for nearly a quarter of an hour, and at last, after a well-directed throw from touch by Morris, the ball was carried through the Wanderers' posts in a scrimmage.

The Sporting Life. The Engineers scored a goal out of a bully that ensued immediately after an excellent throw in by Morris.

Bell's Life in London. The Sappers were not to be denied, however, and a throw in by Morris was so well directed that out of a scrummage which ensued, the ball was forced through. Matters were thus equalised.

NOTE: No sources, contemporary or modern, have identified the scorer of this goal by the Royal Engineers.

2-1 (35 mins.): *The Sportsman*. The Engineers held a momentary advantage, but the Wanderers were not to be settled, and at length they carried the ball down the ground in fine style, just missing another score. Shortly after the Wanderers again made a sharp attack, and after a free kick by Kinnaird the ball was a second time driven between the Engineers' posts.

The Field. The Wanderers forwards, who had the pace of their opponents, steadily succeeded in clearing their lines, some fine runs being made by Denton and Kenrick on the lower side of the ground. A free kick soon fell to Kinnaird, and, after a short scrimmage, a second goal was secured for the Wanderers. During the ten minutes that remained of the first half some spirited play was shown on both sides, but no further result was obtained.

The Sporting Life. During the first portion of the game the Wanderers secured two goals (the first kicked by Kenrick, and the second resulting from a free kick by Kinnaird), the ball being forced through out of a bully in front of the posts.

Bell's Life in London. Before half-time a second goal was secured by the Wanderers out of a short tussle in front of the Wanderers' posts. [a mistake in the report: it should be Engineers' posts]

NOTE: Modern publications credit **KINNAIRD** with this goal but no sources are given and he cannot be confirmed from contemporary reports.

3-1 (65 mins.): *The Sportsman*. The Wanderers, as they have always done on previous occasions, improved as time advanced, and after a very fine run by Heron, **KENRICK** landed the third goal for them. This third score was obtained about twenty-five minutes before the finish.

The Field. The Wanderers now began to press rather heavily on their adversaries, and a miss-kick by Morris enabled Heron to get well away on the upper side, the result of a neat middle being another goal for the Wanderers from the foot of **KENRICK**.

Bell's Life in London. A splendid piece of play by **KENRICK** and Heron enabled the former to again score, and as this was the last point of importance, the Wanderers were at the call of time left masters of the situation.

The Sporting Life. Some splendid play by **KENRICK** and Heron then resulted in the former adding another notch to the score of the Wanderers.

29th March 1879: Old Etonians 1 Clapham Rovers 0

1-0 (65 mins.): *The Sportsman*. The Rovers' backs never relaxed their efforts for a moment, but as the game advanced the forwards flagged. The Etonians gradually took the lead, and twenty-five minutes before the finish, after a good run along the centre, Goodhart crossed neatly to **CLERKE**, and the latter with a clever shot landed the ball just within the Rovers' posts, this score forming the signal for enthusiastic applause from the partisans of Eton.

The Field. Goodhart ran the ball down, and crossed it judiciously to **CLERKE**, who, amid the enthusiastic cheers of the Etonian partisans, cleverly kicked the ball between the posts.

10th April 1880: Clapham Rovers 1 Oxford University 0

1-0 (84 mins.): *The Sportsman*. Lloyd-Jones was always busy on the lower side for the Rovers, and at last, just six minutes before time, after a good run along the centre by Sparks, a mis-kick by King gave the Clapham forwards a clear shot, and **LLOYD-JONES** took advantage of the opportunity to secure a goal for the Rovers amidst vociferous cheering, throwing up of hats, and other demonstrations of delight from their supporters.
The Field. The play thus proceeded, everyone expecting that the match would be drawn. About six minutes before the call of time, however, Sparks conducted the ball up to within about six yards of the University goal; and, as King made a very weak kick, **LLOYD-JONES**, who had followed well up, shot it between the posts. This feat quite 'brought down the house.'
The Sporting Life. The game was now carried on so evenly that a draw appeared imminent, but about ten minutes before 'time' a splendid run by Sparks enabled **LLOYD-JONES** to kick a goal for the Rovers, amid tremendous enthusiasm and excitement.

9th April 1881: Old Carthusians 3 Old Etonians 0

1-0 (25 mins.): *The Sportsman*. Play for a time was pretty even, until the O.C.'s got the leather well into their opponents' ground, and at ten minutes past four **WYNYARD** kicked a goal.
The Field. Whitfeld effected some wonderfully fine runs along the left side of the ground, but each time he was well stopped by Richards. Goodhart and Foley also made determined incursions, but the Carthusian backs proved equal to the occasion. At length the latter's forwards organised a well-timed rush, and the ball went into touch about ten yards from their opponents' lines. Prinsep took the throw in, which he did so cleverly that **WYNYARD** was able to send the ball between the posts, thus securing the first goal for Charterhouse within half an hour's play.
The Sporting Life. When the game had lasted half an hour, from a corner kick by Prinsep the ball was sent through out of a general bully in front of the Etonians' goal.
The Carthusian. A corner then fell to the Carthusians, and Wynyard almost headed the ball through. After two more close but ineffectual attempts to score, Prinsep threw the ball well in, and **WYNYARD** kicked it between the posts.
2-0 (75 mins.): *The Sportsman*. The play for some time was carried on first one side, then on the other, until Prinsep made a capital run down, passing to Page, who took his kick and sent the ball into Rawlinson's hands, when the latter middling gave **PARRY** an easy chance, and at 5 p.m. he obtained a goal.
The Field. Repeated attacks were made by the Carthusians, but for a considerable time the capital defensive play of the Etonians prevented any mishap. At length, however, the determined play of their rivals received its reward. Page and Parry passed and repassed the ball capitally to each other, and Rawlinson just contrived to save the first attack. **PARRY**, however, returned to the charge, and at the second attempt the ball was shot between the posts.
The Sporting Life. On ends being changed Parry quickly gained a goal for his side, but the score was disallowed on the plea of off-side. **PARRY**, however, shortly was the means of adding another goal to the Carthusians' account.
The Carthusian. The sides changed ends. Eton now had the wind at their backs, and a corner nearly caused the downfall of their opponents' goal. Charterhouse, however, quickly reasserted themselves, and a combined run on the part of Page and **PARRY** ended in a goal being kicked by the latter.
3-0 (80 mins.): *The Sportsman*. Within a few minutes Page again distinguished himself with a telling run, and passing to **TOD**, the latter obtained a goal.
The Field. All hopes of Eton retrieving their losses now seemed groundless, and their misfortunes were increased by a third disaster, as Richards made a kick at goal, and the ball glanced between the posts off **TOD**'s breast, thus giving a third score to Charterhouse.
The Sporting Life. A third was scored, the ball going between the posts off the body of one of the Etonians.

The Carthusian. This was soon followed by a third disaster for the Etonians, as the ball glanced between the posts off **Tod**'s chest.

25th March 1882: Old Etonians 1 Blackburn Rovers 0

1-0 (8 mins.): *The Sportsman.* The brothers Hargreaves, Strachan and Douglas showed some beautiful form, when 'hands' were given to the Rovers in the centre. McIntyre took the kick, and a general scrimmage followed close to the Eton goal, the result being a corner to the Rovers. Douglas was entrusted with the kick, and middled well, but Kinnaird once more relieved his side, and passing to Macaulay the latter made a splendid run down the left, being assisted by Dunn. The latter passed to **Anderson**, who, with a splendid side-shot with the wind, kicked the first goal for Eton, amid wild enthusiasm, just ten minutes from the start.

The Sporting Life. The Southerners made a rapid succession of vigorous attacks, and keeping the ball well down in the neighbourhood of the Northern goal-posts, were rewarded after about a quarter of an hour's play, with a goal, the result of a brilliant run down the left side by Novelli, who finally centred the ball well to the front of the posts, through which it was kicked out of a loose and brief bully.

Bell's Life in London match report. The Etonians, with the wind, scored a goal (**Anderson**) in eight minutes from the start.

Bell's Life in London comment column. The Eton forwards were favoured, of course, in having the wind with them for the first half, and the goal got in the first eight minutes by **Anderson**, which proved to be the winning point, was due in some small measure to the rashness of the Blackburn backs.

The Field. Macaulay taking the ball on, passed to Dunn, who finished up a very fine run by crossing to **Anderson**, who took the ball before it reached the ground, and sent it through the Rovers' goal about a yard from the post low down. This was a very smartly obtained goal, and no blame could possibly by attached to Howarth, as the ball, assisted by the wind, went through with great force.

The Times. At last Dunn effected a fine run down the ground and passed the ball over to **Anderson**, who kicked it between the posts.

Note: There seems confusion about the players who made the run down the left. In a tribute paid in *The Times* at the time of his death in 1937 Macaulay is mentioned as liking to recall that he outpaced the Blackburn players and helped towards the goal, so the sequence Macaulay-Dunn-Anderson is the most likely one. The account in *The Sporting Life* crediting the run to Novelli appears to be inaccurate, as does that newspaper's estimate of the time at which the goal was scored.

31st March 1883: Blackburn Olympic 2 Old Etonians 1 (after extra time)

0-1 (30 mins.): *The Sportsman.* Bully after bully in front of the visitors' goal resulted, but it was not until just half an hour after the start that Chevalier and Macaulay ran the leather down and passed to **Goodhart**, who shot it under the tape amid a scene of wild applause.

The Field. Eton kept the ball for some time close to the Blackburn goal, through which it was forced by **Goodhart** out of a bully in which all the forwards took part.

The Field comment. At length, after a concerted run on the part of Chevalier, Goodhart and Macaulay, the Etonians gained the first point, which proved the only one in the opening half.

1-1 (65 mins.): *The Sportsman.* An attack by Yates was warded off by Rawlinson using his hands in defence of his charge. A minute or two later **Matthews** dribbled down, and taking a good shot from the wing equalised the score, Rawlinson being unable to prevent the leather from going through.

The Field. Then ensued a series of Eton rushes, in one of which Dunn was so injured as to be unable to continue. This seemingly upset the calculations of the Etonians, for the Olympians broke through their lines continually, and out of a bully a goal was kicked by **Matthews**.

The Field comment. Dunn, who had shown as much or more ability than any forward on the field, received an injury which prevented him again assisting his side. The blow seemed literally to confuse the holders, and it was surprising, so persistent were the attacks of the Olympians, that their goal was only captured once, making the score level.

2-1 (108 mins.)**:** *The Sportsman.* During the first half (quarter of an hour) the old boys kept their goal intact, but shortly after changing ends Dewhurst ran down and passed to **Crossley**, who scored the winning point.

The Field. Everything was against the Etonians, as Goodhart and Macaulay were both hurt. Still, no disaster befell them during the first quarter, though they were very much pressed. On change of ends they fought pluckily, but the odds were too much for them, and, after a run by Dewhurst, the second Blackburn goal was obtained by **Costley**.

The Field comment. It was not until ends were changed for the second time that the Blackburn players obtained the goal which gave them victory; but subsequently they were within an ace several times of improving upon their position, so thoroughly exhausted were several members of the losing team.

NOTE: The name of the scorer of the winning goal was **Costley** but *The Sportsman* transcribed it inaccurately as Crossley though *The Field* got it right.

1871-72

Date: Saturday 16th March, 1872
Venue: Kennington Oval
Attendance: 2,000
Toss: Wanderers
End chosen: Harleyford Road
Kick-off: 3.05 pm
Youngest player: Vidal 18 years 195 days
Oldest player: Bowen 35 years 352 days
Average ages: Wanderers 23 years 294 days; Royal Engineers 24 years 108 days; joint 24 years 19 days

Wanderers 1 (Betts 15)			Royal Engineers 0	
Goal	1	RC Welch	Goal	Capt. W Merriman
Full-back	2	E Lubbock	Full-backs	†Capt. FA Marindin
Half-back	3	AC Thompson		Lieut. GW Addison
Forwards	4	†CW Alcock	Half-back	Lieut. AG Goodwyn
	5	EE Bowen	Forwards	Lieut. H Mitchell
	6	AG Bonsor		Lieut. EW Creswell
	7	MP Betts		Lieut. HW Renny-Tailyour
	8	WP Crake		Lieut. HB Rich
	9	TC Hooman		Lieut. HH Muirhead
	10	RWS Vidal		Lieut. EW Cotter
	11	CHR Wollaston		Lieut. A Bogle

Referee: A Stair (Upton Park)
Umpires: JH Giffard (Civil Service) for Royal Engineers; J Kirkpatrick (Civil Service) for Wanderers

Injuries: Creswell broke his collar-bone in a charge after ten minutes play but, despite severe pain, refused to leave the field and completed the match.
Other comments: M.P. Betts played under the pseudonym A.H. Chequer. The Engineers, who were favourites, began the match with the wind and sun in their faces. Alcock had a goal disallowed after 20 minutes because of a handling offence by Wollaston; The Wanderers also hit a post; Royal Engineers had only two chances; a fine run by Muirhead brought the ball within a few yards of the centre of the Wanderers' posts. The admirable and faultless kicking of Lubbock and Thompson repulsed all of the attacks by the Engineers; the admirable way they worked together was the great feature of the match.

It was 'the fastest and hardest match that has ever been seen at The Oval ... some of the best play on their [Wanderers] part, individually and collectively, that has ever been shown in an Association game.': *The Field*.

The Cup was presented by the President of the F.A., Mr E.C. Morley, at the annual dinner of the Wanderers at the Pall Mall Restaurant, Charing Cross, on 11th April. The F.A. also gave each player in the winning team a silken badge commemorating the victory and they also received an inscribed gold medal from the committee of the Wanderers.

PATHS TO THE FINAL

Wanderers			Royal Engineers	
R1	Harrow Chequers (scratched)		Reigate Priory (scratched)	
R2	16/12/71 v Clapham Rovers	3-1	10/1/72 v Hitchin	5-0†
R3	20/1/72 v Crystal Palace	0-0*	27/1/72 v Hampstead Heathens	3-0
SF	5/3/72 v Queen's Park	0-0	17/2/72 v Crystal Palace	0-0
replay	Queen's Park (scratched)		9/3/72 v Crystal Palace	3-0

*Both teams allowed through under rule 8.   †Only 50 minutes played; result stood

1872-73

Date: Saturday 29th March, 1873
Venue: Amateur Athletic Club grounds, Lillie Bridge, West Brompton
Attendance: 3,000
Toss: Wanderers
End chosen: not found
Kick-off: 11.30 am
Youngest player: Vidal 19 years 207 days
Oldest player: Bowen 36 years 364 days
Average ages: Wanderers 25 years 44 days; Oxford University 21 years 300 days; joint 23 years 172 days

Wanderers 2
(Kinnaird 27, Wollaston 80)

			Oxford University 0	
Goal	1	RC Welch	Goal	AJ Leach
Full-back	2	LS Howell	Full-back	CC Mackarness
Half-back	3	EE Bowen	Half-back	FH Birley
Forwards	4	CHR Wollaston	Forwards	CJ Longman
	5	RK Kingsford		†AK Smith
	6	AG Bonsor		RWS Vidal
	7	Capt. WS Kenyon-Slaney		FB Maddison
	8	CM Thompson		CJ Ottaway
	9	JR Sturgis		HB Dixon
	10	†Hon. AF Kinnaird		WB Paton
	11	Rev. HH Stewart		JRE Sumner

Referee: A Stair (Upton Park)
Umpires: JH Clark (Maidenhead) for Wanderers; JR Dasent (Gitanos) for Oxford University

Comments: The morning kick-off was arranged in order for spectators to be able to watch the Boat Race later. Oxford were below full strength as their regular goalkeeper, C.E.B. Nepean, could not play. The Wanderers had to play without the half-backs, A.C. Thompson or F.H. Wilson, and the forwards, W.P. Crake and T.C. Hooman.

Early on, Smith made a series of brilliant runs for Oxford; Kenyon-Slaney had a goal disallowed when both umpires agreed an offside offence; an Oxford corner kick was foiled by Howell; after about 40 minutes Oxford moved their goalkeeper, Leach, into the attack and left the goal unattended. The second goal was blamed on this move; Oxford had several chances to score but tried to force their way through the middle and failed each time. Kinnaird showed the best form of the match with extreme brilliance in dribbling.

PATHS TO THE FINAL

Wanderers			**Oxford University**	
Exempt until final under rule 9		R1	19/10/72 v Crystal Palace	3-2
		R2	23/11/72 v Clapham Rovers	3-0
		R3	9/12/72 v Royal Engineers	1-0
		R4	3/2/73 v Maidenhead	4-0
		SF	Queen's Park (scratched)	

1873-74

Date: Saturday 14th March, 1874
Venue: Kennington Oval
Attendance: 2,000
Toss: Oxford University
End chosen: Harleyford Road
Kick-off: 3.15 pm
Youngest player: W.S. Rawson 19 years 151 days
Oldest player: Merriman 35 years 346 days
Average ages: Oxford University 23 years 146 days; Royal Engineers 25 years 86 days; joint 24 years 116 days

Oxford University 2
(Mackarness 10, Patton 20)

				Royal Engineers 0	
Goal	1	CEB Nepean	Goal		Capt. W Merriman
Full-back	2	CC Mackarness	Full-back		†Major FA Marindin
Half-backs	3	FH Birley	Half-backs		Lieut. GW Addison
	4	FT Green			Lieut. GCP Onslow
Forwards	5	RH Benson	Right side		Lieut. PG von Donop
	6	FB Maddison			Lieut. JE Blackburn
	7	WS Rawson	Centres		Lieut. HE Rawson
	8	†CJ Ottaway			Lieut. HW Renny-Tailyour
	9	Rev. AH Johnson			Lieut. HD Olivier
	10	RWS Vidal	Left side		Lieut. CK Wood
	11	FJ Patton			Lieut. T Digby

Referee: A Stair (Upton Park)
Umpires: A Morten (Crystal Palace) for Royal Engineers; CHR Wollaston (Wanderers) for Oxford University

Comments: The Rawsons were brothers in opposition; it was Birley's 24th birthday. The Engineers had spent the previous fortnight in special training for the match. They were without their best back, A.G. Goodwyn, who had been posted to India at the start of 1874; unknown to the players at the time, Goodwyn actually died in India on the day this final was played from injuries suffered in a riding accident.

A threatening run by Ottaway and Vidal was stopped by von Donop who then dribbled along the right wing as far as the Oxford back; Renny-Tailyour struck a post; a free-kick from the corner flag went between the posts of the Engineers' goal but no claim was made nor was there an appeal so the incident was ignored; late assaults by the Engineers were frustrated by the activity of Nepean.

PATHS TO THE FINAL

	Oxford University			Royal Engineers	
R1	29/10/73 v Upton Park	4-0		11/10/73 v Brondesbury	5-0
R2	22/11/73 v Barnes	2-0		26/11/73 v Uxbridge	2-1
R3	6/12/73 v Wanderers	1-1		10/12/73 v Maidenhead	7-0
replay	31/1/74 v Wanderers	1-0			
SF	28/2/74 v Clapham Rovers	1-0		28/1/74 v Swifts	2-0

1874-75

Date: Saturday 13th March, 1875
Venue: Kennington Oval
Attendance: 3,000
Toss: Old Etonians
End chosen: Gasometer
Kick-off: 3.35 pm by Onslow
Extra time: Eton won toss and chose Gasometer end
Youngest player: Stafford 20 years 84 days
Oldest player: Merriman 36 years 345 days
Average ages: Royal Engineers 23 years 331 days; Old Etonians 26 years 23 days; joint 24 years 359 days

Royal Engineers 1			Old Etonians 1 *(aet; 90 mins 1-1)*	
(Renny-Tailyour 35)			(Bonsor 30)	
Goal	1	†Major W Merriman	Goal	CE Farmer
Full-back	2	Lieut. GH Sim	Full-back	FH Wilson
Half-backs	3	Lieut. GCP Onslow	Half-backs	AC Thompson
	4	Lieut. RM Ruck		E Lubbock
Right side	5	Lieut. PG von Donop	Right side	RH Benson
	6	Lieut. CK Wood		Capt. WS Kenyon-Slaney
Centres	7	Lieut. HE Rawson	Centres	FJ Patton
	8	Lieut. WFH Stafford		AG Bonsor
	9	Lieut. HW Renny-Tailyour		CJ Ottaway
Left side	10	Lieut. AL Mein	Left side	†Hon. AF Kinnaird
	11	Lieut. CV Wingfield-Stratford		JH Stronge

Referee: CW Alcock (Wanderers)
Umpires: JR Dasent (Gitanos) for Old Etonians; JH Giffard (Civil Service) for Royal Engineers

Injuries: Ottaway had to be carried off after 37 minutes with a sprained ankle after receiving a severe kick. He was unable to return.
Other comments: The Engineers wore scarlet and blue jerseys and stockings with blue serge knickerbockers while the Etonians were in blue and white. A strong, north-easterly wind spoiled the kicking of the backs. Benson missed a fine chance from a centre by Ottaway near the start; Merriman just saved a shot from Kinnaird; in extra-time there were good rushes from Mein, Patton and Kinnaird. Onslow's neat and effective defensive play was the feature of the match.

PATHS TO THE FINAL

Royal Engineers			Old Etonians	
R1	7/11/74 v Marlow	3-0	5/11/74 v Swifts	0-0
replay			14/11/74 v Swifts	1-1
rep. 2			26/11/74 v Swifts	3-0
R2	5/12/74 v Cambridge Univ.	5-0	A bye	
R3	30/1/75 v Clapham Rovers	3-2	23/1/75 v Maidenhead	1-0
SF	27/2/75 v Oxford University	1-1	27/2/75 v Shropshire Wanderers	1-0
replay	5/3/75 v Oxford University	1-0 aet		

1874-75 replay

Date: Tuesday 16th March, 1875
Venue: Kennington Oval
Attendance: 3,000
Toss: Royal Engineers
End chosen: Harleyford Road
Kick-off: 3.05 pm
Youngest player: Stafford 20 years 87 days
Oldest player: Merriman 36 years 348 days
Averages ages: Royal Engineers 23 years 334 days; Old Etonians 26 years 26 days; joint 24 years 362 days

Royal Engineers 2			**Old Etonians 0**	
(Renny-Tailyour 15 and 75)				
Goal	1	†Major W Merriman	Goal	Capt. HE Drummond Moray
Full-back	2	Lieut. GH Sim	Full-back	MG Farrer
Half-backs	3	Lieut. GCP Onslow	Half-backs	E Lubbock
	4	Lieut. RM Ruck		FH Wilson
Right side	5	Lieut. PG von Donop	Right side	TAH Hamond
	6	Lieut. CK Wood		A Lubbock
Centres	7	Lieut. HE Rawson	Centres	FJ Patton
	8	Lieut. WFH Stafford		CE Farmer
	9	Lieut. HW Renny-Tailyour		AG Bonsor
Left side	10	Lieut. AL Mein	Left side	†Hon. AF Kinnaird
	11	Lieut. CV Wingfield-Stratford		JH Stronge

Referee: CW Alcock (Wanderers)
Umpires: JR Dasent (Gitanos) for Old Etonians; JH Giffard (Civil Service) for Royal Engineers

Changes from the first match: Royal Engineers were unchanged but Old Etonians had to replace Ottaway (sprained ankle), Benson, Kenyon-Slaney and AC Thompson (all unavailable). Drummond Moray replaced Farmer in goal and the latter went into attack; Farrer, Hamond and A. Lubbock were the other newcomers.
Injuries: Bonsor injured a knee early on but though lame continued to the end.
Other comments: The Lubbocks were brothers. There was little wind this time, in comparison with the first match. Shortly before the first goal Patton or Hamond (reports differ) handled in front of the Eton goal and the ball was put through but a goal was disallowed for offside; soon after the first goal the Engineers again had a goal disallowed for offside; Farmer went close to equalising. It was a slow game with a lot of erratic kicking compared to the first match.

1875-76

Date: Saturday 11th March, 1876
Venue: Kennington Oval
Attendance: 3,500
Toss: Wanderers
End chosen: Harleyford Road
Kick-off: 3.23 pm by AC Meysey-Thompson
Youngest player: Hon. A Lyttelton 19 years 33 days
Oldest player: Hogg 31 years 26 days
Average ages: The Wanderers 24 years 336 days; Old Etonians 25 years 78 days; joint 25 years 25 days

Wanderers (1) **1**			**Old Etonians** (0) **1**	
(Edwards 35)			(?Bonsor 50)	
Goal	1	WDO Greig	Goal	Q Hogg
Full-backs	2	AH Stratford	Full-back	JEC Welldon
	3	W Lindsay	Half-backs	AC Meysey-Thompson
Half-backs	4	FB Maddison		Hon. E Lyttelton
	5	†FH Birley	Right side	HP Alleyne
Right side	6	CHR Wollaston		AG Bonsor
	7	GHH Heron	Centres	JR Sturgis
Centres	8	CFW Heron		Hon. A Lyttelton
	9	JH Edwards		Capt. WS Kenyon-Slaney
Left side	10	TB Hughes	Left side	†Hon. AF Kinnaird
	11	J Kenrick		CM Meysey-Thompson

Referee: WS Buchanan (Clapham Rovers)
Umpires: RAMM Ogilvie (Clapham Rovers) for Old Etonians; WH White (South Norwood) for Wanderers

Injuries: Kinnaird was suffering from lameness and with 30 minutes left went into goal and CM Meysey-Thompson was also lame in the later stages.
Other comments: Bonsor is shown as the Etonian scorer in modern publications but no sources are given and he cannot be confirmed from contemporary reports. Three pairs of brothers were in the match; the Herons for Wanderers and the Lytteltons and the Meysey-Thompsons for Old Etonians. CM Meysey-Thompson appeared as 'Meysey' and AC Meysey-Thompson as 'Thompson'. The wind was blowing 'great guns'; early on, the Wanderers had three successive corner kicks but two were misdirected though one hit a post; they also won several free kicks for 'hands'; a corner taken by Maddison saw the wind blow the ball out of play; the Wanderers several times missed out on good scoring chances by hesitation; when the Etonians equalised the goalposts were overturned in the rush. There were many frivolous and needless calls for 'hands' from both sides.

PATHS TO THE FINAL

Wanderers			**Old Etonians**	
R1	23/10/75 v 1st Surrey Rifles	5-0	9/11/75 v Pilgrims	4-1
R2	11/12/75 v Crystal Palace	3-0	11/12/75 v Maidenhead	8-0
R3	29/1/76 v Sheffield Club	2-0	29/1/76 v Clapham Rovers	1-0
SF	26/2/76 v Swifts	2-1	19/2/76 v Oxford University	1-0

1875-76 replay

Date: Saturday 18th March, 1876
Venue: Kennington Oval
Attendance: 3,500
Toss: Old Etonians
End chosen: Gasometer
Kick-off: 3.30 pm by Birley
Youngest player: Hon. A Lyttelton 19 years 40 days
Oldest player: Kinnaird 29 years 31 days
Average ages: The Wanderers 24 years 343 days; Old Etonians 25 years 89 days; joint 25 years 34 days

Wanderers (2) **3**			**Old Etonians** (0) **0**	
(Wollaston 30, Hughes 33, 50)				
Goal	1	WDO Greig	Goal	FH Wilson
Full-backs	2	AH Stratford	Full-back	E Lubbock
	3	W Lindsay	Half-backs	MG Farrer
Half-backs	4	FB Maddison		Hon. E Lyttelton
	5	†FH Birley	Right side	HP Alleyne
Right side	6	CHR Wollaston		AG Bonsor
	7	GHH Heron	Centres	JR Sturgis
Centres	8	CFW Heron		Hon. A Lyttelton
	9	JH Edwards		Capt. WS Kenyon-Slaney
Left side	10	TB Hughes	Left side	†Hon. AF Kinnaird
	11	J Kenrick		JH Stronge

Referee: WS Rawson (Oxford University)
Umpires: RAMM Ogilvie (Clapham Rovers) for Old Etonians; AH Savage (Crystal Palace) for Wanderers

Changes from the first match: The Wanderers were unchanged but Old Etonians had to replace CM Meysey-Thompson (injured), Hogg, AC Meysey-Thompson and Welldon; Farrer, Lubbock, Stronge and Wilson were the replacements.
Injuries: Kinnaird played though still lame from the first match; Lubbock played though only just recovered from illness and therefore out of practice.
Other comments: A set of brothers on each side, the Herons and the Lytteltons. The weather was bitterly cold with an occasional threat of snow. The Etonians started with the emphasis on charging, their play being 'more rough than scientific'; Greig was in action several times early on 'to save the Wanderers' goal'; Alleyne made a splendid run from his own goal-line straight through to the Wanderers' goal. Free kicks abounded through too many appeals for 'hands'. Birley was of great service with his accurate and judicious kicking; Edward Lyttelton kicked with marvellous precision throughout; Alfred Lyttelton was always a source of trouble, his dribbling being very close and effective. Again, there were too many unnecessary claims for 'hands'. The Surrey CCC presented the winning XI with a gold medal apiece.

1876-77

Date: Saturday 24th March, 1877
Venue: Kennington Oval
Attendance: 3,000
Toss: Oxford University
End chosen: Harleyford Road
Kick-off: 3.15 pm by Birley
Extra time: Wanderers won toss and chose Harleyford Road end
Youngest player: Waddington 19 years 262 days
Oldest player: Kinnaird 30 years 36 days
Average ages: The Wanderers 26 years 23 days; Oxford University 21 years 179 days; joint 23 years 283 days

Wanderers (2) **2**
(Kenrick 86, Lindsay 97)

Goal	1	Hon. AF Kinnaird
Full-backs	2	AH Stratford
	3	W Lindsay
Half-backs	4	†FH Birley
	5	FT Green
Right side	6	TB Hughes
	7	CHR Wollaston
Centres	8	GHH Heron
	9	H Wace
Left side	10	CA Denton
	11	J Kenrick

Oxford Univ. (1) **1** *(aet; 90 mins 1-1)*
(Kinnaird own goal 15)

Goal	EH Alington
Full-backs	OR Dunell
	WS Rawson
Half-backs	E Waddington
	JH Savory
Right side	PH Fernandez
	†EH Parry
Centres	HS Otter
	Arthur H Todd
Left side	AF Hills
	J Bain

Referee: SH Wright (Great Marlow)
Umpires: BG Jarrett (Cambridge University); C Warner (Upton Park)

Injuries: Wollaston was hurt early in the second half and replaced Kinnaird in goal.
Other comments: Sleet and rain made the conditions very unpleasant; Oxford were aided by a stiff breeze at the start but it eased considerably later on.

Kinnaird caught the ball from Waddington's corner but stepped back over his line and a goal was awarded. Some time after the match this goal was annulled and this final appeared in all subsequent records as a 2-0 win for the Wanderers after extra time. However, without the goal, extra time would not have been necessary and so it has been reinstated by the F.A. in modern times.

After going behind the Wanderers soon obtained a corner but Fernandez put it behind; Birley took an indirect free kick for hands and put the ball between the posts but the score was ruled out; Bain shot over; Wollaston diverted a goalbound shot by Rawson; at the start of the second half the ground was becoming greasy following a heavy shower; Heron shot just over for the Wanderers then an Oxford corner placed the Wanderers' goal 'in serious jeopardy.'

PATHS TO THE FINAL

Wanderers			Oxford University	
R1	Saffron Walden (scratched)		Old Salopians (scratched)	
R2	16/12/76 v Southall	6-0	14/12/76 v 105th Regiment	6-1
R3	20/1/77 v Pilgrims	3-0	Queen's Park (scratched)	
R4	A bye		24/2/77 v Upton Park	1-0
SF	20/3/77 v Cambridge University	1-0	A bye	

1877-78

Date: Saturday 23rd March, 1878
Venue: Kennington Oval
Attendance: 4,500
Toss: Wanderers
End chosen: Harleyford Road
Kick-off: 3.40 pm by Hedley
Youngest player: Heath 20 years 30 days
Oldest player: Kirkpatrick 37 years 1 day
Average ages: The Wanderers 27 years 217 days; Royal Engineers 22 years 179 days; joint 25 years 15 days

Wanderers (2) **3**			**Royal Engineers** (1) **1**	
(Kenrick 5, 65, ?Kinnaird 35)			(unknown 20)	
Goal	1	J Kirkpatrick	Goal	Lieut. LB Friend
Full-backs	2	AH Stratford	Full-backs	Lieut. JH Cowan
	3	W Lindsay		Lieut. WG Morris
Half-backs	4	†Hon. AF Kinnaird	Half-backs	Lieut. CB Mayne
	5	FT Green		Lieut. FC Heath
Right side	6	CHR Wollaston	Right side	Lieut. HH Barnet
	7	GHH Heron		Lieut. HEM Lindsay
Centres	8	JG Wylie	Centres	Lieut. CE Haynes
	9	H Wace		†Lieut. RS Hedley
Left side	10	CA Denton	Left side	Lieut. FG Bond
	11	J Kenrick		Lieut. OE Ruck

Referee: SR Bastard (Upton Park)
Umpires: BG Jarrett (Old Harrovians) for Royal Engineers; C Warner (Upton Park) for Wanderers

Injuries: Kirkpatrick broke his left arm during a scrimmage after 15 minutes but he managed to clear the ball and continued in goal to the end
Other comments: Kinnaird is shown as scoring the second goal for the Wanderers in modern publications but no sources are given and he cannot be confirmed from contemporary reports; no attribution of the scorer for the Engineers appears in either contemporary or modern sources. The Wanderers were the firm favourites while the Engineers were 4-1. Kinnaird had an unsuccessful shot early on; after the equaliser the Wanderers just missed regaining their lead; just after the start of the second half Hedley had a goal disallowed for offside.

This was the third consecutive Cup final success for the Wanderers, which meant that the trophy became their absolute property under rule 10. However, they handed it back to the F.A. with the stipulation that it could never be won outright again.

PATHS TO THE FINAL

Wanderers			**Royal Engineers**	
R1	7/11/77 v Panthers	9-1	v Union (scratched)	
R2	15/12/77 v High Wycombe	9-0	8/12/77 v Pilgrims	6-0
R3	12/1/78 v Barnes	1-1	30/1/78 v Druids	8-0
replay	26/1/78 v Barnes	4-1		
R4	16/2/78 v Sheffield Club	3-0	15/2/78 v Oxford University	3-3
replay			27/2/78 v Oxford University	2-2 aet
rep. 2			12/3/78 v Oxford University	4-2
SF	A bye		16/3/78 v Old Harrovians	2-1

1878-79

Date: Saturday 29th March, 1879
Venue: Kennington Oval
Attendance: 5,000
Toss: Old Etonians
End chosen: Gasometer
Kick-off: 3.27 pm by Ogilvie
Youngest player: Prinsep 17 years 245 days
Oldest player: Kinnaird 32 years 41 days
Average ages: Old Etonians 24 years 75 days; Clapham Rovers 23 years 46 days; joint 23 years 242 days

Old Etonians (0) **1**
(Clerke 65)

Goal	1	JP Hawtrey	Goal		RH Birkett
Full-backs	2	E Christian	Full-backs		†RAMM Ogilvie
	3	L Bury			E Field
Half-backs	4	†Hon. AF Kinnaird	Half-backs		NC Bailey
	5	E Lubbock			JFM Prinsep
Right side	6	CJ Clerke	Right side		FL Rawson
	7	MH Beaufoy			AJ Stanley
Centres	8	HC Goodhart	Centres		EF Growse
	9	JBT Chevalier			CE Keith-Falconer
Left side	10	N Pares	Left side		HS Bevington
	11	H Whitfeld			SW Scott

Clapham Rovers (0) **0**

Referee: CW Alcock (Wanderers)
Umpires: SR Bastard (Upton Park); CE Leeds (South Norwood)

Injuries: Major Marindin had kept goal for the Etonians in the earlier rounds but missed the semi-final through an injury which also ruled him out of the final. However, Hawtrey was praised for his clever play and adjudged to be a good substitute.

Other comments: Prinsep's record of being the youngest player to appear in a Cup final was surpassed in 2004 by Curtis Weston of Millwall, aged 17 years 119 days. In addition to Prinsep, Clapham had three other players aged below 20 (Keith-Falconer 18 years 169 days, Growse 18 years 264 days and Rawson 19 years 245 days). Bevington had missed much of the season through injury.

The Etonians were slight favourites; it hailed at half-time; Bailey took three fine corners which put Old Etonians under pressure; then the Old Etonians had three corners without success and from the second of these Birkett managed to tip the ball onto the crossbar; just before half-time Bevington missed an easy chance.

PATHS TO THE FINAL

Old Etonians			Clapham Rovers	
R1	9/11/78 v Wanderers	7-2	Finchley (scratched)	
R2	18/12/78 v Reading	1-0	7/12/78 v Forest School	10-1
R3	11/1/79 v Minerva	5-2	2/2/79 v Cambridge University	1-0 aet
R4	13/2/79 v Darwen	5-5	8/3/79 v Swifts	8-3
replay	8/3/79 v Darwen	2-2 aet		
replay 2	15/3/79 v Darwen	6-2		
SF	22/3/79 v Nottingham Forest	2-1	A bye	

1879-80

Date: Saturday 10th April, 1880
Venue: Kennington Oval
Attendance: 6,000
Toss: Clapham Rovers
End chosen: Gasometer
Kick-off: 3.15 pm by Heygate
Youngest player: Rogers 19 years 223 days
Oldest player: Birkett 31 years 13 days
Average ages: Clapham Rovers 24 years 169 days; Oxford University 21 years 185 days; joint 22 years 360 days

Clapham Rovers (0) 1			**Oxford University** (0) 0	
(Lloyd-Jones 84)				
Goal	1	RH Birkett	Goal	PC Parr
Full-backs	2	†RAMM Ogilvie	Full-backs	CW Wilson
	3	E Field		CJS King
Half-backs	4	VE Weston	Half-backs	FAT Phillips
	5	NC Bailey		BMH Rogers
Right side	6	H de V Brougham	Right side	†RT Heygate
	7	AJ Stanley		EH Hill
Centres	8	F Barry	Centres	FD Crowdy
	9	FJ Sparks		J Eyre
Left side	10	CA Lloyd-Jones	Left side	JB Lubbock
	11	EA Ram		GB Childs

Referee: Major FA Marindin (Old Etonians)
Umpires: CW Alcock (Wanderers); R Barker (Herts Rangers)

Comments: Clapham were slight favourites. At the start a strong, cold north-easterly wind blew into the faces of Oxford whereas after half-time it eased considerably.

The Oxford backs began in good form but the wind neutralised the force of their kicks though some huge heaves were made by King; after only a few minutes Phillips shot just wide; Lloyd-Jones, Ram and Stanley shared in some neat passing moves; Lloyd-Jones hit a post shooting from the left; the ball hit the crossbar from a shot by Ram; a good centre by Lloyd-Jones was foiled when Parr caught the ball and cleared; Brougham shot just over the bar; Birkett made three good saves in close succession; a good run by Childs down the left wing looked threatening. There was not one frivolous appeal in the match.

At the end the crowd had special cheers for Lloyd-Jones and Ogilvie, the latter not just for his play but for his 11 years of work in building up the Clapham Rovers club.

PATHS TO THE FINAL

Clapham Rovers			**OxfordUniversity**	
R1	8/11/79 v Romford	7-0	6/11/79 v Marlow	1-1
replay			10/11/79 v Marlow	1-0
R2	20/12/79 v South Norwood	4-1	19/1/80 v Birmingham	6-0
R3	17/1/80 v Pilgrims	7-0	Aston Villa (scratched)	
R4	14/2/80 v Hendon	2-0	14/2/80 v Maidenhead	1-0
R5	21/2/80 v Old Etonians	1-0	5/3/80 v Royal Engineers	1-1 aet
replay			15/3/80 v Royal Engineers	1-0
SF	A bye		27/3/80 v Nottingham Forest	1-0

1880-81

Date: Saturday 9th April, 1881
Venue: Kennington Oval
Attendance: 4,500
Toss: Old Carthusians
End chosen: Gasometer
Kick-off: 3.45 pm by Macaulay
Youngest player: Norris 18 years 1 day
Oldest player: Kinnaird 34 years 52 days
Average ages: Old Carthusians 20 years 310 days; Old Etonians 23 years 149 days; joint 22 years 42 days

Old Carthusians (1) **3**
(Wynyard 25, Parry 75, Tod 80)

Goal	1	LF Gillet
Full-backs	2	EG Colvin
	3	WH Norris
Half-backs	4	J Vintcent
	5	JFM Prinsep
Right side	6	WE Hansell
	7	LM Richards
Centres	8	WR Page
	9	EG Wynyard
Left side	10	†EH Parry
	11	Alexander H Tod

Old Etonians (0) **0**

Goal	JFP Rawlinson
Full-backs	CW Foley
	TH French
Half-backs	†Hon. AF Kinnaird
	B Farrer
Right side	WJ Anderson
	JBT Chevalier
Centres	RH Macaulay
	HC Goodhart
Left side	H Whitfeld
	PC Novelli

Referee: W Pierce Dix (Sheffield FA)
Umpires: EH Bambridge (Swifts); CHR Wollaston (Wanderers)

Comments: Two of the Old Carthusians, Prinsep and Wynyard, went on to win civilian awards for bravery, both involving attempts to rescue men from drowning. Parry became the first overseas-born player to captain a winning Cup final side. This is the only F.A. Cup final to be fought out by public school old boy teams. The Carthusians were the favourites; the Etonians had the wind against them at the start.

Richards shot behind, then Parry shot about a foot over the bar; Foley conceded a corner from which Wynyard headed over; Gillet saved a shot from Anderson; Rawlinson stopped a shot from Parry and Wynyard followed up to put the ball through but Parry was ruled offside; Kinnaird took an excellent corner but Tod cleared.

The Carthusians were in the pink of condition whereas the state of the Etonians' fitness was painfully evident after half-time.

PATHS TO THE FINAL

Old Carthusians			Old Etonians	
R1	23/10/80 v Saffron Walden	7-0	6/11/80 v Brentwood	10-0
R2	11/12/80 v Dreadnought	5-1	4/12/80 v Hendon	2-0
R3	A bye		5/2/81 v Herts Rangers	3-0
R4	19/2/81 v Royal Engineers	2-0	19/2/81 v Grey Friars	4-0
R5	19/3/81 v Clapham Rovers	3-1 aet	19/3/81 v Stafford Road	2-1
SF	26/3/81 v Darwen	4-1	A bye	

1881-82

Date: Saturday 25th March, 1882
Venue: Kennington Oval
Attendance: 6,500
Toss: Old Etonians
End chosen: Harleyford Road
Kick-off: 3.05 pm by Brown
Youngest player: Brown 19 years 237 days
Oldest player: Kinnaird 35 years 37 days
Average age: Old Etonians 23 years 324 days

Old Etonians (1) **1**
(Anderson 8)

Goal	1	JFP Rawlinson
Full-backs	2	TH French
	3	PJ de Paravicini
Half-backs	4	†Hon. AF Kinnaird
	5	CW Foley
Right side	6	WJ Anderson
	7	JBT Chevalier
Centres	8	RH Macaulay
	9	HC Goodhart
Left side	10	ATB Dunn
	11	PC Novelli

Blackburn Rovers (0) **0**

Goal	R Howarth
Full-backs	H McIntyre
	F Suter
Half-backs	†FW Hargreaves
	H Sharples
Right side	J Duckworth
	J Douglas
Centres	J Brown
	T Strachan
Left side	G Avery
	J Hargreaves

Referee: JC Clegg (Vice-President Sheffield FA)
Umpires: C Crump (President Birmingham & District FA); CHR Wollaston (Wanderers)

Injuries: French charged Avery who fell and had to retire for nearly ten minutes before half-time. His play was affected for the rest of the match.
Other comments: Blackburn were quoted as 6-4 favourites. The Hargreaves's were brothers. A stiff breeze in the first half hampered Blackburn.

Foley shot over after a Chevalier corner; a Dunn shot forced Howarth to save; Anderson sent a hurried shot wide; Novelli twice shot over after an Anderson throw-in; Dunn shot about a yard wide; Brown centred to Strachan who headed over; Anderson centred to Goodhart whose shot went between a post and the rope that supported it; Duckworth sent a side-shot right across the goal; Douglas made an excellent shot but de Paravicini jumped in to concede a corner; Rawlinson repeatedly saved the Etonians in the final 15 minutes by some excellent goalkeeping.

Bell's Life said there was not a single case of offside. It was Blackburn's first defeat of the season. The first mention of the referee's whistle in a Cup final report, *The Sportsman* stating "The whistle of the referee put an end to the game."

PATHS TO THE FINAL

Old Etonians			Blackburn Rovers	
R1	5/11/81 v Clapham Rovers	2-2	29/10/81 v Blackburn Park Road	9-1
replay	19/11/81 v Clapham Rovers	1-0		
R2	A bye		19/11/81 v Bolton Wanderers	6-2
R3	17/12/81 v Swifts	3-0	A bye	
R4	14/1/82 v Maidenhead	6-3	30/1/82 v Darwen	5-1
R5	A bye		11/2/82 v Wednesbury Old Ath.	3-1
SF	4/3/82 v Marlow	5-0	6/3/82 v Sheffield Wednesday	0-0
replay			15/3/82 v Sheffield Wednesday	5-1

1882-83

Date: Saturday 31st March, 1883
Venue: Kennington Oval
Attendance: 8,000
Toss: Old Etonians. Extra time toss not found
End chosen: Harleyford Road
Kick-off: 3.34 pm by Wilson
Youngest player: Ward 18 years 3 days
Oldest player: Kinnaird 36 years 43 days
Average age: Old Etonians 24 years 161 days

Blackburn Olympic (0) **2**			**Old Etonians** (1) **1** *(aet; 90 mins 1-1)*	
(Matthews 65, Costley 108)			(Goodhart 30)	
Goal	1	TJ Hacking	Goal	JFP Rawlinson
Full-backs	2	JT Ward	Full-backs	TH French
	3	†SA Warburton		PJ de Paravicini
Half-backs	4	TK Gibson	Half-backs	†Hon. AF Kinnaird
	5	W Astley		CW Foley
	6	J Hunter	Right side	WJ Anderson
Right side	7	T Dewhurst		JBT Chevalier
	8	A Matthews	Centres	RH Macaulay
Centre	9	G Wilson		HC Goodhart
Left side	10	JT Costley	Left side	ATB Dunn
	11	J Yates		HW Bainbridge

Referee: C Crump (President Birmingham & District FA)
Umpires: MP Betts (Old Harrovians); W Pierce Dix (Hon. Treasurer Sheffield FA)

Injuries: Dunn had to retire with a knee injury about 15 minutes into the second half and the Etonians played with ten men from then on. Goodhart and Macaulay were both injured near the end of 90 minutes but played on through extra time.
Other comments: Blackburn had spent time in special training at Blackpool and stayed at Richmond from the Thursday in order to avoid a long journey so close to the match.

Goodhart and Macaulay both shot over the bar early on; the Blackburn forwards used heads as well as feet in an effective spell of passing though Yates headed over; Dunn just missed the target with a left-foot shot; Hacking made a fine save from a corner; Foley conceded a corner to prevent Dewhurst scoring; Kinnaird shot an indirect free kick through the Blackburn posts; the better physical condition of the Blackburn players told towards the end of the 90 minutes and especially in extra time.

Olympic's tactics came under fire in *The Field*: 'When, however, the winners began to play foul – they several times incurred the penalty for charging from behind, which done upon two occasions, at least, most deliberately, and attempts at tripping were, if not always successful, pretty frequent – the Etonians were greatly discomfited.'

The Cup and medals were publicly presented by Major Marindin on the stand adjoining the pavilion for the first time. Earlier presentations had been at the annual dinner of the successful club.

PATHS TO THE FINAL

Blackburn Olympic			**Old Etonians**	
R1	4/11/82 v Accrington	6-3	4/11/82 v Old Foresters	1-1
replay			18/11/82 v Old Foresters	3-1
R2	9/12/82 v Lower Darwen	8-1	2/12/82 v Brentwood	2-1
R3	16/12/82 v Darwen Ramblers	8-0	16/12/82 v Rochester	7-0
R4	3/2/83 v Church	2-0	24/1/83 v Swifts	2-0
R5	24/2/83 v Druids	4-1	3/3/83 v Hendon	4-2
SF	17/3/83 v Old Carthusians	4-0	17/3/83 v Notts County	2-1

OVERALL PLAYING RECORDS 1871-72 TO 1882-83
Clubs playing ten games or more

	p	w	d	l	f	a	w	d	l	f	a	%won
Royal Engineers	51	24	3	1	109	16	9	4	10	28	27	64.71
Old Etonians	44	17	5	0	75	22	14	3	5	45	21	70.45
Oxford University	41	17	3	0	66	10	10	4	7	33	23	65.85
Clapham Rovers	38	20	2	2	107	16	4	1	9	20	25	63.16
Wanderers	30	12	3	2	65	14	9	2	2	31	8	70.00
Upton Park	29	12	1	4	45	17	2	3	7	19	29	48.28
Swifts	28	9	3	0	32	13	6	1	9	19	29	53.57
Maidenhead	27	9	1	3	25	11	5	1	8	16	36	51.85
Marlow	25	6	0	3	16	5	4	3	9	15	27	40.00
Darwen	23	10	1	1	50	9	3	3	5	23	31	56.52
Barnes	22	5	2	2	16	11	2	2	9	11	30	31.82
Cambridge University	22	9	1	1	22	9	1	4	6	15	21	45.45
Sheffield	21	6	3	2	26	17	2	2	6	13	18	38.10
Pilgrims	20	6	1	0	19	4	2	1	10	9	41	40.00
Old Carthusians	17	10	0	1	51	12	4	0	2	16	6	82.35
Old Harrovians	17	5	2	1	26	7	3	1	5	12	18	47.06
Notts County	16	3	3	2	23	18	3	1	4	23	19	37.50
Aston Villa	16	8	1	1	33	15	2	2	2	13	13	62.50
Sheffield Wednesday	16	5	1	1	32	10	4	3	2	19	14	56.25
Hendon	15	4	1	1	26	9	3	1	5	16	16	46.67
Blackburn Rovers	14	8	0	1	48	14	1	1	3	5	9	64.29
Nottingham Forest	14	5	1	1	24	7	3	0	4	15	11	57.14
Old Foresters	14	3	2	1	11	6	0	3	5	5	14	21.43
Stafford Road	12	3	1	1	17	6	2	2	3	17	16	41.67
Crystal Palace	12	2	0	2	8	4	0	5	3	1	8	16.67
South Norwood	11	2	0	2	8	15	1	0	6	3	16	27.27
Rochester	11	3	0	2	9	8	0	0	6	3	28	27.27
Turton	11	4	1	2	19	9	1	2	1	9	9	45.45
Remnants	10	3	1	2	15	7	0	1	3	4	11	30.00
Hotspur	10	2	2	0	4	1	2	0	4	6	14	40.00
Druids	10	3	2	0	9	2	2	1	2	5	13	50.00

Byes, walkovers and games ordered to be replayed are not included.
Games played on a neutral ground are included in the 'away' totals.

WHO'S WHO

Notes on the text
The gross amount of capital a player left on his demise according to the Probate records is shown in brackets after the date of death.

The symbol † against an appearance date indicates captain; the second half of the football season may be shown: e.g., 1872=1871-72.

The contemporary quotations on a player's style are usually from Alcock's *The Football Annual* but a few have been taken from newspapers and school magazines. Some of the phrases used in these have become obsolete and modern equivalents are: middling = centring; side = wing as in right side or 'good down a side' etc; 'last' = stamina or staying power.

The phrase 'international cap' at this period is a solecism and has therefore been avoided as a synonym for international appearances as England did not award caps until 1886. Before then, a player was said to have 'won his colours.'

A player's career details begin with school and university sides, then clubs and finally representative teams. International appearances are listed in more detail. At a time before registrations and transfers it should not be inferred that the sequence shown here means that the player moved from club to club in that order. Sometimes they made intermittent appearances for other clubs while continuing to play with their main one.

The pre-official international appearances in the career details are the five arranged by the F.A. in London 1869-70 to 1871-72 in which 'Scotland' comprised London-based players with Scottish affiliations.

The playing position or positions shown are the ones the player took in the Cup finals or filled most frequently though they often made ad hoc appearances elsewhere in the line-up; for instance a goalkeeper one week might be a centre-forward the next. See under C.E. Farmer in the Who's Who for an example of this in a drawn Cup final and its replay.

The title, military rank or clerical position that appears with the player's name at the head of each Who's Who entry is the highest one he eventually reached. Earlier ones, where known, are detailed in the entry. Civil or military honours and degrees along with some organisations are usually shown in abbreviated form.

Key to abbreviations
(commonly used ones such as JP or MP are omitted here):
AAA = Amateur Athletic Association; AAG = Assistant Adjutant General; ADC = Aide-de-camp; AMICE = Associate Member of the Institute of Civil Engineers; BA = Bachelor of Arts; BD = Bachelor of Divinity; CB = Companion of the Bath; CBE = Companion of the Order of the British Empire; CiC = Commander-in-Chief; CIE = Companion of the Order of the Indian Empire; CMG = Companion of the Order of St Michael and St George; CSI = Companion of the Order of the Star of India; CVO = Commander of the Royal Victorian Order; DAAG = Deputy Assistant Adjutant General; DD = Doctor of Divinity; D.Sc = Doctor of Science; DSO = Distinguished Service Order; FRGS = Fellow of the Royal Geographical Society; FRS = Fellow of the Royal Society; GoC = General officer Commanding; KBE = Knight of the British Empire; KC = King's Counsel; KCB = Knight Commander of the Bath; KCMG = Knight Commander of St Michael and St George; LL.B = Bachelor of Laws; LL.D = Doctor of Laws; LL.M = Master of Laws; LRCP = Licentiate of the Royal College of Physicians; LSA = Licentiate of the Society of Apothecaries; MA = Master of Arts; matric. = Matriculated; MB = Bachelor of Medicine; MCC = Marylebone Cricket Club; MD = Doctor of Medicine; MRCS = Member of the Royal College of Surgeons; MVO = Member of the Royal Victorian Order; OBE = Officer of the Order of the British Empire; Ph.D = Doctor of Philosophy; QC = Queen's Counsel; RA = Royal Academy; RAMC = Royal Army Medical Corps; RMA = Royal Military Academy; RMC = Royal Military College.

ADDISON, Lieut.-Col. George William:

b. Chestnut Cottage, Manningham, Bradford, Yorkshire, 18 September 1849;
d. 16 Ashburn Place, South Kensington, London SW7, 8 November 1937 (£52,908).
Education: Cheltenham College (Jan.1863-Dec.1866); RMA, Woolwich (1867-69).
FA Cup runner-up (2): Royal Engineers 1872, 1874.
Career: Cheltenham; RMA, Woolwich; Royal Engineers.

Full-back who, along with A.G. Goodwyn and then G.C.P. Onslow, made up a formidable defensive partnership for the Royal Engineers in their peak years. He was described as 'a very sound back' and 'playing beautifully at back.' Addison was also a useful cricketer who was a member of MCC.

Addison joined the Royal Engineers as a lieutenant on 7th July 1869, was promoted to captain in July 1881, major on 1st April 1888 and lieut.-colonel on 29th March 1895. He was in the torpedo service in Malta November 1875 to August 1877, ADC at the War Office to the Inspector-General of Fortifications August 1880-November 1882; secretary to the Royal Engineers Committee December 1882-July 1885; and Assistant Private Secretary at the War Office to the Rt. Hon. W.H. Smith, Secretary of State, August 1885-February 1886. He was assigned to the Board of Trade for telegraphic and general electrical development in July 1894 and retired from the army on 4th October 1899 to join the Guinness Company as the 1st Earl of Iveagh's personal assistant in England, retiring from this post in 1927. He was buried at Gunnersbury.

ALCOCK, Charles William:

b. 10 Norfolk Street, Bishopwearmouth, Sunderland, 2 December 1842;
d. 7 Arundel Road, Brighton, 26 February 1907 (£3,186).
Education: Harrow School.
FA Cup winner (1): Wanderers 1872†.
FA Cup final referee (2): 1875; 1879; umpire (1): 1880.
Career: Harrow (not in the XI); Forest Club; Wanderers; Upton Park; Crystal Palace; Harrow Chequers; Old Harrovians; Harrow Pilgrims; London; Middlesex; Surrey; The North. Full internationals (1): England v Scotland 1875†. Pre-official internationals (5): England v Scotland 1870†; 1871 (both matches: captain in first); 1872† (both matches).

Forward who was said to be 'a hard-working forward player, and usually a safe shot at goal', also 'a good shot in the neighbourhood of goal' and 'second to none in every department of the game.' Alcock's important place in the development of football as administrator and journalist has tended to overshadow his prowess as a player. In addition, he was at his peak during the 1860s, a period hardly looked at in detail by football historians. It is clear from contemporary match reports that he was a powerful, robust performer who often got on the scoresheet during a time when goals were relatively scarce.

He was a founder of the Forest Club at the start of the 1859-60 season and over the next decade usually took part in two or three matches a week for a variety of teams. He founded and ran the Wanderers from 1864-65, continuing as secretary until 1873-74. When a special match was arranged between the F.A. President's XIV and the F.A. Secretary's XIV on 9th January 1864 in order to try out the rules of the newly formed Association, it was Alcock who registered both goals in the 2-0 victory of the President's XIV and so became the first man to score in association football. Alcock also scored a goal in his only full international and a hat-trick when the Wanderers beat Barnes 5-0 in the 1874-75 Cup second round. His final season as a player was 1875-76, his retirement following a series of injuries over the previous couple of seasons.

Alcock also took part in other sports though here he was of only average ability. He played once in first-class cricket, for MCC v Middlesex at Lord's in 1862 when he made a duck in his only innings and did not bowl. He also played for Essex v Norfolk in 1865 when the teams were all-amateur. As a young man he took part in athletics and rackets while in later life he was a golfer, becoming vice-president of the Mid-Surrey Golf Club.

Alcock's role in the development of football ensured his place in the game's history books when most of his contemporaries had been forgotten. He was on the F.A. committee 1866-69, then hon. secretary 1870-87 which included acting as treasurer 1872-77 and finally paid secretary 1887-95. When he retired from this post he was elected an F.A. Vice-President, a position he filled until his death. Alongside the day-to-day running of F.A. affairs he was responsible for such important initiatives as the launch of genuine international matches in 1872-73, the institution of the F.A. Cup in 1871-72 and the legalisation of professionalism in 1885. After resigning as F.A. secretary in 1895 he became President of the Surrey F.A., President of the Sussex F.A., and Vice-President of the London F.A.

As if this were not enough, Alcock was also an important cricket administrator. He was secretary of Surrey CCC from 1872 until his death and was the man who established Test cricket in England when he arranged a match against the touring Australians at The Oval in 1880. It is true that three matches played earlier by English touring sides in Australia have been counted as the first Test matches but those teams were not at all representative of England's best team. Only in 1880 did a full-strength England XI oppose Australia. Alcock also had much to do with the introduction of county qualification rules in 1873, an important development in the history of the County Championship. When he took over at Surrey, the county were a struggling outfit but gradually things improved until, by the late 1880s and during the 1890s, they became the most powerful side in the country. Alcock later became chairman of the Richmond Town Cricket Ground and Athletic Association.

There was yet another side to Alcock which involves his sporting journalism. In fact it was as a 'journalist' that he described himself on census returns and the birth certificates of his children rather than as a sporting administrator. He worked for two of the leading sporting newspapers of the day, *The Sportsman* and *The Field*, was editor of *The Football Annual* 1868-1906, editor of *James Lillywhite's Cricketers' Annual* 1872-1900 and editor of *Cricket, a Weekly Record of the Game* 1882-1906. He wrote numerous articles in various books and magazines and was himself the author of several books, the most important of which were *Football, Our Winter Game* (1874) and *Surrey Cricket: Its History and Associations* (1902, jointly with Lord Alverstone).

Away from sport, Alcock began in business as a shipbroker and insurance broker but by his mid-twenties had moved into sports journalism. When he settled in Richmond in 1891 he was soon elected to the town council but he did not stand for re-election after 1894. He was also a JP. In 2002 a full-scale biography of Alcock by Keith Booth was published with a title which sums him up exactly: *The Father of Modern Sport*.

ALINGTON, Rev. Edward Hugh:

b. Candlesby, near Spilsby, Lincolnshire, 9 April 1857;
d. Bardwell Court, Bardwell Road, Oxford, 11 September 1938 (£8,146).
Education: Uppingham School (August 1867-70); Westminster School (1870-75; captain of school 1875); Hertford College, Oxford (matric 1876; BA 1880; MA 1883).
FA Cup runner-up (1): Oxford University 1877.
Career: Westminster (XI 1872-75; 1875-76†); Hertford College XI; Oxford University (Blue 1877, 1878); Old Westminsters.

Goalkeeper in his Cup final appearance but later featured as an attacker. He was described as 'a good goalkeeper; can also play forward well, though not very fast.' Alington was a capable cricketer who was in the Westminster XI 1873-75 and the Hertford College XI, earning a brief obituary in *Wisden's Cricketers' Almanack*.

Alington was the son of the rector of Candlesby and was himself a clergyman-schoolmaster. He was ordained in 1884, becoming curate at St Mark's Church, Leicester, 1884-87, then curate at St John the Baptist's Church, Summertown, Oxford, 1887-98 when he resigned his curacy. Alington was a master at Summer Fields Prep School, Oxford, in 1883, returning as assistant master 1887-1918 and finally headmaster 1918-27 when he retired. He was buried at Wolvercote Cemetery, Oxford. One of his sons was a once well-known novelist, Adrian Alington.

ALLEYNE, Herbert Percy:
b. 2 Litfield Place, Clifton, Somerset, 5 March 1855;
d. Darley Hall, Two Dales, Derbyshire, 25 November 1884 (£17,710).
Education: Eton College; Merton College, Oxford (matric. 1873; BA 1877).
FA Cup runner-up (1): Old Etonians 1876 (both matches).
Career: Eton; Oxford University (no Blue).

Forward in the Eton tradition who was praised for his 'fine runs', good play and 'hard work'. Alleyne was also a fair cricketer who was in the Eton XI in 1873.

Alleyne was a barrister who was called to the bar at the Inner Temple in 1878. He died from haematemesis (vomiting blood), probably caused by a duodenal ulcer. On his birth certificate, his second name is given as Piercy but all other sources give Percy.

ANDERSON, William Joseph:
b. Liverpool, 12 August 1861;
d. Johannesburg, South Africa, 23 June 1903 (£19,688).
Education: Eton College; Trinity College, Cambridge (matric. 1880).
FA Cup winner (1): Old Etonians 1882; runner-up (2): Old Etonians 1881, 1883.
Career: Eton (XI 1880); Cambridge University (no Blue); Old Etonians; Corinthians; Surrey; London; The South.

Outside-right categorised as a 'very hard-working forward, and of great use to his side.' He was on the original committee of the Corinthians when that club was formed in 1882.

Anderson was a man of independent means who was free to travel the world. He spent some years in Montana in the United States and later in South Africa where he died. At the time of his death his London home was at 23 Albermarle Street while in the 1890s he lived at the family property of Waverley Abbey, Farnham, where the ruins of a Cistercian monastery are still a tourist attraction.

AVEBURY, Lord:
see LUBBOCK, John Birkbeck

BAILEY, Norman Coles:

b. Streatham, Surrey, 23 July 1857;
d. The Beeches, Cowley, Middlesex, 13 January 1923 (£5,704).
Education: Westminster School (1866-74).
FA Cup winner (1): Clapham Rovers 1880; runner-up (1): Clapham Rovers 1879.
Career: Westminster (XI 1874); South Norwood; Wanderers; Clapham Rovers; Old Westminsters; Swifts; Corinthians (1886-89); Surrey; London; The South; Probables (v The Rest); England (v The Rest); Amateurs (v Professionals). Full internationals (19): England v Scotland 1878; 1879; Wales 1879; Scotland 1880; 1881†; 1882†; Wales 1882†; Scotland 1883†; Wales 1883†; Scotland 1884†; Ireland 1884†; Wales 1884†; Scotland 1885†; Ireland 1885†; Wales 1885†; Scotland 1886†; Wales 1886†; Scotland 1887†; Wales 1887†. Also selected three times for England but unavailable: v Ireland 1882; v Ireland 1883†; v Ireland 1886.

Half-back who was England's first choice in the position for ten seasons, Bailey was described as 'a very safe half-back with plenty of dash and judgment; has both strength and pace, and never misses his kick.' He played against Scotland ten times, against Wales seven times and against Ireland twice, being captain on 15 of his 19 appearances. Bailey was a founder-member of the Corinthians in 1882, on the F.A. committee 1882-84, then was an F.A. Vice-President 1887-90 when he resigned at the same time as Major Marindin as he was unhappy at the growing representation of directors of professional clubs in the F.A. council chamber. He had been a good cricketer at school and was in the Westminster XI in 1873 and 1874.

Bailey was a solicitor by profession who was admitted in March 1880 and spent his career with the London firm of Baileys, Shaw and Gillett of 5 Berners Street, which was still in existence in the 1970s.

BAIN, John:
b. Bothwell, Lanarkshire, 15 July 1854;
d. Mount Pleasant, St Davids, Pembrokeshire, Wales, 7 August 1929 (£3,690).
Education: Sherborne School; Winchester College; New College, Oxford (matric. 1873; BA 1877; MA 1882).
FA Cup runner-up (1): Oxford University 1877.
Career: Sherborne; Winchester; Oxford University (Blue 1876); Swifts; London. Full internationals (1): England v Scotland 1877.

Forward and a good team man who was said to be 'a fast, hard-working forward, always near the ball, and plays well for his side.'

Although Bain qualified as a barrister who was called to the bar at Lincoln's Inn in 1880 he did not practise. Instead he was a schoolmaster by profession who had two spells as master at Marlborough College, from 1879-83 and from 1886-1913 when he retired.

BAINBRIDGE, Herbert William:

b. Ghowhatti, Assam, India, 29 October 1862;
d. Eastwood Lodge, 55 Binswood Avenue, Leamington, Warwicks, 3 March 1940 (£69,134).
Education: Eton College (1876-82); Trinity College, Cambridge (matric. 1882; BA 1886).
FA Cup runner-up (1): Old Etonians 1883.
Career: Eton; Cambridge University (no Blue); Old Etonians.

Outside-left who was a regular with the Old Etonians throughout the 1880s though he failed to win a Blue in what was a very strong Cambridge team; however, he did play in other matches for his university. He was described as 'possessed of wonderful speed, and plays a good, fast game. Charges well.' At Eton he was a member of the Field Game and Wall Game teams.

However, it was as a first-class cricketer that Bainbridge made his mark. He played for Surrey 1883-85 under a residential qualification, then moved to Warwickshire (his father was born in Solihull) where he played 1886-1902, being captain 1888-1902, then secretary in 1903. Warwickshire were promoted to first-class status in 1894 and Bainbridge's career record at that level was 6,878 runs, average 25.76 with seven centuries. In 1897 Bainbridge was 11th in the national first-class batting averages with 998 runs at 41.58 while in 1895 he was 19th, scoring 1,162 runs at 34.17. He was in the Eton XI 1879-82 and won his Blue at Cambridge 1884-86. In addition he was captain at both school (1882) and university (1886), and also a member of MCC. He was also a good scratch golfer and at Eton won every event at the school athletic sports.

Bainbridge by profession was a merchant in Birmingham associated with the Sutton and Ash, Iron and Steel Works as well as a director of the Mitchells and Butlers brewery there. He was also a JP and owned a large collection of British birds' eggs.

BARNET, Colonel Horace Hutton:
b. Kensington, London, 6 March 1856;
d. 9 Lincoln House, Basil Street, Knightsbridge, London, 29 March 1941 (£15,000).
Education: Rugby School; RMA Woolwich.
FA Cup runner-up (1): Royal Engineers 1878.
Career: Rugby; RMA Woolwich; Royal Engineers; London; Middlesex; The South.
Full internationals (1): England v Ireland 1882.

Outside-right who was described in his early days as a 'very promising player, possessing great speed, and very useful along the side' then as 'plays right wing, very fast and clever, but middles weakly, and is a bad shot at goal.' Barnet was on the F.A. committee April 1883. He was also a good cricketer who played regularly for the Royal Engineers XI and was a member of MCC. In addition he was proficient at athletics, being a first-rate sprinter. In India he became a notable big game hunter with ten tigers to his credit.

He joined the Royal Engineers as a lieutenant on 28th January 1875, was promoted captain on 28th January 1886, major on 24th October 1894, lieut.-colonel on 1st October 1901 and retired with the rank of colonel in 1909. Barnet was posted to Bombay in 1878 then saw active service in the Afghan war of 1879 but was invalided home because of a bad sunstroke. After six months sick leave he served at Chatham Depot until 1883 when he returned to India to join the railways department then had more active service in the Burmese war of 1885-87 (medal with two clasps and mentioned in despatches). After this Barnet joined the Indian military works department where he remained until retirement. He was Executive Engineer at Quetta where he built the garrison church which was later destroyed in an earthquake. He also served at Allahabad, Multan, Calcutta, Barrackpore, Hansi and was Commanding R.E. at Lucknow and later Meerut. He was recalled from retirement for the Great War 1914-18 when he served in the intelligence branch of the War Office.

BARRY, Felix:
b. Leytonstone, Essex, 5 September 1858;
d. Holywell, Cliff Road, Eastbourne, 23 December 1933 (£5,903).
Education: Forest School.
FA Cup winner (1): Clapham Rovers 1880.
Career: Forest School (XI 1873, 1874, 1875); Old Foresters; Clapham Rovers; Essex; London.

Centre-forward with a goal-scoring penchant, Barry had a short but brilliant career and must have been in the running for international honours at times, being described as 'a hard-working and useful centre, being a sure shot at goal.' In his last year at Forest, his captain, G.B. Childs, summed him up at some length in the school magazine: 'A middle forward who dribbles excellently, has plenty of pluck, and good speed; is very successful in getting goals and very good in passing the enemy's backs. His only fault is that he sometimes goes over a great deal of unnecessary ground by dribbling from side to side instead of adopting a straighter course. Has great powers of dribbling through a 'mob' but should avoid taking the ball back into a scrimmage when in front of goal, instead of kicking it through the posts.' Ironically, when Barry gained his Cup medal in 1880, Childs was in the losing Oxford University team. Barry was also a useful cricketer and was in the Forest School XI.

After leaving school he went into a City office as a merchant's clerk to learn about business, then he spent some time in Germany at Bonn. By 1901, the census reports him to be manager of the Arundel Hotel, Arundel Street, The Strand, London, definitely an up-market establishment in the heart of the West End. However, when he made his will in 1921 he was living off income at The Wynd, Gibson Place, St Andrews, Fifeshire, and his death certificate shows him as of 'independent means'. At the time of his death his home was still at The Wynd. He died from cerebral thrombosis after developing arterio sclerosis.

BEAUFOY, Mark Hanbury:
b. South Lambeth, London, 21 September 1854;
d. Coombe House, Shaftesbury, Dorset, 10 November 1922 (£79,001).
Education: Eton College; Trinity Hall, Cambridge (matric. 1874).
FA Cup winner (1): Old Etonians 1879.
Career: Eton; Cambridge University (no Blue); Clapham Rovers; Old Etonians; Surrey.

Outside-right with the usual dash and flair shown by forwards produced via the Eton Field Game.

By profession he was a vinegar brewer with the family firm, Mark Beaufoy & Co., of Vauxhall, London, which he inherited from his father at the age of 10. Beaufoy was MP for Kennington 1889-1895, High Sheriff of Wiltshire in 1900 and a JP in Wiltshire, Surrey and London. He supported the reduction of working hours in the day to eight, a measure that he introduced into his own factory.

BENSON, Robert Henry:

b. Stang End, Fairfield, Manchester, 24 September 1850;
d. Walpole House, Chiswick Mall, Middlesex, 7 April 1929 (£116,481).
Education: Eton College; Balliol College, Oxford (matric. 1869; BA 1874).

FA Cup winner (1): Oxford University 1874; runner-up (1): Old Etonians 1875 (first match).
Career: Eton; Oxford University (Blue 1874); Old Etonians; Wanderers.

Outside-right who was said to be 'a brilliant forward at times, but a little wanting in strength; has great pace, and is a clever dribbler' also 'a good forward and very useful as a wing player; fast and dribbles well.' But Benson was better known as an athlete who won the Amateur Athletic Club (forerunner of the AAA) mile championship in 1870. He was president of the Oxford University Athletic Club in 1872 and earned his athletics Blue in 1870, 1872 and 1873. In 1870 he won the mile race, in 1872 the three miles, while in 1873 he was fourth in the mile.

Benson was the senior partner in Robert Benson & Co., merchant bankers, London. He was a collector of object d'art which included early Italian paintings and early Chinese porcelain. Benson was a Trustee of the National Gallery from 1912, a member of the council of the Royal College of Music and a JP. He had a country home, Buckhurst, at Withyham, Sussex.

BETTS, Morton Peto:

b. 29 Tavistock Square, St Pancras, London, 30 August 1847;
d. Villa Massa, St Anne, Garavan, near Mentone, France, 19 April 1914 (£40 in England).
Education: Harrow School (1862-65).
FA Cup winner (1): Wanderers 1872.
FA Cup final umpire (4): 1883, 1886, 1888, 1890.
Career: Harrow; West Kent; Wanderers; Old Harrovians; Kent; London; The South. Full internationals (1): England v Scotland 1877. He was selected for the first-ever full international v Scotland in 1872-73 but was unavailable. Pre-official internationals (3): England v Scotland 1871 (both matches); 1872.

Forward and occasional back who was summed up as 'a neat and effective dribbler, useful in any position, can play back well too' and also as 'useful in any part of the field; a safe back and a skilful dribbler; a good goalkeeper.' Betts had a long career in the game both as a player and an administrator. As usual for a product of the game in the 1860s, he excelled as a dribbler while in defence he exhibited the robust charging expected of a full-back. After serving on the F.A. committee 1871-72, Betts returned to off-the-field work throughout the 1880s. He was on the F.A. committee 1881-86, then served on its replacement F.A. Council 1887-90 and was finally a F.A. Vice-President 1890-91.

Betts was also involved in cricket almost to the same degree. He was in the Harrow XI, then played for Middlesex in 1872, Kent from 1872-81, was a member of MCC and was Hon. Secretary of Essex CCC 1887-1890.

By profession he was a civil engineer, though how he found the time to fit this in with his sporting activities has not been recorded, though he was working in South America 1873-76 and Copenhagen in 1878-80. His father was a partner in a leading firm of railway construction engineers.

Betts achieved fame perhaps above his ability by scoring the first and only goal in the first Cup final when he played under the pseudonym 'A.H. Chequer' and thus ensured that he was given a paragraph in most histories of the competition. The point of the pseudonym was that it stood for A Harrow Chequer, the club for old Harrovians of which Betts was a member. The Chequers had entered for the Cup that year, were drawn against the Wanderers in the first round but then scratched to give their opponents a walkover and leave the way clear for Betts to switch to the eventual winners.

BEVINGTON, Herbert Shelley:
b. Brunswick Square, Camberwell, Surrey, 15 December 1852;
d. 16 Becmead Avenue, Streatham, Surrey, 9 August 1926 (£5,991).
Education: Harrow School; Trinity College, Cambridge (matric. 1871; BA 1875; MA 1878).
FA Cup runner-up (1): Clapham Rovers 1879.
Career: Harrow; Cambridge University (no Blue: he was elected captain for the first University match in 1873-74 but was unable to play); Clapham Rovers; Old Harrovians; London; Middlesex; Surrey.

Inside-left who made an impression as 'a very hard-working forward, persevering and undaunted; does not play solely for himself.' Injury kept him out of much of the 1878-79 season but he was back in time for the Cup final.

Bevington was a leather manufacturer, being a partner in the firm of Bevington and Morris. At the time of his death his home was at Strathmore, 81 West Side, Clapham Common, Surrey.

BIRKETT, Reginald Halsey:

b. Bishopsgate, London, 28 March 1849;
d. Grangeside, Wimbledon, 30 June 1898 (£7,488).
Education: Lancing College.
FA Cup winner (1): Clapham Rovers 1880; runner-up (1): Clapham Rovers 1879.
Career: Lancing (XI 1866, 1867); Lancing Old Boys; Clapham Rovers; Surrey. Full internationals (1): England v Scotland 1879.

Goalkeeper who was both steady and fearless, Birkett earned the description 'a most brilliant and reliable goalkeeper; knows how to use his hands, but is apt to run out too much.' As with a number of his goalkeeping contemporaries, he operated at times as an outfield player, both in defence and attack, summed up as 'a useful man in any position, good either forward or back' and also as 'a fine half-back, being fearless, a sure kick, fast and firm on his legs, plays well, too, forward.'

He was equally outstanding as a rugby back with Clapham Rovers which played both codes. He achieved double international status as he played four times for England at rugby, against Scotland in 1871, 1875 and 1876, and v Ireland in 1877. He was a member of the original committee of the Rugby Union in 1871, while his brother, L. Birkett, and his son J.G.G. Birkett, were also England rugby internationals.

By profession Birkett was a hide and skin broker in the City of London. His death was a tragic one, following an accident sustained while suffering from delirium during an attack of typhoid fever.

BIRLEY, Francis Hornby:

b. Chorlton, Manchester, 14 March 1850;
d. Claridge's, Dorman's Land, near Lingfield, Surrey, 1 August 1910 (£37,420).
Education: Winchester College; University College, Oxford (matric. 1868; BA 1873).
FA Cup winner (3): Oxford University 1874; Wanderers 1876† (both matches), 1877†; runner-up (1): Oxford University 1873.

Career: Winchester; Oxford University (Blue 1874); Wanderers; Middlesex; London. Full internationals (2): England v Scotland 1874; 1875. Selected as captain for England v Scotland 1875-76 but unavailable.

Half-back who was considered the best of his period. It was said of Birley: 'A very fine half-back, kicking well with either foot and very difficult to pass; plays the game thoroughly.' He captained the Wanderers to two Cup final successes. Birley was also a good cricketer who was in the Winchester XI 1867 and 1868 (captain), then played for Lancashire from 1870-72 and Surrey in 1879 as well as for Cheshire. He won an athletics Blue in 1872 when he was unplaced in throwing the hammer.

Birley was a barrister by profession who was called to the bar at the Inner Temple on 26th January 1876 and then practised on the Northern circuit. He was a Surrey JP and married a sister of Jarvis Kenrick, his Cup final teammate of 1876 and 1877. Birley was a great student of ornithology.

BLACKBURN, Colonel John Edward:

b. Edinburgh, 30 April 1851;
d. 183 Ashley Gardens, Victoria, London, 29 September 1927.
Education: Trinity College, Glenalmond; Eton College; RMA, Woolwich.
FA Cup runner-up (1): Royal Engineers 1874.
Career: Eton; RMA, Woolwich; Royal Engineers. Full internationals (1): Scotland v England 1873 (2nd match).

Wing forward praised for the accuracy of his ball distribution. Blackburn gained his call-up for Scotland in his solitary international appearance because the Scottish F.A. were short of funds and could afford to send only eight players to London, relying on three already based there to make up the side. Luckily, Blackburn, the Hon. A.F. Kinnaird and H.W. Renny-Tailyour, the three concerned, were high-quality performers.

Blackburn joined the Royal Engineers as a lieutenant in 1871, was promoted to captain in 1883, major in 1890, lieut.-colonel in 1898 and colonel in 1902. He was on active service in Egypt 1882-83 and 1884-85 (medal with three clasps and large bronze star, also mentioned in despatches). He retired in 1908 but was recalled for the Great War 1915-16. Blackburn was made a CB in 1917. He was the son of a former Sheriff of Stirlingshire.

BOGLE, Major Adam:
b. Glasgow, 21 June 1848;
d. Collyers, Petersfield, Hampshire, 3 March 1915 (£26,742).
Education: Harrow School (1862-65); RMA, Woolwich.
FA Cup runner-up (1): Royal Engineers 1872.
Career: Harrow; RMA, Woolwich; Royal Engineers; Gitanos.

Forward who displayed the vigour and robust play typical of the Royal Engineers' attackers with their combined rushes on opposing defences. His career was coming to a close at the time of the first F.A. Cup competition.

Bogle joined the Royal Engineers as a lieutenant on 15th July 1868, was promoted to captain on 25th November 1880, major on 23rd July 1887 and retired on 25th May 1892 without having seen any active service. He was in Bermuda 1874-76, Gibraltar 1876-79, spent 1882-89 as instructor in fortifications at the Royal Military College, Sandhurst, and was posted to Jamaica 1889-90.

BOND, Maj.-Gen. Sir Francis George:
b. Marlborough, Wiltshire, 10 August 1856;
d. Stowe, Brackendale Road, Camberley, Surrey, 15 August 1930 (£4,753).
Education: Marlborough College; RMA, Woolwich.
FA Cup runner-up (1): Royal Engineers 1878.

Career: Marlborough (rugby); RMA, Woolwich; Royal Engineers.

An inside-left whose early involvement on active service meant that his football career was a brief one. However, after his Cup final appearance it was said of him: 'Did good service for the Engineers in the Cup-ties, keeping well on the ball and rarely missing a shot.'

Bond joined the Royal Engineers as a lieutenant in 1876, then served in the Zulu war 1879 (medal with clasp); Egypt 1882, including Kassassin and Tel-el-Kebir engagements (medal with clasp; Khedive's Star); Hazara Expedition 1891 as field engineer, 1st Brigade (medal with clasp, mentioned in despatches); NW Frontier, India, 1897-98 with Tirah Expeditionary Force where he was wounded (medal with two clasps); Boer War 1901-04 as DAAG and Chief Staff Officer, Eastern Transvaal (CB 1902, medal with three clasps, mentioned in despatches); commanded 2nd QO Sappers and Miners 1902-04; Assistant Quartermaster General in Punjab 1904-06; Deputy Quartermaster General in India 1906-08; Director-General Military Works in India 1908-11; retired 1913.

Bond was recalled for the Great War in 1914 as Assistant Director of Quartering at the War Office, becoming Director 1917-19. He was created a KBE in 1919 and other honours included CMG 1918, Knight of Grace Order of St John of Jerusalem 1918 and the American Distinguished Service Medal. He was the son of a clergyman.

BONSOR, Alexander George:
b. Polesden Lacey, near Great Bookham, Surrey, 7 October 1851;
d. 56 Rue-Locquemhein, Brussels, Belgium, 17 August 1907 (£5 in England).
Education: Eton College (1865-68).
FA Cup winner (2): Wanderers 1872, 1873; runner-up (2): Old Etonians 1875 (both matches), 1876 (both matches).
Career: Eton; Wanderers; Gitanos; Old Etonians; Surrey; London. Full internationals (2): England v Scotland 1873 (2nd match); 1875. Pre-official internationals (2): England v Scotland 1872 (both matches).

Forward of the strong bustling type, Bonsor was usually thereabouts when goalscoring opportunities turned up. He was described as 'a hard worker and excellent dribbler, his weight too tells most effectively; altogether a valuable forward'; then 'a most valuable forward, playing a straight game. His weight, too, often stands him in good stead.' Later he was 'an indefatigable forward with weight and pace; plays hard and close on the ball, though rather apt to tire towards the finish.' He was also a useful cricketer and was a member of MCC.

By profession Bonsor was a brewer with the family firm of Combe and Delafield which was incorporated with Watneys as Watney, Combe and Reid in 1898, but he spent the latter part of his life abroad in Europe where he died. He was a younger brother of Henry Cosmo Orme Bonsor who was created baronet in 1925 after many years in politics, having been MP for Surrey North-East 1885-1900. Cosmo had also played for the Old Etonians in an early round of the Cup.

BOWEN, Edward Ernest:

b. Glenmore, Co. Wicklow, Ireland, 30 March 1836;
d. Moux, near Dijon, department-de-la-Nieme, France, 8 April 1901 (£67,899).
Education: Blackheath Proprietory; King's College, London; Trinity College, Cambridge (matric. 1854; BA, 4th Classic, 1858; MA 1861).
FA Cup winner (2): Wanderers 1872, 1873.
Career: Blackheath; King's College; Cambridge University (pre-university match); Wanderers;

Old Harrovians. Pre-official internationals (1): England v Scotland 1870.

Half-back, a sturdy defender and a real veteran at the time of the first Cup final; he was aged 35 years 352 days when he played in it and 36 years 364 days at the time of his second and last appearance in 1872-73. He was a useful cricketer who was a member of MCC but in his only first-class match, for Hampshire in 1864, he bagged a pair (out for nought in each innings, for the benefit of non-cricketers). He was an all-round sportsman who also excelled at rowing, athletics, shooting, skating, cycling and mountaineering.

Bowen was a schoolmaster who began his career as an assistant master at Marlborough College in 1858, then moved to Harrow School in 1859 where he stayed until his death, a remarkable 42-year span. He was author of the Harrow School song '40 Years On' which appeared in his publication *Harrow Songs and Other Verses*. While at university he was president of the Cambridge Union in 1856, was a Fellow of Trinity in 1859 and a Bell University Scholar. In 1858 he gained a 4th Classic, in 1861 he was on the staff of the *Saturday Review* and in 1880 contested Hertford unsuccessfully in the General Election. He was the son of a clergyman and died while on a cycling holiday in France. At the time of his death his home was at The Grove, Harrow School and his body was brought back to Harrow for burial.

BROUGHAM, Harold de Vaux:

b. West Derby, Liverpool, 17 August 1858;
d. St John's House, Ryde, Isle of Wight, 26 March 1930 (£3,644).
Education: Malvern College.
FA Cup winner (1): Clapham Rovers 1880.
Career: Malvern (XI 1876 and 1877); Barnes; Clapham Rovers.

Outside-right and half-back of whom it was said 'plays a good game just behind the ups, is very fast on his legs and quick at recovering himself and getting away the ball.'

Brougham was a barrister who was called to the bar at Lincoln's Inn on 26th January 1881. He became the Senior Registrar in Bankruptcy, sometimes known as the Senior Official Receiver of Companies, and retired in 1921.

BURY, Lindsay:

b. Withington, near Manchester, 9 July 1857;
d. Stanford Wood, Bradfield, near Reading, Berks, 30 October 1935 (£52,944).
Education: Eton College; Trinity College, Cambridge (matric. 1876; BA 1880).
FA Cup winner (1): Old Etonians 1879.
Career: Eton (XI 1875-76); Cambridge University (Blue 1877, 1878); Swifts; Old Etonians; The South; England (v The Rest).
Full internationals (2): England v Scotland 1877; Wales 1879. He was also selected for England v Scotland in 1877-78 but was unavailable; for England v Scotland in the match called off because of snow on 1st March 1879 and was unavailable on the rearranged date; and for England v Scotland in 1879-80 when he was again unavailable.

Full-back who had an accurate kick plus great power, he would have played in more international games but for unavailability as can be seen above. He was said to be 'a very good back; a splendid kick; plays at times most brilliantly, but is uncertain.' He might have continued as a Cambridge Blue in 1879 and 1880 but was not selected as he preferred to play for Old Etonians in the F.A. Cup. He was on the F.A. committee in 1878. Bury was a good cricketer who was in the Eton XI in 1876, won his Blue in 1877 and also played for Hampshire that same season. In addition he gained his athletics Blue in 1878, 1879 and 1880 for throwing the hammer in which he was third in 1878, third also in 1879 and fourth in 1880.

Bury spent a period in Florida as an orange planter, then resided for a time in Wiltshire and later retired to Berkshire where he was a JP. During the Great War he served with the French Red Cross when approaching the age of 60.

CHAPPELL, Frederick Patey:
See **MADDISON, Frederick Brunning**.

CHEVALIER, John Barrington Trapnell:
b. Aspall Hall, Suffolk, 10 January 1857;
d. Aspall Hall, 17 February 1940 (£10,049).
Education: Eton College; King's College, Cambridge (matric. 1876; BA 1880; MA 1886).
FA Cup winner (2): Old Etonians 1879, 1882; runner-up (2): Old Etonians 1881, 1883.
Career: Eton (XI 1876); Cambridge University (Blue 1879); Swifts; Old Etonians; Derby County.

Centre-forward and inside-right who was described as 'a hard-working forward, possessing weight and pace' and a 'hard-working, energetic forward, very useful to his side.' It was during Chevalier's time as a master at Repton School that he turned out occasionally for the newly-formed Derby County.

After leaving university Chevalier became a schoolmaster, being assistant master at Lancing College 1880-83, then at Repton School 1883-85. On 8th May 1885 he inherited the family property in Suffolk where he established himself as a fruit grower and cider maker as well as a noted breeder of Red Polls. He was a Suffolk JP, president of the Suffolk Chamber of Agriculture in 1899 and a director of the Mid-Suffolk Light Railway. His father was a clergyman. His name sometimes appears as Chevallier but the version given here is correct.

CHILDS, Rev. George Borlase:
b. Winchmore Hill, London, 11 August 1857;
d. Brooke House, Upper Clapton, Middlesex, 4 March 1909 (£1,002).
Education: Forest School; Magdalen College, Oxford (matric. 1876; BA 1880).
FA Cup runner-up (1): Oxford University 1880.
Career: Forest School (XI 1872-74, 1875[†], 1876[†]); Oxford University (Blue 1879, 1880); Old Foresters; Swifts; Essex; London. He was selected for England against Scotland in 1878-79 but the match was postponed because of snow and he was unavailable on the rearranged date.

Attacking wing forward who was a fine exponent of the traditional dribbling style. He scored the only goal of the 1879-80 fifth round Cup replay against the Royal Engineers that put Oxford into the semi-finals and then repeated the feat in the victory over Nottingham Forest which gave the University a place in the final. He was said to be 'a useful wing player, dribbles well, but is apt to get too far forward'. This last attribute perhaps indicating that he was caught in an offside position a number of times.

He was the son of a clergyman but was only a child when his father died. Subsequently his mother owned The Green Draper's Shop in Edmonton. Childs also took holy orders and was heavily involved in missionary work. He was ordained deacon in 1881 and priest 1883.

His career was: curate at St Mary the Less, Lambeth, London, 1881-82; curate at Yorktown, Hants., 1883-86; then to Canada for Society for Propagation of the Gospels; missionary at Moosomin 1886-87, Qu'Appelle 1888, Selkirk and Winnipeg 1889-90; Organising Secretary to the SPG in the dioceses of Lichfield and Chester 1890; later curacies at Christ Church, Reading, 1896-97, Holy Trinity, East Finchley, London, 1897-1900 and St Paul's, Harringay, London; also served on SPG deputations 1890-95 and 1900-04. At the time of his death his home was at Tudor House, East Deal, Kent.

CHRISTIAN, Edward:

b. Malvern, Worcs, 14 September 1858;
d. 29 Wimpole Street, Marylebone, London, 3 April 1934 (£240,665).
Education: Eton College; Trinity College, Cambridge (matric. 1877; BA 1881).
FA Cup winner (1): Old Etonians 1879.
Career: Eton; Cambridge University (no Blue); Old Etonians. Full internationals (1): England v Scotland 1879.

Full-back who was praised as 'a fine back, kicking well with either foot'. However, Christian was soon lost to the game as he moved to Ceylon in 1881 where he spent 23 years in business. While there he featured as a prominent member of the Colombo Jockey Club. He was also a useful cricketer and was a member of MCC.

During his years in Ceylon he amassed a considerable fortune as a member of Messrs H.M. Robertson and Co. of Colombo; a director of the Bengal and North-Western Railway of India; and a director of the Pundaloga Tea Co of Ceylon. He returned to England in 1904, settling at Otterbourne House, near Winchester, where he was Lord of the Manor and a frequent prize-winner at agricultural shows. At the time of his death his home was still at Otterbourne House.

CLERKE, Charles John:

b. St George's, Hanover Square, Westminster, London, 8 September 1857;
d. Rush House, Farnborough Park, Hants, 7 November 1944 (£56,036).
Education: Eton College.
FA Cup winner (1): Old Etonians 1879.
Career: Eton; Old Etonians. He was selected for England v Wales in 1880 but was unavailable.

Inside-right and outside-right who earned praise as 'fast down a side, and a good shot when near the goal.' Clerke was also a decent cricketer who played for Herefordshire and was a member of MCC and Free Foresters.

By profession Clerke was a farmer in Hampshire where he owned an extensive number of acres.

COLVIN, Sir Elliot Graham:

b. Almora (150 miles N-E of Delhi), India, 18 July 1861;
d. Gang Bridge, St Mary Bourne, Andover, Hampshire, 2 August 1940 (£5,826).
Education: Charterhouse School (1875-78); King's College, Cambridge (matric. 1880).
FA Cup winner (1): Old Carthusians 1881.
Career: Charterhouse (XI 1878); Cambridge University (Blue 1881, 1882); Old Carthusians; The South.

Full-back who was praised as 'a good back, difficult to pass, as he has plenty of pace and always sticks to his man. At different times has filled both posts of back and half-back, and always satisfactorily.' He was also said to be 'a really first-class back; fast, clever, and a powerful kick.' Colvin was in the Charterhouse cricket XI 1876-78 (captain in 1878), also played cricket for Norfolk from 1878 and was a member of MCC. He was lost to English sport when he moved to India the year after his Cup final appearance.

Colvin followed in his father's footsteps by joining the Indian Civil Service in 1882 and over the next 36 years filled a variety of posts. Assistant magistrate in Bengal 1883; assistant in the Political Department 1884; political assistant in Rajputana 1885; private secretary to the Lieut.-Governor of Bengal 1887; first assistant agent to the Governor-General in Baluchistan 1889; Settlement Officer Saran and Champaran 1891; magistrate and collector in Champaran 1895; settlement commissioner in Alwar and Sharatpur 1896; political agent in Eastern Rajputana States 1897; Revenue and Judicial Commissioner in Baluchistan 1897; General Superintendent in Thagi and

Dakaiti 1901; Resident in Kashmir 1902; agent to the Governor-General in Rajputana and Chief Commissioner in Ajmer-Merwara 1905-17; retired in 1918.

At the end of the Great War Colvin was appointed British Delegate on the Inter-Allied Commission for War Reparations in Sofia, Bulgaria, 1920-24 and then on the Inter-Allied Commission for Assessment of Damages suffered to Turkey with headquarters in Paris 1926-30. He was created a CSI in 1906 and received a knighthood of that order in 1911.

COTTER, Colonel Edmond William:

b. Valletta, Malta, 13 February 1852;
d. 97 Cranleigh Road, Bournemouth, 23 August 1934 (£470).
Education: RMA, Woolwich (1868-71).
FA Cup runner-up (1): Royal Engineers 1872.
Career: RMA, Woolwich; Royal Engineers.

Forward and another typical Royal Engineer who revelled in rushes and scrimmages. His career, though, was restricted by military requirements; by 1873 he was involved in the Ashanti War. He was also a good cricketer who appeared for the Royal Engineers.

Cotter joined the Royal Engineers as a lieutenant on 2nd August 1871, was promoted to captain on 2nd August 1883, major on 18th January 1890, lieut.-colonel on 1st October 1897 and colonel on 1st October 1901. He saw active service in the Ashanti War on the Gold Coast 1873-74 including the defence of Quarman (medal with clasp); the Zhob Valley Expedition 1884 (field engineer); the Sudan Expedition on the Nile 1885; and the Burmese Expedition 1887-88 (medal with clasp). He was assistant engineer in India 1874-76, was in Gibraltar 1878-80, India 1883-91 with a break for the Sudan Expedition, and was back in Egypt 1892-97. Cotter went on the half-pay list on 1st October 1902 and retired on 12th October 1904. His father was an Army major who had risen from the ranks in the Crimean War.

COWAN, Colonel James Henry:

b. Chiswick, 28 September 1856;
d. Moffat, Dumfriesshire, 7 August 1943.
Education: Edinburgh Academy; Cheltenham College; RMA, Woolwich.
FA Cup runner-up (1): Royal Engineers 1878.
Career: Cheltenham; RMA, Woolwich (rugby); Royal Engineers; London.

Full-back and half-back of whom it was said 'is a very good back; is very quick and never misses his kick; very difficult to pass.' Cowan originally played rugby but as a sportsman he was most prominent in rifle shooting. While still at Cheltenham he won the Spencer Cup at Wimbledon and from 1891 onwards he shot six times in the Scottish team for the Elcho Shield. In 1893 he was one of the founders of the Army Rifle Association and that year won the Gold Jewel at the Army Championships. From then until 1905, except for two years when he was serving in South Africa and China, he always gained a high place. On 13 occasions he shot for the Army Eight and was captain 1908-11. He was a member of the team that represented Britain at the Hague in 1899.

Cowan shot for the Old Cheltonians in the Public Schools' Veterans' Trophy 41 times and led them to victory on ten occasions. His last appearance for this team was just before his 79th birthday when he scored nine consecutive bulls but dropped to an inner with his last shot, this after his usual lunch of two apples and a glass of milk. A colleague recalled: 'He was always wonderfully fit and active, and when nearing 80 thought nothing of cycling 50 miles a day.'

At the Royal Military Academy he passed out top of his batch, winning the Sword of Honour and the Pollock Medal. He joined the Royal Engineers as a lieutenant in February 1876, was promoted to captain in 1887, major in 1895, and colonel in 1908. After going through the submarine mining course at Chatham, he served in Malta with the 33rd (S.M.) Company, then at the War Office 1885-87, first in the Submarine Mining and later in the Fortifications branches. He then became instructor in fortification at the RMA, Woolwich. Cowan saw active service in the Boer War in 1899 (mentioned in despatches) before being appointed Commanding R.E., Wei-Hai-Wei, China, 1901-02, then returned home to become a member of the Ordnance Committee 1902-05. In 1906-07 he was Commanding R.E. Chatham, then assistant director of fortifications and works at the War Office, 1908-13, when he retired.

He was retained at the War Office to superintend the provision of rifle ranges for the Territorial Army and continued this work throughout the Great War. In all he arranged for the construction of 200 ranges in Britain, including ranges for the Royal Flying Corps and on not one of these ranges was there a casualty during the whole war period. He was created a CB in 1917. In 1918 he finally retired and settled at Moffat. He also had property at Boghall, Linlithgow and altogether owned about 1,300 acres. In 1880 he married the daughter of a general who was then Commanding R.E. at Chatham.

CRAKE, William Parry:
b. Madras, India, 11 February 1852;
d. 31 Norfolk, Crescent, Hyde Park, London, 1 December 1921 (£23,765).
Education: Harrow School (1866-70).
FA Cup winner (1): Wanderers 1872.
Career: Harrow (XI 1868, 1869); Barnes; Harrow Chequers; Wanderers; Middlesex; The South. Pre-official internationals (4): England v Scotland 1870; 1871 (both matches); 1872.

Forward who was a regular choice for the important matches of the early 1870s when he was said to be 'one of the neatest dribblers of the day, slow but very sure and a most skilful player' and 'very useful on the side.' Crake sometimes appeared under the pseudonym of 'W. Parry'. He was also a useful cricketer who was in the Harrow XI 1869-70 and later a member of MCC and Free Foresters.

Later in the 1870s he returned to his birthplace, India, where his father had been in business, setting up as a merchant but on retirement in 1892 came back to England. He was buried at Kensal Green Cemetery.

CRESWELL, Colonel Edmund William:

b. Gibraltar, 7 November 1849;
d. Copse Hill, Ewhurst, Surrey, 1 May 1931 (£2,322).
Education: Bruce Castle School, Tottenham, London; RMA, Woolwich.
FA Cup runner-up (1): Royal Engineers 1872.
Career: Bruce Castle; RMA, Woolwich; Royal Engineers.

Forward whose name went into the record books in the first F.A. Cup final when he broke his collar bone early on but bravely continued to the end to establish a tradition of Cup final heroism which extended at least until Manchester City's Bert Trautmann in the 1955-56 final. *The Sportsman* said 'too much praise cannot be accorded to him for the pluck he showed in maintaining his post, although completely disabled and in severe pain, until the finish.' At the time Creswell was secretary of the R.E. However, he had a short football career but was an active sportsman for a long period. He played cricket for the Royal Engineers for many years as well as for Hampshire in 1889 when that county was not ranked as first-class.

Creswell joined the Royal Engineers as a lieutenant on 8th January 1870, was promoted to captain on 8th January 1882, major on 1st August 1888, lieut.-colonel on 12th August 1895 and colonel on 12th August 1899. He was involved mainly in administrative and staff work and did not see active service before he retired on 2nd August 1900. He was assistant engineer in India 1872-80, spent 1881-88 working on ordnance survey, was posted to South Africa 1888-92 and was in the military works department in India 1897-1900. One of his sisters was married to teammate Hugh Mitchell in 1878. His father was Gibraltar's chief postmaster.

CROWDY, Francis Demainbray:
b. Donnington, Berkshire, 17 July 1857;
d. Byways, Pinhoe, Exeter, Devon, 12 February 1939 (£3,702).
Education: Westminster School (1871-76); Oriel College, Oxford (matric. 1877; BA 1881; MA 1885).
FA Cup runner-up (1): Oxford University 1880.
Career: Westminster (XI 1874-76); Oxford University (Blue 1877, 1880); Old Harrovians (guest); Old Westminsters.

Forward who earned both praise and criticism: 'Dribbles neatly, and is a good shot at goal; might do more work' and 'at times plays well forward, but very uncertain, and wants to work more.' He seems to have given up the game at a high level after leaving university, perhaps in order to concentrate on his medical studies.

Crowdy was a doctor by profession. He took his MB in 1885 and MD in 1889. He gained his MRCS England and LSA in 1885 at Oxford and St Thomas's Hospital. Then he served as a surgeon at the West Ham and South Essex Dispensary; and house surgeon and house physician at St Thomas's Hospital. He became hon. physician at St Luke's Convalescent Home & Erith House in Torquay where he was in practice in the partnership Crowdy & Dunn, at Belvedere House. Crowdy was the author of an 1898 article in the *British Medical Journal* 'Pneumothorax – paracentesis – incision – Recovery.'

DENTON, Charles Ashpitel:
b. St Bartholomew's Vicarage, Moor Lane, Cripplegate, City of London, 24 October 1852;
d. Grand Hotel, Folkestone, Kent, 28 September 1932 (£12,289).
Education: Bradfield College; Trinity College, Oxford (matric. 1872; BA 1876).
FA Cup winner (2): Wanderers 1877, 1878.
Career: Bradfield (XI 1869-72, captain 1872); Oxford University (no Blue); Swifts; Wanderers.

Inside-left and outside-left whose main weakness was pointed out in this contemporary comment: 'A fast wing player; not a good shot at goal.' Denton was also a useful cricketer who was a member of MCC.

He was admitted a solicitor in 1880 and became assistant secretary of the Union Bank of London. In 1891 he was appointed secretary of the London Assurance Corporation Royal Exchange, retiring in 1921.

At the time of his death his home was at Grosvenor Place, Westminster. His father was vicar of St Bartholomew's Church.

DE PARAVICINI, Percy John:

b. Kensington, London, 15 July 1862;
d. Hillfield, Pangbourne, Berks, 11 October 1921 (£9,323).
Education: Aldin House School, Slough; Eton College; Trinity College, Cambridge (matric. 1881).
FA Cup winner (1): Old Etonians 1882; runner-up (1): Old Etonians 1883.
Career: Eton (XI 1880, 1881); Cambridge University (Blue 1883); Old Etonians; Windsor; London; Berks & Bucks; Corinthians 1885; The South. Full internationals (3): England v Scotland 1883; v Ireland 1883; v Wales 1883. Selected for England v Ireland 1883-84 but unavailable.

Defender who was regarded as a leading exponent of his position in the early 1880s when he was said to be 'one of the best full-backs at the present time; a splendid kick with either foot; is also very fast'. He also earned praise for his 'cool judgment.' De Paravicini was on the F.A. committee in 1885 and he retired from football that year because of a sprained knee. At Eton he was Keeper of the Field and of the Wall. He was also an outstanding schoolboy cricketer who never quite fulfilled his potential in the adult game. He was in the Eton XI 1878-81 (captain 1880-81), was a Cambridge Blue 1882-85 and played for Middlesex from 1881-92. Altogether he scored 2,699 first-class runs, average 15.51, and took 32 wickets at 32.75 but he earned his greatest cricketing renown as the most brilliant fielder of his day. De Paravicini also played for Buckinghamshire and was a member of MCC. His brother, Harry Farquhar de Paravicini, also played first-class cricket.

He was the third son of Baron Prior de Paravicini and married a sister of the 4th Marquis of Cholmondeley. In 1908 he was created MVO and in 1921 a CVO. He was also a Buckinghamshire JP and for years presided over Datchet Parish Council. As chairman of the King Edward VII Hospital in Windsor he found scope for his powers of management. Ironically, De Paravicini died following an operation.

De Paravicini's most quoted feat on the cricket field came in a minor match when 15 runs were needed to win with only a few balls to go. 'Percy Para' as he was known, hit his first ball for eight and the next one for seven!

DIGBY, Colonel Thomas:

b. 20 October 1851;
d. Woodlands, Orchard Hill, Northam, Bideford, Devon, 10 June 1919 (£11,048).
Education: RMA, Woolwich.
FA Cup runner-up (1): Royal Engineers 1874.
Career: RMA, Woolwich; Royal Engineers.

Forward who had a brief football career but earned a high reputation during it. He was said to be 'most conspicuous in attack' and deserved 'extra praise' for his display in his Cup final appearance.

He joined the Royal Engineers as a lieutenant on 2nd May 1872, was promoted to captain on 2nd May 1884, major on 13th August 1891 and lieut.-colonel on 8th March

1899, retiring with the rank of colonel. He was on active service in the Afghan war 1879-80 including the Action of Besud, (mentioned in despatches) and on the North-West Frontier of India 1897-98 where he served as Commanding R.E. in the Tochi action (medal with clasp; mentioned in despatches).

Digby died as the result of a bicycle accident on 29th May 1919 near Westward Ho! golf course. A witness told an inquest that Digby was cycling not very fast down Bone Hill when he was thrown over the handlebars, falling heavily on the road. He was unconscious when the witness reached him and the bicycle was broken in two. A doctor who was called said Digby had a cut over the right eyebrow and abrasions on his elbows and hands. He regained consciousness for only a day or so about a week after the accident but could say nothing about how it happened. Medical evidence agreed that death was due to cerebral haemorrhage, probably caused by the impact when he struck the ground. Digby was buried at Northam Church.

DIXON, Harold Baily:
b. Marylebone, London, 11 August 1852;
d. Lytham St Annes, Lancashire, 18 September 1930 (£11,188).
Education: Westminster School (1865-71); Christ Church, Oxford (matric. 1871; BA 1875; MA 1878).
FA Cup runner-up (1): Oxford University 1873.
Career: Westminster (1870-71); Oxford University (no Blue); Wanderers; Middlesex.

Forward in the traditional public school style who was a founder member of the Oxford University Association Football Club when it was formed on 9th November 1871. Dixon made more of an impact in the world of mountaineering though. He undertook exploring climbs in the Canadian Rocky Mountains and was a member of the Alpine Club, the Rucksack Club, Manchester, and the Canadian Alpine Club. At school he was a good cricketer who was in the Westminster XI 1869-71 and was captain in his final season.

Dixon became a front-rank scientist who was appointed Hon. Professor of Chemistry at Manchester University in 1922 and supervised research on the ignition of gases for the Safety in Mines Research Board in 1927. He took a First Class Honours in Natural Science with his 1875 degree; was Millard Lecturer at Trinity College, Oxford, 1879-86; Bedford Lecturer at Balliol College, Oxford, 1881-86; Fellow of Balliol 1886; then succeeded Sir H.E. Roscoe at Owens College, Manchester, in 1886. He was chairman of the Royal Technical College, Salford, from 1916; chairman of Salford Higher Education Committee from 1919; and chairman of the Selective Committee for North-West District, Ministry of Labour, from 1922.

In 1891-94 he served on the Royal Commission on Explosions of Coal Dust in Mines; Royal Commission on Coal Supplies 1902-05; member of the Home Office Executive Committee on Explosions in Mines 1911-14; and member of the Alcohol Fuel Committee 1918. In 1915 he was appointed deputy inspector of High Explosives for the Manchester area during the Great War. Dixon was made a CBE in 1918, was awarded the Royal Medal of the Royal Society in 1913 and was also a D.Sc., Ph.D. and FRS. In 1907-08 and again in 1923-25 he was president of the Manchester Literary and Philosophical Society as well as president of the Chemical Society in 1909-11.

He published many works on scientific matters, especially to do with explosions of gases. These included the Bakerian Lecture for 1893, 'The Rate of Explosion in Gases'. At the time of his death Dixon's home was at The Meadows, 7 Carill Drive, Fallowfield, Manchester.

DRUMMOND MORAY, Lieut.-Col. Henry Edward (H. E. Stirling-Home-Drummond from 1884):

b. Edinburgh, 15 September 1846;
d. Blair Drummond, Perthshire, 16 May 1911.
Education: Eton College.
FA Cup runner-up (1): Old Etonians 1875 (replay).
Career: Eton; Scots Guards; Gitanos; Old Etonians.

Goalkeeper as an emergency call-up in his Cup final but usually appeared as a half-back in other matches, receiving praise for 'excellent play throughout' more than once.

As a young man he was in the Scots Guards but settled down at the family estates of Blair Drummond and Ardoch, Braco, in Perthshire. He entered Parliament as its second youngest member when he won a by-election against the Hon. Sir Fulke Greville in 1878 standing as a Conservative and had the honour of seconding the Queen's Speech that year. He was therefore only three years off being the only sitting MP to play in a Cup final. In the 1880 General Election when Disraeli's Government was ousted, he lost his seat to Sir Donald Currie, the shipping magnate and donor of the Currie Cup for South African cricket.

After that he concentrated on local politics, being Convenor of Perthshire County Council at the time of his death, was also chairman of the Western District Committee of the council, president of the Perthshire Unionist Association and a JP. He took an active part in Kincardine School Board and parish council work and was also chairman of the Ardoch Agricultural Association. In addition he was chairman of directors of the General Accident Assurance Corporation. Drummond Moray was related to some of the noblest Scottish families. His mother was a daughter of the 5th Marquess of Queensberry and he was a cousin of both the Duke of Atholl and the Earl of Mansfield. He married a daughter of the 5th Marquess of Hertford. On inheriting the Blair Drummond estate he changed his name to reflect his ancestral links.

Home Drummond died of a heart attack at Blair Drummond house after appearing to be on the mend from earlier heart trouble and on the day of his death had felt sufficiently well to attend the council's Western District committee meeting in Dunblane. He was described as 'a perfect country squire, a gentleman who took the most whole-hearted interest in his tenantry' and again 'he endeared himself to every heart through this genial, kindly, courteous manner of his.'

As a landowner he had a forward-looking attitude towards public access to the beautiful grounds of his Blair Drummond estate. One trespasser who met him near the house and hoped he would be excused for being there was told: 'Not at all. There is no harm; in fact we rather like to see people taking the pleasure of walking.' No doubt he would be pleased that today a part of the estate, which was sold by the family in 1913, is a safari park.

DUNELL, Owen Robert:

b. Port Elizabeth, South Africa, 15 July 1856;
d. Lyons, France, 21 October 1929 (£6,461).
Education: Eton College; Trinity College, Oxford (matric. 1875; BA 1878; MA 1883).
FA Cup runner-up (1): Oxford University 1877.
Career: Eton; Oxford University (Blue 1877, 1878).

Full-back who was described as 'a very safe and neat kick; a thoroughly reliable back, though a little wanting, perhaps, in pace.' Dunell was on the F.A. committee in 1878. He was a fine cricketer who captained South Africa in that country's first Test match, against England in 1888-89 when he scored 26 not out in his side's first innings total of 84. In addition, he was a member of MCC and Free Foresters. He also won his Blue at real tennis in 1878 when he was beaten in both the singles and doubles.

Dunell spent a period in business in Natal and later lived for a time at New Alresford, Hants. He died while on a visit to France and at the time his home was at 14 Brompton Square, South Kensington, London.

DUNN, Arthur Tempest Blakiston:

b. Whitby, Yorks, 12 August 1860;
d. Ludgrove, Cockfosters, near Barnet, Hertfordshire, 20 February 1902 (£24,807).
Education: Eton College; Trinity College, Cambridge (matric. 1880; BA 1884; MA 1887).
FA Cup winner (1): Old Etonians 1882; runner-up (1): Old Etonians 1883.
Career: Eton; Cambridge University (Blue 1883, 1884); Old Etonians; Granta; Corinthians (1886-92); London; Cambridgeshire; Norfolk; The South. Full internationals (4): England v Ireland 1883; 1884; Scotland 1892†; Wales 1892†.

Inside-left in the early years of his career when it was said of him: 'A good centre, rather light, but has plenty of pluck, and is a sure shot at goal' and 'has great pace, and both dribbles and middles well.' Later he moved into the defence, appearing at right-back in his two England appearances of 1891-92. Dunn was also a good cricketer at Minor County level with appearances for Norfolk from 1886 and Hertfordshire in 1898. He was a member of Free Foresters.

By profession Dunn was a schoolmaster who started as tutor to the Dunville family in Ireland 1884-85, then was at Elstree School 1885-92 and in May 1892 opened Ludgrove School of which he was headmaster. Dunn died suddenly at the early age of 41 only a few days after he had refereed a match between his own XI and Oxford University. Two days before his death he had played a game of hockey on the ice at Trent Park near the school and complained of tiredness. His final day included a visit to the House of Commons with another Etonian Cup finalist, the MP Col. W.S. Kenyon-Slaney whose son was a pupil at Ludgrove. Dunn died soon after retiring to bed for the night and was buried at the village where he had spent his childhood, Little Shelford, near Cambridge. His father was a Cambridge University maths professor and his mother the daughter of a clergyman. Dunn's daughter, Mary, born in 1900, became a well-known satirical writer.

Dunn had on his Ludgrove staff the famous England and Corinthian centre-forward of the 1890s, G.O. Smith, who took over as joint headmaster along with fellow England-Corinthian W.J. Oakley. In 1937 the school relocated to a site near Wokingham, Berks. The Arthur Dunn Cup for competition among old boy teams was instituted in his memory in 1902 a few weeks after his death, picking up on an idea that Dunn himself made shortly before.

EDWARDS, John Hawley:
b. Pride Hill, St Alkmund's, Shrewsbury, 21 March 1850;
d. Old Colwyn, Denbighshire, 14 January 1893.
Education: Shifnal Grammar School.
FA Cup winner (1): Wanderers 1876 (both matches).
Career: Shropshire Wanderers (1873-80); Wanderers; Shrewsbury (1876-80); North Wales; Birmingham & District F.A.; Staffordshire. Full internationals (2): England v Scotland 1874; Wales v Scotland 1876.

Forward who was praised as 'a useful man; being a hard worker, a strong dribbler, and an unselfish player, is apt to get a little in front of the ball.' The *Shrewsbury Chronicle* added: 'There are few better dribblers in this part of the country, his only fault being that he prefers a crooked course to a straight one.' Edwards played in full internationals for both England and Wales though at the time of his England appearance as a late replacement for J.G. Wylie, Wales had no national team. On the formation of the F.A. of Wales in 1876 he became treasurer and had a spell on the committee of the Birmingham & District F.A. He was the founder and captain of the Shropshire Wanderers who reached the Cup semi-final in 1875 and became known as 'the godfather of Shropshire football'. He captained the Shrewsbury team who won both the Birmingham Senior Cup and the Shropshire Cup in 1877-78 two years before his playing career was ended by a series of knee injuries.

Edwards was also a good cricketer who played for Shropshire 1867-76, Warwickshire (not first-class) and Shrewsbury CC, being also secretary of Shropshire for a few years. Later he became a keen angler. In 1889 he officiated as starter at the Shrewsbury Whit Monday Athletics Fete as well as at subsequent ones in 1890 and 1892. This was a major event which drew competitors from all over the country, raising money for local institutions such as Shrewsbury Town FC who benefited in 1896.

Edwards followed in his father's footsteps professionally, being admitted a solicitor in September 1871. He was Clerk to Shrewsbury Magistrates for 19 years, 1874-93, up to his death which came from a throat infection while he was convalescing at Old Colwyn.

He was always keen for a game of football and became well known across Shropshire and the north Wales border area, so much so that an attempt by Druids to strengthen their side by including Edwards under the name of 'Jones' sparked a bitter dispute with their opponents, Wrexham.

EYRE, John:
b. Shaw House, near Newbury, Berks, 29 October 1859;
d. Cleveland Square, Bayswater, London, 24 November 1941 (£721).
Education: Winchester College; Keble College (1879) & Christ Church (1880), Oxford (matric. 1878).
FA Cup runner-up (1): Oxford University 1880.
Career: Winchester; Oxford University (Blue 1879, 1880); Berkshire.

Centre-forward whose form appears to have been rather in-and-out according to this estimate of his prowess: 'A somewhat uncertain centre; at times works very hard, but hardly consistent.' He was a useful cricketer whose obituary featured in *Wisden's Cricketers' Almanack*. He played one first-class match, for MCC in 1887, of which club he was a member, and was in the Winchester XI 1876-78.

By profession Eyre was a land agent but he also undertook many civic duties for which he received the OBE. He was a Buckinghamshire JP and county councillor and also sat on the boards of a number of local hospital authorities. For a period after the Great War he resided in Switzerland.

FARMER, Charles Edward:
b. Nonsuch Park, Surrey, 26 May 1847;
d. 34 Sloane Court, Chelsea, London SW, 23 December 1935 (£8,866).
Education: Cheam School; Eton College.
FA Cup runner-up (1): Old Etonians 1875 (both matches).
Career: Eton; Gitanos; Old Etonians; Surrey; London.

Farmer had the unusual experience of being goalkeeper in the drawn 1874-75 Cup final and centre-forward in the replay! He was summed up as 'an excellent goalkeeper, being very safe and cool; plays well too as a forward.' Farmer founded and ran the Gitanos club, mainly made up of old Etonians, and served on the F.A. committee 1874-77. He was an honorary auditor of the MCC and also on the committees of MCC, Free Foresters CC and Eton Ramblers CC as well as on the committee of the All England Lawn Tennis Club. For many years he was a member of the Alpine Club while shooting and golf were also among his recreations.

He was a member of the legal profession, being admitted a solicitor in November 1872. Farmer became a clerk in the Chancery Registrar's office of the Supreme Court. He was promoted to Registrar in November 1889 then Senior Registrar in 1912 and retired in 1920. He served on the Board of the Great Northern Central Hospital; the Hospital for Sick Children in Great Ormond Street; and was chairman of the Board of Management of the British Lying-in Hospital in Endell Street. Farmer was buried at Cheam Parish Church and was brother-in-law to W.P. Crawley (first-class cricket for MCC; minor county for Somerset).

FARRER, Bryan:
b. Westminster, London, 25 November 1858;
d. Binnegar Hall, Wareham, Dorset, 23 April 1944 (£58,762).
Education: Eton College; Trinity College, Oxford (matric. 1878; BA 1883).
FA Cup runner-up (1): Old Etonians 1881.
Career: Eton; Oxford University (Blue 1881, 1882); Swifts; Old Etonians; Clapham Rovers.

Half-back who was summed up as a 'good half-back; tackles well, and plays to his forwards.' He was also a useful cricketer who was a member of MCC.

Bryan Farrer became a barrister by profession, being called to the bar at Lincoln's Inn on 20th February 1884. He practised at the Chancery Bar and retired in 1925 to the family property at Binnegar Hall. He was a Dorset JP.

FARRER, Matthew George (usually known as Matt Farrer):

b. Marylebone, London, 14 February 1852;
d. Kennington, near Oxford, 27 January 1928 (£340).
Education: Eton College; Brasenose College, Oxford (matric. 1870).
FA Cup runner-up (2): Old Etonians 1875 (replay), 1876 (replay).
Career: Eton; Oxford University (no Blue); Old Etonians; Gitanos.

Full-back or half-back, Matt Farrer was considered a doughty exponent of the former position though not so effective at half-back. He was an Oppidan in the Eton Wall Game of 1868 but was better-known as a first-class oarsman who gained his Blue in the 1873 Boat

Race. He was in the Eton eight in 1869; captained the Brasenose College boat to victory in the Ladies' Plate at Henley; won the Oxford Boat Club pairs with his brother William (Balliol) in 1873 and with H.W. Benson in 1874; and he was in the Old Etonians' crew which won the Grand Challenge at Henley in 1871.

Farrer was possibly the classic case of a square peg in a round hole. His father was a clergyman, his mother the daughter of a general and he himself became a barrister by profession, being called to the bar at Lincoln's Inn on 15th May 1878. But his heart was not really in the law, instead his real interests lay in farming affairs and country life. Accordingly he emigrated to New Zealand where he played a major role in the development of the fruit industry in the North Island. He eventually returned to England in 1906.

FERNANDEZ, Rev. Philip Hosken:

b. Madras, India, 20 February 1854;
d. Brislington House, near Bristol, 13 August 1932 (£1,227).
Education: Winchester College; Trinity College, Oxford (matric. 1873; BA 1877; MA 1880).
FA Cup runner-up (1): Oxford University 1877.
Career: Winchester; Oxford University (Blue 1876).

Forward praised for his 'excellent runs' and for backing up well. He was in the Winchester cricket XI in 1872 and achieved a short obituary in *Wisden's Cricketers' Almanack*.

Fernandez was another clergyman-schoolmaster who was ordained deacon in 1885 and priest in 1886. His educational posts were assistant master at Uppingham School 1882-89; chaplain at Sunningdale School, Berks., 1890-93; and finally assistant master at Hereford Cathedral School 1906-10. He had curacies at Newcastle, Maritzburg, 1894-95; Dundee, Natal, 1895-96; Sellack with King's Capel, Herefordshire, 1897-1904; Stretton Grandison with Ashperton, Herefordshire, 1904-05; and Thruxton with Kingstone, Herefordshire, 1905-12. He then became vicar of Hewelsfield, Gloucs., 1912-18 with a final post as rector of Dewsall with Callow, Herefordshire, 1918-26. He was granted permission to officiate in the Dioceses of Bath & Wells and Bristol & Sarum from 1927. At the time of his death his home was at Southside, The Cloisters, Bath.

FIELD, Edgar:
b. Wallingford, Berks, 29 July 1854;
d. 7 Fairfield Road, Derby, 11 January 1934 (£648).
Education: Lancing College.
FA Cup winner (1): Clapham Rovers 1880; runner-up (1): Clapham Rovers 1879.
Career: Lancing (XI 1870-71); Reading; Clapham Rovers; Berkshire; London; The South; An England XI; Berks & Bucks. Full internationals (2): England v Scotland 1876; 1881.

Full-back who usually featured on the left but occasionally played on the right. He was summed up as follows: 'A very powerful but somewhat erratic kick; charges well, but is rather slow'. He had a lengthy career, switching from Reading to Clapham Rovers in the late 1870s and then back to Reading a few years later. Field was a chartered accountant by profession.

FOLEY, Charles Windham:

b. Wadhurst, Sussex, 26 December 1856;
d. 80 Kensington Court, London, 20 November 1933 (£157,702).
Education: Eton College; King's College, Cambridge (matric. 1876; BA 1880).
FA Cup winner (1): Old Etonians 1882; runner-up (2): Old Etonians 1881, 1883.
Career: Eton; Cambridge University (Blue 1880); Old Etonians; Middlesex; London; Berks & Bucks.

Full-back and half-back who was praised because he was 'to be relied on as half-back; works hard, and plays well for his forwards.' It was also said that he 'kicked with great accuracy.' He was on the F.A. committee 1883-84. Foley also played first-class cricket, winning his Blue in 1880, the same year in which he obtained his football Blue. He was in the Eton XI in 1876, became a member of MCC and his final first-class match was for them in 1891. He was also a proficient oarsman, being captain of King's College Boat Club while at university.

Foley was admitted a solicitor and spent the years 1892-1919 in India in practice with Morgan & Co. at Hastings Street, Calcutta. He retired in 1919.

FRENCH, Thomas Harvey:
b. Worlingworth Rectory, Suffolk, 22 December 1859;
d. Lansdowne Cantonment, (now in Uttar Pradesh) India, 8 November 1908 (£4,774).
Education: Eton College; Merton College, Oxford (matric. 1879; BA 1883; MA 1886).
FA Cup winner (1): Old Etonians 1882; runner-up (2): Old Etonians 1881, 1883.
Career: Eton; Oxford University (Blue 1880, 1882, 1883†); Remnants; Old Etonians; Berks & Bucks; London.

Full-back who was praised for his 'brilliant kicking' and described as a 'good back; sure and powerful kick, with plenty of dash.' He came from a sporting family as his father was the Rector of Worlingworth, the Rev. Frederic French who played cricket for Cambridge Town Club in 1858, while his uncle was the Rev. Thomas Lee French who played cricket for Cambridge University in 1841.

French was a master at Wellington College 1884-89, then Boston Spa Preparatory School. He moved to India as tutor to a Maharajah, then was appointed Principal of Rajhumar College, Raipur, Central Provinces (now Madhya Pradesh), a post he still held at the time of his death.

FRIEND, Maj.-Gen. Rt. Hon. Sir Lovick Bransby:
b. Penhill, Halfway Street, Kent, 25 April 1856;
d. 20 Glazbury Road, West Kensington, London, 19 November 1944 (£1,537).
Education: Cheltenham College; RMA, Woolwich.
FA Cup runner-up (1): Royal Engineers 1878.
Career: Cheltenham; RMA, Woolwich; Royal Engineers.

Goalkeeper who was praised as 'a splendid goalkeeper, always cool, and a sure kick.' Friend was also a first-class cricketer who played for Kent 1886-87 and MCC 1891 as well as for Northumberland. In his six first-class matches his highest score was 72. He was also a regular choice in the Royal Engineers XI and a member of MCC.

He joined the Royal Engineers as a lieutenant in 1873 and became an instructor at Sandhurst 1883-84. He was promoted to captain in 1885 when he became secretary to the Royal Engineers Experimental Committee until 1889. Friend became a major in 1893 and saw active service in the Omdurman campaign of 1898 (medal with clasps, 3rd class Osmanieh, 3rd class Medjidieh and mentioned in despatches). In 1900 he attained the rank of lieut.-colonel and became Director of Works and Stores Egyptian Army 1900-04; Egyptian Public Works 1905; Assistant-Director Fortification Works 1906-07; commander Scottish Coast Defences 1908-12; then major-general in charge of Administration Irish Command 1912-14; and General Officer commanding in Ireland 1914-16.

Friend was appointed President of the Claims Commission British Armies in France 1916-19 (mentioned in despatches) before retiring in 1920. He was a Commander of the Legion of Honour and a Commander of the Belgian Couronne and Croix de Guerre. In 1908 he was made a CB, was on the Privy Council Ireland in 1916 and was created KBE in 1919. At the time of his death his home was at 7 Park Place, St James's, London.

GILLET, Leonard Francis:

b. Derby, 21 January 1861;
d. Austin's Close, Harbertonford, near Totnes, Devon, 23 November 1915 (£14,994).
Education: Charterhouse School (1874-79); Pembroke College, Oxford (matric. 1879; BA 1882).
FA Cup winner (1): Old Carthusians 1881.
Career: Charterhouse (XI 1879); Oxford University (Blue 1882); Old Carthusians; Notts County.

Goalkeeper who earned plaudits as 'a most sure goalkeeper, very sharp.' During his schooldays the school magazine said of him: 'Has been of infinite service to the Eleven.' He played for Notts County in the 1882-83 season including a losing F.A. Cup semi-final against the Old Etonians.

By profession Gillet became a civil and mining engineer but in later years ceased to practise as he was able to live off his income. His name sometimes appears as Gillett or Gillette but the correct version is the one given here.

GOODHART, Harry Chester:
b. Wimbledon, 17 July 1858;
d. 2 Drumsheugh Gardens, Edinburgh, 21 April 1895 (£3,016 in England).
Education: Eton College; Trinity College, Cambridge (matric. 1877; BA, 2nd Classic, 1881; MA 1884).
FA Cup winner (2): Old Etonians 1879, 1882; runner-up (2): Old Etonians 1881, 1883.
Career: Eton (XI 1877); Cambridge University (no Blue); Runnymede; Old Etonians; London; The South. Full internationals (3): England v Scotland 1883; Ireland 1883; Wales 1883.

Centre-forward who was highly praised: 'A very good forward, dribbles well and unselfishly; always in front of goal when required' and also 'a hard-working forward; sticks close to the ball, and is very dangerous in front of goal.' Among his scoring feats were a hat-trick in the Old Etonians' famous 5-5 draw with Darwen in the 4th round of the 1878-79 Cup, another in 1879-80 when the Etonians beat West End 5-1 in the Cup fourth round, three more in 1880-81 as the Etonians humbled Brentwood 10-0 in the Cup first round, a repeat performance for the OEs in the 1881-82 Cup, this time a 5-0 semi-final thrashing of Marlow, and his fifth Cup hat-trick in 1884-85 as the Etonians beat Middlesbrough 5-2 in the fourth round. Goodhart was also a lawn tennis Blue in 1881 when he won 2, lost 1 in the singles, and lost 3 in the doubles. He was also a good cricketer and was in the Eton XI in 1876 and 1877.

Goodhart had a successful academic career, launched when he was awarded several prizes at Cambridge: Brown Medal 1880;

Members' Prize 1881; 1st Chancellor's Medal 1881; Fellow of Trinity College 1881. He was a Cambridge University lecturer 1884-90 before becoming Professor of Humanities at Edinburgh University 1890-95 and was appointed to the Latin Chair at Edinburgh in 1891. Among his publications was an edition of Thucydides Book VIII.

He was one-time tutor to the Duke of Clarence who was best man at his wedding. Goodhart's death came after he had been ill for six weeks with influenza which was followed by complications. He was buried at Lower Beeding Church, Horsham, Sussex. A friend summed him up in an obituary tribute as follows: 'He combined the artist's brain with the skill and strength of an artisan.'

GOODWYN, Lieut. Alfred George:

b. Roorhir, Bengal, India (now Ruhea in Bangladesh), 13 March 1850;
d. Roorkee 14 March 1874 ('below £1,000').
Education: RMA, Woolwich.
FA Cup runner-up (1): Royal Engineers 1872.
Career: RMA, Woolwich; Royal Engineers. Full internationals (1): England v Scotland 1873 (2nd match).

Full-back and half-back, one of the earliest players to earn a big reputation as a defender who was described as 'a very fine half-back, being a sure as well as a good kick' and 'has proved himself to be a faultless back; kicking with great skill, and rarely allowing himself to be passed.' Goodwyn had played in the early rounds of the 1873-74 F.A. Cup competition, his last appearance being the third round victory over Maidenhead on 10th December 1873. He then took part in the northern tour of the Royal Engineers at Christmas, playing his last game against Nottingham Forest at Trent Bridge on 23rd December 1873. He was 'a most zealous and admirable' club secretary for a time in which role it was said he had much to do with the success of the Royal Engineers.

He joined the Royal Engineers as a lieutenant on 2nd August 1871, then on 28th January 1874 he was posted to India and after a few weeks there he had a fall from his horse, from the effects of which he died after two days illness. His death took place only one day after his 24th birthday and on the same date as the 1873-74 F.A. Cup final in which the Royal Engineers were involved. His obituarist noted: 'On Saturday last during the struggle with Oxford University (and when we little thought he was in his grave), many were the wishes that he was in his old place.' Goodwyn also played cricket for the Royal Engineers where he earned a reputation as a fine fielder at leg. His father was also an officer in the Royal Engineers (Bengal).

GREEN, Frederick Thomas:
b. Wrexham, 21 June 1851;
d. The Uplands, Church Stretton, Shropshire, 6 July 1928 (£997).
Education: Winchester College; New College, Oxford (matric. 1869; BA 1874).
FA Cup winner (3): Oxford University 1874; Wanderers 1877, 1878.
Career: Winchester; Oxford University (no Blue); Wanderers; London; Middlesex. Full internationals (1): England v Scotland 1876.

Half-back of great consistency whose ability is proved by his three Cup-winning medals, Green was described as 'a reliable half-back, being a sure kick and never irresolute.' He was a useful cricketer who was in the Winchester XI in 1869.

Green was to begin with a barrister by profession who was called to the bar at the Inner Temple on 25th April 1877 but he left the legal world in 1880 to take up a post as H.M. Inspector of Schools and moved up to the Education Office in 1890. He was buried at Church Stretton and his father was Rector of Lydham, Shropshire.

GREIG, William Dallas Ochterlony:
b. Dundee, 31 October 1852;
d. not found (last traced in April, 1901).
Education: Brighton College (1866 to summer 1868).
FA Cup winner (1): Wanderers 1876 (both matches).
Career: Brighton; Farningham; Wanderers; London.

Goalkeeper and earlier an outfield player, Greig filled the latter position for the Farningham team who lost to the Wanderers 16-0 in the first round of the F.A. Cup on 31st October 1874, a score described at the time as the biggest ever made under F.A. rules. Greig's brother, Alexander, was also in the Farningham line-up but despite the result, William must have made an impression on the Wanderers officials for they recruited him for their own club where he soon graduated to the position of goalkeeper. In this position he was noted for his activity in saving the goal while as an outfield player his good runs and good kicks were praised.

He filled the goalkeeper's role throughout the Cup-winning season of 1875-76, keeping clean sheets in each of the first three rounds. The first goal he let in came in the semi-final when Wanderers won 2-1, then there was one further concession in the 1-1 drawn final but the replay ended with a 3-0 victory so that, all told, Greig conceded just two goals in six Cup ties. However, after playing for London v Sheffield a week later, Greig disappears from sight as far as football is concerned.

His later life in general is also mysterious. No clues have been found which point to his profession and he has no entry in the 1881 census. He does, however, turn up in the 1901 census where he is shown as living at Coptfold Hall, Margaretting, near Chelmsford, Essex, with his widowed sister, Elizabeth O. Jupp, and her family. Greig's entry under 'profession' has been left blank. Coptfold Hall was part of the extensive Petre family estate of that area of Essex and by the time of the 1907 electoral register, the Jupps and Greig were no longer there.

Extensive searches, including the death registers and probate records for England/Wales and Scotland 1901-52, have failed to produce any further information on Greig's later life or his death. The most likely theory is that he went abroad after 1876, hence his absence from the 1881 census, and was home on leave when the 1901 census was compiled, which would explain why he was living with his widowed sister and her family. If this hypothesis is the correct one, then he almost certainly died abroad.

GROWSE, Edward Frederic:

b. Brentwood, Essex, 8 July 1860;
d. on board ship, Red Sea, 10 November 1905 (£5,148).
Education: Charterhouse School; Balliol College, Oxford (matric. 1879).
FA Cup runner-up (1): Clapham Rovers 1879.
Career: Charterhouse (XI 1876-77 & 1877-78†); Oxford University (no Blue); Clapham Rovers; Old Carthusians; Essex; London.

Centre-forward summed up as 'a fast forward, at times brilliant. Works hard though is occasionally rather too excitable; must learn not to get offside when backing up.' Growse was a good cricketer who was in the Charterhouse XI 1875-78 (captain in 1877) and played for Essex in 1880 in the period before they were promoted to first-class status. He was also an excellent sprinter who won his athletics Blue in 1880 and 1881, finishing second in the 440 yards on both occasions.

Growse was yet another whose sporting career ended early because he went abroad to help to run the British Empire, in his case as a magistrate with the Indian Civil Service. He died at sea while returning from India to England where his home was at 'Pallas', The Park, Cheltenham, Gloucs.

HAMOND, Thomas Astley Horace:
b. High House, West Acre, Norfolk, 17 August 1845;
d. The Abbey, West Acre, Norfolk, 5 February 1917 (£37,500).
Education: Eton College; Magdalene College, Cambridge (matric. 1864; BA 1868; MA 1871).
FA Cup runner-up (1): Old Etonians 1875 (replay).
Career: Eton; Cambridge Eton Club; Cambridge University (pre-university match); Old Etonians.

Outside-right and an exponent of the dashing Eton Field Game style, the bulk of Hamond's playing career fell into the period before the F.A. Cup really got under way. He also played cricket and was a member of MCC.

Hamond was admitted a solicitor and was in practice in Lincoln's Inn Fields in London. His family could trace its line back to the Norman Conquest and through his status in the landed gentry he was Lord of the Manor at Swaffham, Norfolk. It should be noted that the spelling of his surname is as given here and not Hammond.

HANSELL, Walter Edward:

b. Norwich, 15 November 1860;
d. Heigham Hall, Norwich, 25 May 1938 (£9,144).
Education: Charterhouse School (1873-78).
FA Cup winner (1): Old Carthusians 1881.
Career: Charterhouse (XI 1878); Old Carthusians.

Outside-right, perhaps somewhat inconsistent as this contemporary comment shows: 'A fast wing, who shows some very good play but uncertain, and sometimes appears to get nervous in matches' though later he was 'very fast and clever on the wing.' He served on the F.A. Council 1897-1900 as the representative for Norfolk. Hansell was also a useful cricketer who appeared for Norfolk in 1889 and was a member of MCC.

By profession Hansell was a solicitor and Notary Public in Norfolk from 1886. He was a partner in Hansell & Hales of Norwich and later became Under-Sheriff of Norfolk. He joined the Norfolk Infantry Volunteer Battalion in 1879, reaching the rank of captain in the 3rd Battalion in 1899. At the time of his death his home was at Pegg's Close, Sheringham, Norfolk.

HAWTREY, John Purvis:
b. Eton, Berks, 19 July 1850;
d. Hammersmith, London, 17 August 1925.
Education: Eton College 1857-64; Clifton College 1864-68.
FA Cup winner (1): Old Etonians 1879.
Career: Remnants; Old Etonians; Swifts; Berks & Bucks; London. Full internationals (2): England v Scotland 1881; Wales 1881.

Goalkeeper summed up pithily as a 'good' one and 'very fine', though others noted inconsistency of form. Strangely, he did not play association football at school (Clifton was a rugby college) but eventually reached the top around the age of 30 with his Cup-winner's medal and his international appearances. He was also a useful cricketer who was a member of MCC.

He was for several years a schoolmaster at Aldin House, Slough, which was run by his father, then in turn actor, producer and playwright, this last under the pseudonym 'John Trent-Hay'. Finally he went into journalism, becoming editor of the *Sporting World* newspaper. Hawtrey was a brother of the famous Victorian actor Charles Hawtrey. In more modern times a young, aspiring actor read the latter's memoirs and decided to take 'Charles Hawtrey' for his own stage name. As such, he later achieved fame as a member of the regular 'Carry On' film comedy team.

HAYNES, Colonel Charles Edward:
b. Hampstead, Middlesex, 8 July 1855;
d. Mount Stuart Nursing Home, Torquay, 29 October 1935 (£24,137).
Education: RMA, Woolwich.
FA Cup runner-up (1): Royal Engineers 1878.
Career: RMA, Woolwich; Royal Engineers.

Centre-forward who career was a short one as the year after his Cup final appearance he was taking part in the Zulu War in South Africa. He was succinctly described as a 'useful centre; plays unselfishly.'

Haynes joined the Royal Engineers as a lieutenant in 1875, was promoted to captain in 1886, major in 1894, lieut.-colonel in 1901 and colonel in 1907. He saw active service in the Zulu War 1879 (medal with clasp and mentioned twice in despatches); and the Bechunanaland Expedition 1884-85. He was on the Coast Defence Eastern Command 1908-12 when he retired. Haynes was recalled for the Great War and was with the British Expeditionary Force 1915-17. He had been made a CB in 1911.

He married the daughter of a lieut.-general and at the time of his death his home was at Roborough House, Furze Hill Road, Torquay. Charles Haynes should not be confused with his contemporary army officer, the Gloucestershire cricketer Carleton Haynes.

HEATH, Maj.-Gen. Frederick Crofton (from 1913 Heath-Caldwell)**:**
b. Mersham House, Bitterne, Hants., 21 February 1858;
d. Linley Wood, Talke, Staffordshire, 18 September 1945 (£24,058).
Education: RMA, Woolwich.
FA Cup runner-up (1): Royal Engineers 1878.
Career: RMA, Woolwich; Royal Engineers.

Half-back with a vigorous style and yet another member of the 1878 Cup final team who saw plenty of active service.

Heath joined the Royal Engineers as a lieutenant in 1877, was promoted to captain in 1888, brevet major in 1888, major in 1895, lieut.-colonel in 1903 and colonel in 1906. He served in Egypt 1882 (medal with clasp, bronze star); Sudan 1885 (clasp and mentioned in despatches); the Boer War 1899-1902 (Queen's medal with two clasps, King's medal with two clasps, mentioned in despatches). He was AAG South Africa 1900-02, AAG R.E. Headquarters of Army 1906-08, Inspector of R.E. 1908-13, Commanding Scottish coast defence 1913-14, Director Military Training War Office 1914-15, GoC. Portsmouth Garrison 1916-18, then GoC South-East area RAF 1918. He retired in 1919 with the rank of Major-General.

Heath was the son of Admiral Sir Leopold George Heath KCB, and took the name of Heath-Caldwell on succeeding his great-uncle J.S. Caldwell to the property at Talke. He became a JP County Palatine of Chester and had been made a CB in 1910.

HEDLEY, Lieut. Robert Shafto:

b. Taunton, Somerset, 17 January 1857;
d. Trincomalee, Ceylon, 29 January 1884.
Education: Reading School; RMA, Woolwich.
FA Cup runner-up (1): Royal Engineers 1878†.
Career: Reading School (1871-73: he played for the school aged 15 against the present Reading FC in its first season of 1871-72); RMA, Woolwich; Royal Engineers.

Centre-forward, described as 'a useful centre, combining considerable speed and weight with no small amount of energy'. Early comment on him suggested he 'should study shooting at goal', which he obviously did as he was in particularly lethal scoring form in the season his team reached the Cup final, 1877-78, with hat-tricks in successive ties against

Pilgrims (R.E. won 6-0 in the second round) and Druids (an 8-0 win in the third round). Selected for England v Scotland 1877-78 but unable to play, he was chosen for England against Scotland on 1st March 1879. The match was postponed because of bad weather and Hedley was unavailable on the rearranged date. He was on the F.A. committee 1878-79.

Hedley became a lieutenant in the Royal Engineers in 1876 and was eventually posted to Ceylon where he was tragically drowned at the age of 27. He was out boating and landed on a rock. Somehow his boat got loose and drifted away so he swam after it but was either seized with cramp or struck his head against the boat or a rock for he sank and was not seen afterwards until his body was recovered by a search party sent out to look for him. At the time of his death, his parents lived at St George's Square, London.

HERON, Charles Francis William (usually known as Frank Heron):
b. Uxbridge Common, Hillingdon, Middlesex, 10 September 1853;
d. 4 New Broadway, Southall, Middlesex, 23 October 1914 (£707).
Education: Mill Hill School (briefly in 1864).
FA Cup winner (1): Wanderers 1876 (both matches).
Career: Windsor Home Park; Uxbridge; Swifts; Wanderers; Middlesex; London. Full internationals (1): England v Scotland 1876.

Forward who was sometimes at a disadvantage with his slight build in view of the robust play of the day as shown in this contemporary comment: 'Dribbles well but is rather too light.' However, it did say he 'is always useful.' In addition to being an expert dribbler, his all-round play was good. He and his brother, Hubert, played together in the 1876 Cup final and notched a 'double' by doing the same against Scotland that season.

Frank Heron was in business as a wine merchant, like his brother and their father. His will contains two fascinating clauses. Firstly he said: 'I give my gold signet ring with the Heron arms engraved upon it; also my gold watch and chain to my son Douglas; and also to him the pictures of the England Team and my football badges and my Association Football Challenge Cup Medal.' The England team picture mentioned would presumably be the one for the 1875-76 match against Scotland in which Frank played and its rediscovery along with his other football memorabilia would certainly be a scoop.

The second item in his will is more bizarre and relates to the then more common fear of being buried alive. Heron says: 'Though not wishing to be kept unnecessarily long after my decease I should like my dear ones to be absolutely certain that I am dead before I am screwed down. The reason for this desire is obvious.' See also under A.J. Stanley for an even more amazing similar request.

HERON, George Hubert Hugh (usually known as Hubert Heron):
b. Uxbridge Common, Hillingdon, Middlesex, 30 January 1852;
d. Crossways, Waldegrave Road, Twickenham, Middlesex, 5 June 1914 (£441).
Education: Mill Hill School.
FA Cup winner (3): Wanderers 1876 (both matches), 1877, 1878.
Career: Mill Hill; Windsor Home Park; Uxbridge; Wanderers; Swifts; Middlesex; London. Full internationals (5): England v Scotland 1873 (2nd match); 1874; 1875; 1876†; 1878.

Centre-forward or inside-right of whom it was said: 'As a wing player is useful and at times brilliant; is fast and dribbles skilfully; used to be a little selfish in his style of play, but of late very much improved in this respect.' To add to his brilliance as a dribbler he was also regularly on the scoresheet. He and his younger brother, Frank, were both in the 1876 Wanderers Cup-winning team as well as in the England side against Scotland that season. His outstanding scoring feat was four goals when the Wanderers cruised to a 9-1 first round Cup victory against Panthers in 1877-78. Heron was on the F.A. committee 1873-76.

He followed his father by going into business as a wine merchant as did his brother. It has been stated that Hubert established his business in Bournemouth but confirmation of this claim has not been discovered.

HEYGATE, Rev. Canon Reginald Thomas:

b. Southend, Essex, 7 January 1857;
d. Shipton Moyne, Tetbury, Gloucs., 1 March 1947 (£4,814).
Education: Lancing College; Keble College, Oxford (matric. 1877; BA 1881; MA 1886); theology at Leeds Clergy School.
FA Cup runner-up (1): Oxford University 1880†.
Career: Lancing; Oxford University (Blue 1880†, 1881†); London; The South.

A wing forward said to be 'fast on the side; never tires' and 'very clever forward; plays on either wing, but apt to play selfishly.' Heygate was also a fair cricketer who was in the Lancing XI 1875-77 and achieved a brief obituary in *Wisden's Cricketers' Almanack*.

Heygate was the son of a clergyman. He was ordained deacon in 1882 and priest in 1883, becoming assistant curate at Leeds Parish Church, curate at St John's Cathedral, Newfoundland 1884-89 (he married a daughter of the Governor of Nova Scotia) and senior curate back at Leeds Parish Church 1889-93. He was then successively vicar of Honley, near Huddersfield, 1893-1900, King Cross, Halifax, 1900-05 and Boston, Lincs., 1905-16.

At that point overwork caused a breakdown in health and Heygate moved to a less strenuous country living as vicar of Shipton Moyne, Gloucs., 1916-23. He was also Rural Dean of Tetbury 1921-23. Continuing ill-health brought retirement in 1923 to the Old Rectory, Staunton, near Coleford, in the Wye Valley near Monmouth. He was offered bishoprics in Colombo and Bermuda but had to decline because of his poor health; nevertheless he lived long enough to see his 90th birthday. During his Yorkshire and Boston years he was noted as an exceptionally fine trainer of curates.

HILL, Rev. Evelyn Henry:
b. Felton Vicarage, Herefordshire, 5 April 1859;
d. Droitwich, 21 April 1915 (£5,838).
Education: Malvern College; Oriel College, Oxford (matric. 1878; BA 1882).
FA Cup runner-up (1): Oxford University 1880.
Career: Malvern (XI 1877, 1878†); Oxford University (Blue 1880, 1881).

Forward after a spell as a schoolboy defender. He was summed up as follows: 'Distinguished himself at first as a behind but latterly played very well forwards.' A later, more detailed comment was 'not necessarily the fastest or most brilliant but with the peculiarity that when he gets a run he seldom fails to send the ball near the enemy's goalposts. He has by example counteracted that fault of last year to make for the side [i.e.: to head towards the wing]. His power of dodging is very good, and when he is past his man he is not to be caught again. His generalship in the field is good; he never flags in his play.' Hill played cricket for Herefordshire, was in the Malvern XI 1876-77 and also in the Oriel College XI.

Hill's father was the vicar of Felton, the Rev. Henry Thomas Hill. The son studied theology at Lichfield College in 1887, then was ordained deacon in 1888 and priest in 1889. He became curate of Rugeley, Staffs., 1888-96 and vicar of Brereton, Staffs., 1896-1911. At the time of his death his home was at 'Felton', Roslin Road, Bournemouth.

HILLS, Arnold Frank:

b. Lambeth, London, 12 March 1857;
d. Hammerfield, Penshurst, Kent, 7 March 1927. (£60,496).
Education: Harrow School; University College, Oxford (matric. 1876; BA 1880).
FA Cup runner-up (1): Oxford University 1877.
Career: Harrow (XI 1874, 1875†); Oxford University (Blue 1877, 1878); Old Harrovians.
Full internationals (1): England v Scotland 1879.

Left sided forward described as 'a fast and energetic forward, works his hardest all through the game. Should endeavour to middle the ball sooner than he does.' Another comment was more critical: 'Very fast along the side, but has a fatal habit of taking the ball over the goal-line instead of taking it to goal.' Hills was also a fine athlete who won his Blue in 1877, 1878, 1879 and 1880, being unplaced in the mile in 1877, second in the mile in 1878 and winner of the three miles in 1879. In 1880 he was President of the University Athletic Club while in 1878 he was the AAA mile champion.

In 1880 Hills joined the board of Thames Ironworks and quickly rose to the position of managing director. While in charge he did much to develop the company. When the industry eventually began to decline in London he fought hard to keep it going but despite his endeavours the firm finally had to close. Hills was responsible for introducing workers' profit-sharing schemes and the eight-hour day. He founded the Thames Ironworks FC which eventually developed into West Ham United though, with his amateur background, he opposed the club's move into professionalism.

Severe overwork eventually led to serious rheumatic illnesses which left Hills a 'helpless cripple tied to his bed chair unable to move a limb without help' (*The Times*), but he continued with his work and ignored his disabilities. He was a keen vegetarian and President of the National Vegetarian Federal Union as well as being involved in the temperance movement. Hills was buried at St Luke's Church, Penshurst. His father was a manufacturing chemist.

HOGG, Quintin:

b. Grosvenor Street, Westminster, London, 14 February 1845;
d. Polytechnic Institute, 309 Regent Street, London, 17 January 1903 (£161,253).
Education: Eton College (1858-63).
FA Cup runner-up (1): Old Etonians 1876 (first match).
Career: Eton; Wanderers; Old Etonians; Civil Service; Hanover United. Pre-official internationals (2): Scotland v England 1871 (both matches).

Goalkeeper and full-back who was described as a 'capital custodian'. Hogg claimed in his *Who's Who* entry 'seven years captain of Old Etonian FC, during which period the club never sustained a defeat; captained the first seven Scotch teams against England, 1864-70.' Pre-official Scotland-

England games have been documented only from 1869-70 so presumably these earlier ones were played in London among players from member clubs of the F.A. Hogg took part in many sports until the end of his life including cricket, fives, cycling and yachting. He played first-class cricket for British Guiana in the 1860s and later appeared for Essex before they were promoted to first-class status.

When Hogg left Eton in 1863 he joined a firm of tea merchants in the City, then two years later he moved to a sugar company with which he rose to the position of a senior partner when it became Hogg, Curtis and Campbell Ltd. Under his direction the business prospered greatly and he built up a huge fortune. He made frequent visits to Demerera in British Guiana where he owned large sugar plantations. When the sugar industry later declined he continued to do well in business as chairman of the North British and Mercantile Insurance Company and at the time of his death was a director of the London Underground Company which had a number of new tube lines under construction. For the period 1889-94 he was an elected Alderman of the first London County Council.

Hogg's interest in philanthropy began early and in the winter of 1864-65 he started a ragged school for boys near Charing Cross, later moving to Castle Street, off Hanover Street. This developed by 1878 into a Youths' Christian Institute at Long Acre where, in addition to technical education courses, he provided opportunity for sporting activities, opening a ground at Mortlake for this purpose. About this time he started his own football club, Hanover United, appearing as captain and taking part in the F.A. Cup. Presumably the name was in memory of the site of his first ragged school and the suffix 'United' may well be the first such ever to be used by a football club (there was a rugby club called simply United and based at Highbury which was formed in 1871).

In 1882 Hogg used his money to found and become president of the Polytechnic Institute in Regent Street where, he said: 'We could gratify any reasonable taste, whether athletic, intellectual, spiritual or social.' The institute opened in September 1882 with 2,000 members and within a year this had risen to 6,800. He also organised holiday tours for the members.

Hogg was found dead in his bath at the institute where he had his own rooms close by his home at 2 Cavendish Place. An inquest brought in a verdict of 'death by misadventure' after the jury heard expert evidence that a gas stove in the bathroom was without a ventilating shaft and the fumes from this would alone account for the manner of death. On his desk in his study was found an unfinished letter in which Hogg had made an appointment for the following Monday.

His funeral was at All Souls, Langham Place, then he was cremated and his ashes buried at Marylebone Cemetery, Finchley. A statue of Hogg, by Sir George Frampton RA was erected in Langham Place in 1906 opposite the Polytechnic Institute. Hogg's father had been an MP as well as twice chairman of the East India Company and he himself was the grandfather of Lord Hailsham, Tory politician and Lord Chancellor under Mrs Thatcher in the 1980s.

He once told an interviewer about his maiden attempt at philanthropy after his first visit to a London slum. There was, he said, one court in which he found that in all the houses there were only two bedsteads, the rest of the people sleeping on bundles of rags, with old brandy cases and the like being used for seats, and two or three old cases serving as a table. 'I had never been brought into contact with real poverty and want before, and felt almost as though I should go mad unless I did something to try and help some of the wretched little chaps I used to find running about the streets.' So he persuaded two young crossing-sweepers to let him teach them to read and they got together one night under the Adelphi arches 'with an empty beer bottle for a candlestick and a tallow candle for illumination, two crossing-sweepers as pupils, your humble servant as teacher and a couple of Bibles as reading books'.

He continued: 'We had not been engaged in our reading very long when, at the far end of the arch, I noticed a twinkling light. "Kool esclop," shouted one of the boys, at the same time dousing the glim [light] and bolting with his companion, leaving me in the dark with my upset beer bottle and my doused candle, forming a spectacle which seemed to arouse suspicion on the part of our friend the policeman, whose light it was that had appeared in the distance. However, after scrutinising me for some time by the light of his bull's-eye, he moved on, leaving me in a state of mental perturbation as to what the mystic words I had heard hollered out meant. Afterwards, when I became proficient in slang, I knew that "kool esclop" was "look (out for the) police" spelt backwards, the last word being evidently the original for the contraction "slop", the word generally applied to the police of London today.'

A statue of Hogg, with figures typical of his work, by Sir George Frampton, RA

HOOMAN, Thomas Charles:

b. The Copse, Hoo Lane, Kidderminster, Worcs., 28 December 1850;
d. 6 Marine Parade, Hythe, Kent, 22 September 1938 (£2,419).
Education: Charterhouse School (1863-68).
FA Cup winner (1): Wanderers 1872.
Career: Charterhouse (XI 1867-68 & 1868-69); Wanderers; Middlesex; London; The North.
Pre-official internationals (4): England v Scotland 1871 (both matches); 1872 (both matches). He was chosen for England v Scotland in both the first full internationals matches of 1872-73 but was unavailable.

Forward who was one of the most highly-rated of his day and among the first choices for the big matches. He was summed up as 'the fastest dribbler of the day, and an accomplished player; can play back, and kicks well.' Hooman was also an excellent cricketer who headed the batting averages while at Charterhouse where he was in the XI 1867-68. In addition he ran in the sprint for England in 1872, rowed in the Grand Final at Henley for Kingston and was also a good boxer, marksman and golfer. In fact he was the father of Walker Cup golfer and Kent cricketer C.V.L. Hooman.

Hooman, whose father was a carpet manufacturer, went into business in London as a merchant ship broker and later as a manufacturer of Portland cement. His death followed an operation. His obituary in *The Times* mentioned a recent interview with him in which he claimed to have scored the winning goal in the 1871-72 Cup final but no contemporary report agrees with this. He also claimed that the final was played without umpires or referee, the captains making all the decisions, but match reports show this not to be the case. As Hooman was 87 at the time it must be assumed that his memory was failing and he was confusing other matches with the Cup final.

HOWELL, Leonard Sidgwick:
b. Herne Hill, Dulwich, 6 August 1848;
d. Lausanne, Switzerland, 7 September 1895 (£710).
Education: Winchester College.
FA Cup winner (1): Wanderers 1873.
Career: Winchester; Wanderers; Old Harrovians; Surrey; London. Full internationals (1): England v Scotland 1873 (2nd match).

Full-back and half-back who was noted for his outstanding kicking, it was said of Howell: 'He excels as a half-back; and his kicking not unfrequently "brings down the house." ' His 'unwearied defence' and 'unvarying precision' were also mentioned while in 1873 he was said to be playing 'better than ever in the position of back' but his career was ended by injury in 1874. He was a good cricketer who was in the Winchester XI 1864-66 (captain 1866) and appeared for Surrey 1869-80. He scored 519 first-class runs, average 18.53, with a highest score of 96.

Howell was a malt factor by profession. Although he was a notable sportsman his health was never good and he died at a Swiss health resort. At the time his home was at Maybury Heath, Woking, Surrey.

HUGHES, Thomas Bridges:
b. Newton Longville, Bucks., 17 September 1851;
d. The Swan Hotel, Wells, Somerset, 10 August 1940 (£4,618).
Education: Highgate School; Winchester College; New College, Oxford (matric. 1870; BA 1874).
FA Cup winner (2): Wanderers 1876 (both matches), 1877.
Career: Highgate; Winchester; Oxford University (Blue 1874); Wanderers; Swifts; Old Wykehamists; Remnants; Berks & Bucks.

Wing forward at home on either flank who scored twice in the 3-0 win by the Wanderers in the 1875-76 Cup final replay against the Old Etonians. Hughes was described as 'a hard-working forward, and good shot at goal.' He was a founder member of the Oxford University Association Football Club when it was formed on 9th November 1871. Hughes was also a good cricketer who just missed first-class status. He was in the Winchester XI 1868-70, played in the Oxford Freshman's match in 1871 and was a member of Free Foresters.

Hughes, the son of a clergyman, was Head of School at Winchester for three years. He became a barrister who was called to the bar at the Inner Temple in 1876 but did not go into practice. Instead, he followed a career as a schoolmaster. He was at Repton School April-December 1878, then Brighton College January-July 1879 before becoming a partner in Evelyn's School, Hillingdon, from September 1879. At the time of his death his home was at Bickington, Lelant, Cornwall.

JOHNSON, Rev. Arthur Henry:
b. Marylebone, London, 8 February 1845;
d. 5 South Parks Road, Oxford, 31 January 1927 (£31,043).
Education: Eton College; Exeter College, Oxford (matric. 1864; BA 1868; MA 1870).
FA Cup winner (1): Oxford University 1874.
Career: Eton; Exeter College; Oxford University (pre-university match).

Forward famed for his speedy runs. Much of his football was played before the introduction of the F.A. Cup and he was not an undergraduate when he appeared in the 1874 final but a Fellow of All Souls College as well as an ordained clergyman. Johnson was a noted athlete who won Blues in 1865 and 1866, finishing second in the two-mile race in the former year though unplaced in the latter. Fishing, hunting and shooting were also among his pursuits.

He was the son of a captain in the Coldstream Guards, was ordained in 1872 but he spent his whole life in academic circles as a lecturer at various Oxford colleges as follows: Fellow of All Souls 1869-74 and 1906 to death (college Chaplain too); Modern History Lecturer at Pembroke College 1874-84, St John's College 1875-84, Wadham College 1875-84, Trinity College 1876-1903, Hertford

College 1876-1903, Worcester College 1883-85, Corpus Christi College 1884-85, Balliol College 1884-90, Merton College 1884-1923, University College 1885 to death; chairman of the Modern History Board 1893-1912; Hon. Secretary to Curators of the University Parks 1911-24; Ford Lecturer for 1909. He also wrote a number of history books including *Europe in the XVI Century* and *The History of the Drapers' Company.*

Johnson died after catching influenza from which pneumonia developed. One of his sons became Deputy Master of the Mint while the other was headmaster at Alleyne's School, Stevenage. Johnson's athletic prowess remained with him for many years. It is related that when he was on late duty and spotted errant students trying to sneak back into college after hours, he surprised them by the speed with which he caught them when they ran away.

KEITH-FALCONER, Lieut.-Col. Cecil Edward:

b. St Leonard's Forest, near Horsham, Sussex, 11 October 1860;
d. in action, near Belmont, South Africa, 10 November 1899 (£3,060).
Education: Charterhouse School.
FA Cup runner-up (1): Clapham Rovers 1879.
Career: Charterhouse (XI 1877-78); Swifts; Clapham Rovers; Old Carthusians.

Centre-forward who earlier featured as a wing forward. As the latter he was described as 'a good wing, is faster than he appears to be; always plays well, and backs up without tiring.' Later he was 'a fair centre, but slow.' Keith-Falconer was also a fair cricketer, being in the Charterhouse XI in 1878.

He joined the army in 1881 with the Sussex Militia until 1883, then was in the 5th Northumberland Fusiliers 1883-87. Keith-Falconer was appointed ADC to the Governor & CiC of Victoria, Australia, 1887-89; and ADC to the Governor, Cape of Good Hope 1889-92. He was promoted to captain in 1892 and passed Staff College with honours. From 1895-98 he was in the 13th Sudanese Battalion, seeing active service with the Dongola Expeditionary Force 1896 and the Nile Expeditions, also 1896. He also took part in a number of battles including Omdurman 1898 where he was Brigade Major, being mentioned three times in despatches for which he was promoted to major in March 1898 and lieut.-colonel in November 1898.

He was killed during Boer War action with the 5th Regiment of Fusiliers while on reconnaissance near Belmont where a battle was fought on 23rd November, 13 days after Keith-Falconer's death. Earlier that same year he had married. Keith-Falconer was the grandson of the 7th Earl of Kintore and his father was an Army major. At the time of his death his home was at 25 Granville Place, Portman Square, London.

KENRICK, Jarvis:
b. Chichester, Sussex, 13 November 1852;
d. Meads Cottage, 39 Westdown Road, Blatchington, Seaford, Sussex, 29 January 1949 (£10,718).
Education: Lancing College.
FA Cup winner (3): Wanderers 1876 (both matches), 1877, 1878.
Career: Lancing (XI 1868-69); Clapham Rovers; Wanderers; Surrey; London. Pre-official internationals (1): England v Scotland 1872.

Inside-left and outside-left who was said to be 'a fine player all round, very quick and sure forward, and careful and safe back' then later in his career 'fair down a side; rather slack at times, but generally near the goal when the ball is there.' He was the first player to score a goal in an F.A. Cup-tie, which he did in the 15th minute of the very first round of the very first competition in 1871-72 as Clapham

Rovers beat Upton Park 3-0. Kenrick scored two of the goals and, along with Young, of Maidenhead, who also notched a couple that afternoon, was also the first to achieve this feat in the Cup. He was on the F.A. committee 1877-78. Kenrick was a good cricketer who played one first-class match, for Surrey in 1876 and was also a member of Free Foresters.

Kenrick was in practice as a solicitor, having been admitted in 1875. His sister was married to F. H. Birley, under whose captaincy he played in the 1875-76 and 1876-77 Cup finals. He died at the age of 96, therefore living long enough to hear about Sir Matt Busby's first big managerial triumph, the Manchester United Cup final victory over Blackpool in 1947-48.

KENYON-SLANEY, Colonel the Rt. Hon. William Slaney:

b. Rajkot, Gujarat, India, 24 August 1847;
d. Hatton Grange, Shifnal, Shropshire, 24 April 1908 (£135,502).
Education: Eton College; Christ Church, Oxford (matric. 1865).
FA Cup winner (1): Wanderers 1873; runner-up (2): Old Etonians 1875 (first match), 1876 (both matches).
Career: Eton; Grenadier Guards; Household Brigade; Wanderers; Gitanos; Shropshire Wanderers; Old Etonians. Full internationals (1): England v Scotland 1873 (2nd match).

Inside-right who earned a reputation for his dashing and effective play; for instance he scored two goals in his single international appearance. According to one contemporary commentator, Kenyon-Slaney 'showed great powers of dribbling' while in 1874 he was acknowledged as 'being the most successful forward of the year.' In 1886 he became President of the Shropshire F.A. but declined to resume the position after that organisation re-formed itself in 1887 as he disagreed with the changes. At his wedding celebrations in 1888 Aston Villa played an exhibition match against Shifnal FC of which Kenyon-Slaney was president. Kenyon-Slaney was a well-known cricketer whose first-class career covered the years 1869-80 with MCC and other major teams. He also played for Shropshire, I Zingari and Household Brigade. In addition he was on the MCC committee. In 1894 he was elected vice-president of the Shropshire Chess Association. Then, in 1908 he was made president of the Severnside Bowling Club, Shrewsbury, but died soon afterwards. However, as a mark of respect, the post was left unfilled for the rest of the season.

Kenyon-Slaney followed a military career as a young man, serving in the Grenadier Guards 1867-88 (captain 1878; major 1883; colonel 1887), which included active service in the Egyptian campaign of 1882 where he fought in the battle of Tel-el-Kebir (medal and Khedive's Star). He then entered politics and was Conservative MP for Newport, Shropshire, 1888-1908. He became a Privy Councillor in 1904. He was the son of an army colonel and married a daughter of the third Earl of Bradford. Altogether he owned about 4,000 acres. His death followed an attack of gout.

KING, Charles James Stuart:
b. New Road Rectory, Leigh-on-Sea, Essex, 2 June 1860;
d. Chardstock, Devon, 23 April 1928.
Education: Felsted; Hertford College, Oxford (matric. 1879; BA 1883).
FA Cup runner-up (1): Oxford University 1880.
Career: Felsted; Oxford University (Blue 1881, 1882); Upton Park; Essex; London.

Full-back noted for his strong, long kicking. A contemporary commented: 'A powerful back, kicks with great vigour, but rather wanting in discretion; is very fast' while another view was 'a very powerful back, difficult to pass; is a little erratic at times.' It was this 'little erratic' factor which led to a bad miskick in his Cup final and let in Lloyd-Jones to score the only goal of the match for Clapham Rovers. His brother was Robert Stuart King, England international of 1882. Charles was also a good cricketer who was in the Felsted XI 1875-78, as captain in his two final seasons.

He was a schoolmaster who had a period as headmaster of a prep school, then spent several years in Minnesota. In retirement at Chardstock King was a manager of the National School there. After his death his son presented the school with a stuffed owl in memory of his father who had shot it in Minnesota! King was buried at St Andrew's, the Chardstock parish church. His father was the Rev. Walker King, Rector of Leigh, to which parish Charles' brother, Robert, returned as Rector for an amazing 58 years, 1892-1950.

KINGSFORD, Robert Kennett:
b. Sydenham Hill, London, 23 December 1849;
d. Adelaide, Australia, 14 October 1895.
Education: Marlborough College.
FA Cup winner (1): Wanderers 1873.
Career: Marlborough; Old Marlburians; Wanderers; Crystal Palace; Surrey; London. Full internationals (1): England v Scotland 1874.

Goal-getting forward who was the leading scorer in England in 1873-74 and was said to be 'a fast and invaluable forward' as well as having 'a happy knack of putting the ball between the posts.' That was certainly the case the following season of 1874-75 when he became the first player on record to notch five goals in a Cup game as Wanderers hammered Farningham 16-0 in the first round, said to be the largest score by any team ever under F.A. rules. Kingsford had a spell as secretary of the Wanderers from 1874. He played cricket for Surrey 1872-74. For some years he studied the law but later moved to Australia where he died.

KINNAIRD Hon. Arthur Fitzgerald (later Lord Kinnaird, 11th Baron: he succeeded to the title in 1887)

b. 35 Hyde Park Gardens, Kensington, London, 16 February 1847;
d. 10 St James's Square, Westminster, London, 30 January 1923 (£250,000).
Education: Cheam Prep School; Eton College; Trinity College, Cambridge (matric. 1865; BA 1869; MA 1873).
FA Cup winner (5): Wanderers 1873†, 1877, 1878†; Old Etonians 1879†, 1882†; runner-up (4): Old Etonians 1875† (both matches), 1876† (both matches), 1881†, 1883†.
FA Cup final umpire (2): 1887, 1889.
Career: Cheam; Eton; Cambridge University (pre-university match); Cambridge Eton Club; Crusaders; Wanderers; Gitanos; Old Etonians; Kent; Middlesex; London; The North. Full internationals (1): Scotland v England 1873 (2nd match). Pre-official internationals (3): Scotland v England 1870; 1871 (both matches).

Half-back in his later Cup finals, but earlier an inside-forward and occasional goalkeeper, Kinnaird is nicely summed up as: 'second to none at any part of the game. A good forward, never away from the ball, keen player, very fast, knows how and when to use his speed, possesses consummate judgment; is a good and safe back' and also as 'without exception the best player of the day; capable of taking any place in the field; is very fast and never loses sight of the ball. An excellent captain.' Later in his career this was condensed to 'very fast, with great pluck, and a good man anywhere.' His record of nine Final appearances will probably stand for ever (11 if one counts two replays as separate appearances), though he shares the record of five winning finals with C.H.R. Wollaston of the Wanderers and J.H. Forrest of Blackburn Rovers.

Unlike C.W. Alcock and F.A. Marindin, his colleagues in the triumvirate who set the F.A. on the road which established it as the supreme body in the game, Kinnaird's role off the field has not eclipsed his feats on it. He had a long career from the early 1860s to the early 1890s and was a well-known figure with his flowing red beard and his long, white flannels.

Nevertheless his role in the administration of the game was a vital one which lasted for 54 years until his death. He was on the F.A. committee 1869-77, then was Treasurer 1878-90 and finally President 1890-1923. In 1911 he was presented with the F.A. Cup (the copy made in 1895 after the theft of the original one) to celebrate his 21st year as President of the F.A. He also became the first President of the London F.A.

Kinnaird was proficient at many other sports, being a real tennis Blue in 1868 and 1869 when he won the singles in both years and he also represented Cambridge at fives and swimming. At the Paris Exhibition of 1867 he won an international canoe race while at Eton he had been a good sprinter. In addition he was a member of MCC.

As a peer of the realm and owner of some 11,900 acres Kinnaird filled many official posts. He was created a Knight of the Thistle in 1914, was Lord High Commissioner to the General Assembly of the Church of Scotland 1907-09, Hon. Colonel of the Tay Division Royal Engineers (volunteers) Submarine Miners from 1893, president of the YMCA, a Deputy Lieutenant, a JP and a FRGS. He also took a prominent part in the House of Lords and was well-known as a philanthropist. His main business interest was as a director of Barclay's Bank.

At the time of his death it was reported that his spirits had been low since the loss of his wife 11 days earlier. He was buried at the family property of Rossie Priory, Inchture, Perthshire.

The way Kinnaird threw himself into the rough and tumble of the game with his vigour and rumbustiousness always worried his mother who felt that one day he would be brought home with a broken leg. 'Pray do not be alarmed', Major Marindin told her: 'If anybody's leg is broken it will not be Arthur's!'

Kinnaird when President of the F.A.

KIRKPATRICK, Sir James (8th Baronet: he succeeded to the title in 1880):
b. Closeburn, Dumfriesshire, 22 March 1841;
d. 296 Stanstead Road, Forest Hill, London, 10 November 1899 (£11,736).
Education: Private.
FA Cup winner (1): Wanderers 1878.
FA Cup final umpire (1): 1872.
Career: Civil Service; Wanderers; Surrey & Kent; Surrey. Pre-official internationals (4): Scotland v England 1870†; 1871 (both matches, the first as captain); 1872.

Goalkeeper in the main but also occasional general utility outfield player who was praised as 'a useful player all round, a good back and excellent goalkeeper' while later he was 'a very useful goalkeeper; fields well, and does not lose his head'. He graduated into goal as he reached his 30s; in 1874 it was reported: 'Is now chiefly known as a goalkeeper, his "flying" days being numbered with the past.' Kirkpatrick had a long career and gained his Cup-winning medal at the age of 37 years and one day. He earned it too, continuing to keep goal to the end of the match despite suffering a fractured left arm after only 15 minutes. He umpired the first Cup final of all, six years before his winning appearance! Kirkpatrick was on the F.A. committee 1869-71.

He was also a good cricketer with the Civil Service club and made one appearance at first-class level, for the Gentlemen of the South in 1867 when he took 3 wickets for 36 runs.

By profession Kirkpatrick held a high rank in the Civil Service as a clerk in the Admiralty, being Private Secretary to Lord George Hamilton, the First Lord of the Admiralty. His baronetcy dated back to 1685.

LEACH, Andrew John:
b. Hampstead, London, 16 September 1851;
d. 'Bel Retiro', Chester Road, Bournemouth, 7 November 1904 (£857).
Education: Highgate School; St John's College, Oxford (matric. 1871; BA 1874).
FA Cup runner-up (1): Oxford University 1873.
Career: Highgate; Oxford University (no Blue).

Goalkeeper in his Cup final appearance but Leach was also proficient as an outfield player where he more frequently featured. He was a founder member of the Oxford University Association Football Club when it was formed on 9th November 1871.

Leach was a member of the legal profession, being a barrister who was called to the bar at Lincoln's Inn on 17th April 1876. Then, like many of his contemporary Cup finalists, he was soon lost to the game through making his career abroad. He established himself in the Far East and eventually reached the rank of Puisne Judge of the Straits Settlement at Shanghai.

LINDSAY, Colonel Henry Edzell Morgan (usually known as Morgan Lindsay):

b. (probably in Dublin),13 February 1857;
d. Ystrad Fawr, Ystrad Mynach, Glamorgan, 1 November 1935 (£7,894).
Education: Royal Academy, Gosport; RMA, Woolwich.
FA Cup runner-up (1): Royal Engineers 1878.
Career: RMA, Woolwich; Royal Engineers; The South.

Inside-right was who said to be 'a useful wing player, being fast and not to be removed from the ball.' He was President of the South Wales F.A. from 1893. Lindsay became well-known in horse racing circles as a National Hunt owner-trainer. He was a member of the NH committee and owned Ego which won the 'blue riband' of steeplechasing, the NH Chase at Cheltenham in 1933.

He joined the Royal Engineers as a lieutenant in 1876 and transferred to the Royal Monmouthshire R.E. in 1892, commanding them until 1917. Lindsay saw active service in South Africa 1880-81; the Sudan expedition of 1885 (medal with two clasps plus Khedive's Star); Boer War 1899-1901 (Queen's Medal with four clasps as well as being mentioned in despatches); and finally the Great War 1914-19 (medal). He was also made a Knight of Justice Order of St John of Jerusalem and a CB in 1911.

Lindsay was a grandson of the first Lord Tredegar, his father was a former Chief Constable of Glamorgan and he himself was later a JP in Glamorgan (senior magistrate for the Caerphilly Petty Sessional Division) as well as County Dublin where the family home was Glasnevin House. He was buried at Ystrad Mynach Church and at his funeral the streets of the district were lined by thousands of people.

LINDSAY, William:
b. India, 3 August 1847;
d. 1 Minor Canon Row, Rochester, Kent, 15 February 1923 (£10,691).
Education: Winchester College.
FA Cup winner (3): Wanderers 1876 (both matches), 1877, 1878.
Career: Winchester; Old Wykehamists; Gitanos; Civil Service; Wanderers; Surrey. Full internationals (1): England v Scotland 1877. Pre-official internationals (5): England v Scotland 1870; 1871 (both matches); 1872 (both matches).

Defender, among the best of his day who won high praise: 'A very good half-back, being a remarkably sure kick, and never "funks"; plays well to his forwards'. He was a good utility man, too, who could play in the attack to some effect and earlier in his career was 'a very fine forward, as well as a good back.'

Lindsay was also a fine cricketer who played 33 matches for Surrey 1876-82, as well as Devon. Altogether he scored 987 first-class runs, average 17.31, being 13th in the national first-class batting averages in 1877 and 19th in 1881. He was in the Winchester XI 1864-65 and later became a member of MCC.

Lindsay was orphaned by the slaughter of his parents in 1857 during the Indian Mutiny and was admitted to Winchester as a Commoner by the headmaster at the beginning of 1858. By profession he became a civil servant who held a clerkship in the India Office from 1865 to 1900 when he retired. While there he acted as private secretary to Lord George Hamilton, the Hon. E. Stanhope, the Marquis of Lansdowne and Viscount Enfield, being promoted to Senior Clerk in 1882.

The street in which he had his final home, Minor Canon Row, Rochester, turns up as Minor Canon Corner, Cloisterham, in Charles Dickens' unfinished last novel, *The Mystery of Edwin Drood*.

LLOYD-JONES, Clopton Allen:
b. Hanwood House, Shropshire, 12 November 1858;
d. Montreux, Belle Vue Gardens, Shrewsbury, 7 March 1918 (£2,444).
Education: Trent College
FA Cup winner (1): Clapham Rovers 1880.
Career: Trent College; Southill Park; Clapham Rovers (1879-84); London; Middlesex; Pontesbury (1884); Shrewsbury Castle Blues (1884-86); Shropshire. Selected for Wales v England 1884-85 but unavailable.

Inside-forward or winger who scored the only goal when Clapham Rovers won the Cup to deserve fully his description as 'a very neat dribbler and dangerous shot at goal.' He had played for the Walthamstow club, Southill Park, in the Cup in 1877-78 and 1878-79 before joining Clapham Rovers. Later he settled in Shrewsbury where he immediately joined up with the Castle Blues, playing mainly at inside-right. However this club disbanded voluntarily in 1886 after being found guilty of violent and dangerous play and Lloyd-Jones ended his active football career. In 1889 and 1890 he was on the committee of the Shropshire Amateur F.A. as one of Shrewsbury's representatives. In the former year he was also a member of the executive committee of the Shropshire Mayor's Charity Cup Association.

His selection for Wales came about because his parents were Welsh and Castle Blues were affiliated to the Wales and Border Counties F.A. Lloyd-Jones had been in the football XI at Trent College where he played against Nottingham Forest and was described as the outstanding player on the field. He also won two athletics cups at the school sports in 1875.

He was also a keen cricketer, playing for Herefordshire in 1886-89, Shropshire in 1887-89 and Radnorshire in 1888. At Shrewsbury area club level he played for Abbey Foregate, Pontesbury, Montgomery and Shrewsbury CC. Earlier he had played for the Stock Exchange XI and for Clapham Rovers who also ran a cricket section as well as fielding association and rugby football teams. The month after his Cup final appearance he won two events at Clapham Rovers' athletic sports. He was also a keen angler and good rifle shot.

Lloyd-Jones became a full member of the Severnside Bowling Club, Shrewsbury, in 1899 and was a player until 1916, winning the club's major prize, the Allcroft Vase, in 1911. He was on the committee 1901-14 and was elected a life member in 1912. He also became involved with the Pengwerne Boat Club, Shrewsbury, from 1885 though not as a competitive rower. He was on the club's committee at various times between 1888 and 1906 and was Deputy-Captain in 1896. In 1894 he was the starter at the club's annual athletics meeting.

He became a familiar sight in general Shrewsbury sporting circles and was involved as organising committee member, judge or more frequently starter at various local athletics events including the Whit Monday Fete between 1890 and 1908; starter (and in 1913 judge) at the annual Shropshire Constabulary Sports held in early September from 1897. He was also starter at sports held to commemorate the marriage of the future King George V in 1893, the 500th anniversary of the Battle of Shrewsbury in 1903 and George V's coronation in 1911.

Lloyd-Jones was in business in London as an indigo broker (1881 census) but during 1884 moved to Shrewsbury where he set up as a commission agent, i.e. a bookmaker (1891 and 1901 census). He was the younger son of Charles Lloyd Jones, who was known as the squire of Hanwood, about two miles from Shrewsbury, and, like his father, his name was not hyphenated on his birth certificate. Lloyd-Jones died from cancer of the bladder after what was described as a long and painful illness. He was buried in Shrewsbury's Longden Road Cemetery where, more recently in 2002, the Football League's all-time leading goalscorer, Arthur Rowley, was also buried.

In 1892 Lloyd-Jones entered a fancy dress ball held by Shrewsbury Amateur Dramatic Society under the name of Clopton Jones and in the character of a member of 'Clapham Rovers C.C.' He did not win a prize but, far from London and during the winter months, his appearance in the gaudy Clapham colours of cerise and French grey would have stood out flamboyantly from his surroundings.

LONGMAN, Charles James:
b. 36 Hyde Park Square, Kensington, London, 14 April 1852;
d. 27 Norfolk Square, Paddington, London W2, 17 April 1934 (£61,624).
Education: Harrow School; University College, Oxford (matric. 1870; BA 1874; MA 1877).
FA Cup runner-up (1): Oxford University 1873.
Career: Harrow; Oxford University (no Blue); Harrow Chequers; Herts. Rangers; Old Harrovians.

Forward whose 'vigour' and hard work attracted notice. He achieved more fame as an archer, being champion of England in 1883 and joint author of the Badminton Library volume on the sport, published in 1894. He was also a useful cricketer, being a member of MCC.

Longman was a member of the famous publishing family and joined the firm, Longmans, Green & Co., in 1877. He was personally responsible for the inception of the Badminton Library of Sports and Pastimes; editor of *Fraser's Magazine* 1881-82; editor of *Longman's Magazine* 1882-1905; and president of the Publishers' Association in 1896, 1897, 1902 and 1903. He retired from the firm in 1928. Longman was a personal friend of Rider Haggard and Andrew Lang, two of the many famous authors published by Longmans. He was a JP and had a country home at Upp Hall, Braughing, Herts.

LUBBOCK, Alfred:

b. 23 St James's Place, Westminster, London, 31 October 1845;
d. Kilmarth Manor, Par, Cornwall, 17 July 1916 (£643).
Education: Eton College (1856-63).
FA Cup runner-up (1): Old Etonians 1875 (replay).
Career: Eton (XI 1860-63, captain 1863); Old Etonians.

Inside-right who played alongside his brother, Edgar, in the replayed 1874-75 Cup final. They were related to John Birkbeck Lubbock, the later 2nd Lord Avebury, who appeared in the 1879-80 Cup final. Alfred was an outstanding schoolboy footballer at the Eton Field Game, becoming a member of the XI in 1860. When playing against other schoolboys, his side never failed to win.

But he achieved more fame as a cricketer and was in the Eton XI 1861-63 (captain 1863). His great feat as a schoolboy was to score 174 not out against Winchester in 1863. He played for Kent from 1863-75 as well as eight times for the Gentlemen v the Players and in all he scored 1,043 first-class runs at an average of 23.70 with two centuries. Lubbock was a member of the English team to Canada in 1872. He was a founder of the Eton Ramblers CC, selecting the club colours, and also a member of MCC.

While at Eton he also featured as an oarsman, being in the Thetis in 1860 and in the Prince of Wales in 1861, then went on to star at Fives, winning the Cup in 1861 (with Lancelot Dent), 1862 (with his brother, Edgar) and 1863 (with Quintin Hogg). He made his mark at athletics in 1862, winning the high jump, putting the shot and throwing the cricket ball. Later, variable health affected the frequency with which he could undertake sporting activities.

Lubbock was the seventh son of a baronet. By profession he was firstly an underwriter and then a banker; in fact the Lubbocks were a family of bankers who had their own firm, Robarts, Lubbock and Co., a business later taken over by the well-known Coutts and Co.

Lubbock's success at the Eton Field Game extended to house matches. His side, Joynes' House, never failed to win though their victory against Stevens' House was by only a rouge. Captain of the opposition in this match was the future Poet Laureate Robert Bridges.

LUBBOCK, Edgar:

b. 23 St James's Place, Westminster, London, 22 February 1847;
d. 18 Hans Court, Chelsea, London, 9 September 1907 (£208,171).
Education: Eton College (1859-66).
FA Cup winner (2): Wanderers 1872; Old Etonians 1879; runner-up (2): Old Etonians 1875 (both matches), 1876 (replay).
Career: Eton; West Kent; Flying Dutchmen; Wanderers; Old Etonians; Gitanos; Kent; Middlesex; The South. Pre-official internationals (5): England v Scotland 1870; 1871 (both matches); 1872 (both matches). He was selected for England in the 1874-75 full international against Scotland but was unavailable.

Lubbock was one of the outstanding defenders of his generation, was usually first choice for the full-back position and was equally good at half-back. He was praised as 'the finest kick anywhere, his aptitude for kicking the ball in the most difficult position being unequalled, would be better still was he faster', also as 'unrivalled as a back; very accurate in his kicking' and 'a wonderful back in any position, and is truly the bane of all forwards.'

He was the youngest of eight famous sporting Lubbocks who was better known to his contemporaries as 'Quintus' because, when he went to Eton, four of his elder brothers were still at the school. In his nine years there he was Keeper of the Wall, three years in the Field XI and three times winner of the Fives. Lubbock was an excellent cricketer who played once for Kent in 1871 as well as for the Gentlemen of Kent in a first-class match in 1866. His top score in five first-class innings was 54. At Eton Lubbock was in the cricket XI in 1864-65-66 (captain 1866) and he later became a member of MCC. He and his brother, Alfred, toured Canada in 1872 with an English team which included W.G. Grace. He was also Master of the Blankney Foxhounds.

Edgar Lubbock, who was a LL.B. and D.L., was a member of the family banking business, became a director of the Bank of England and at the time of his death was the Deputy Governor. He was also in business as a brewer, being a member of Whitbreads and owner of The Brewery, Chiswell Street, Middlesex. At the time of his death his home was at North House, Little Gonerby, Grantham, Lincs., and he also had a residence at Caythorpe, near Grantham. Edgar and his brother, Alfred, played together in the 1874-75 Cup final replay and they were both related to John Birkbeck Lubbock (later 2nd Lord Avebury) who played in the 1879-80 final.

The story has been related that in a match between the Old Etonians and the Wanderers at The Oval, C.W. Alcock, the latter's captain, tried out a special charge of his own against Lubbock, one of the great half-backs of the day. 'By heaven, Alcock!', cried out the towering Lubbock, 'if you do that again I'll hack your legs off!'

LUBBOCK, John Birkbeck (2nd Lord Avebury: succeeded to title 1913)**:**
b. High Elms, Farnborough, Kent, 4 October 1858;
d. High Elms, 26 March 1929 (£522,585).
Education: Eton College; Balliol College, Oxford (matric. 1878; BA 1885; MA also 1885).
FA Cup runner-up (1): Oxford University 1880.
Career: Eton; Oxford University (Blue 1881).

Inside or outside-left who was described as a 'clever dribbler; plays on the wing; good shot at goal.' He was a fair cricketer who was a member of MCC and played while at Eton though he did not get into the XI. However, while there he won the Eton fives with the Hon. Ivo Bligh (England cricket captain of 'Ashes' fame) in 1876. Lubbock won an Oxford real tennis Blue in 1880 when he lost in the doubles. In later life he became a scratch golfer.

He was a banker by profession, becoming a director of the family firm, Robarts, Lubbock and Co., from 1880 until its takeover by Coutts and Co. in 1914, then a director with Coutts. He was also on the boards of the National Provincial Bank and the Australian Mercantile Land & Finance Co.

After succeeding to the title as the 2nd Lord Avebury in 1913, he attended the House of Lords regularly and sat on many of its committees. Lord Avebury was buried at High Elms on the family property. His father received his peerage in 1901 after a prominent political career in which he initiated a major piece of legislation which was of importance to the future pattern of football fixtures, namely the Bank Holidays Act of 1871.

LYTTELTON, Rt. Hon. Alfred:

b. Westminster, London, 7 February 1857;
d. at a nursing home, 3 Devonshire Terrace, Marylebone, London, 5 July 1913 (£49,099).
Education: Eton College; Trinity College, Cambridge (matric. 1875; BA 1879; Hon. MA 1899).
FA Cup runner-up (1): Old Etonians 1876 (both matches).
Career: Eton (XI 1873, 1874); Cambridge University (Blue 1876, 1877, 1878); Old Etonians. Full internationals (1): England v Scotland 1877.

Inside-forward who received the strongest praise: 'A very strong and fast forward, a splendid shot at goal, and perhaps the most dangerous forward out.' He lived up to his reputation in the University Match of 1877-78 when he scored a hat-trick as Cambridge were comprehensive 5-1 victors over Oxford. Alfred and his brother, Edward, were teammates in the 1875-76 drawn final and replay. In a private memoir written after Alfred's death, Edward recalled: 'There have been other players more deft at dribbling, there have been a few, very few, of greater speed, and there have been heavier players, but I never knew one who combined the three great essentials, and added to them a surprising accuracy at kicking goals and "bunting" his opponents.

This last faculty he exercised by dint of a jerk of his hips, not as ordinarily by lowering the shoulder, and so the aggressor could see no signs of the terrific impact coming. Once playing against the Royal Engineers I saw him make a run down from one end of the field to the other and floor four last men on the way – the last two having charged him simultaneously from opposite sides, and both rebounding on to their backs – and shoot the goal at the end ... His method of securing a goal was peculiar and seldom failed, especially in the Association game, at which in those days a great deal more individual play was allowed than is now. He would run towards the corner and then swiftly turn inwards, running parallel to the back line, and some ten yards from it. At this point he was pursued probably by three of the opponents, barely keeping up. This continued till he got opposite the further goal post, and then one huge foot was smartly dropped on the ball, stopping it dead, and of course the pursuers all ran a yard or so too far, not suspecting the sudden pull up; thus he had a clear shot at the goal.'

Despite his prowess at the winter game, Alfred achieved greater fame as a cricketer and in 1880 set a record which can never be beaten when he became the first man to appear for England at both football and cricket, in other words, the first double international at these two sports. He played for England against Australia at The Oval in the first Test match to be played in England to add to his 1877 football appearance which was also at The Oval!

Altogether Lyttelton played in four Tests, while in the first-class game he appeared for Middlesex 1877-87 and was a Cambridge Blue 1876-79, being captain in 1879. His career record was 4,429 first-class runs, average 27.85 with 7 centuries and as a wicket-keeper he caught 134 and stumped 70, a total of 204 dismissals. He was third in the national first-class batting averages in 1879 with 688 runs at 28.66 while in 1878 he was seventh and in 1877 12th. In addition Lyttelton played for Worcestershire 1874-85 (before their promotion to first-class status) and had been in the Eton XI 1872-75, captain in his final season when he scored 102 against

Winchester and 59 against Harrow. He was a member of MCC, served on the committee 1881-85, was President in 1898 and returned to the committee 1899-1903.

Lyttelton was truly an all-round sportsman of distinction who won an athletics Blue in 1876 when he was second in throwing the hammer; a rackets Blue in 1877, 1878, 1879 when he registered victories in all three years; a real tennis Blue in the same period, winning the doubles in all three years and the singles in 1879; and holder of the MCC Gold Real Tennis Prize in 1882, 1884-85, 1887-1895 as well as the Silver Prize in 1880-81, 1883 and 1896. Later in life he took up golf, though not to the level he achieved in other sports.

After being President of Pop at Eton, he had a distinguished professional career which culminated in Cabinet office. He was a barrister who was called to the bar at the Inner Temple on 29th June 1881, going on to become a QC and later KC. Lyttelton was Legal Private Secretary to the Attorney-General, Sir Henry James, 1882-86; Recorder of Hereford 1893-94; Recorder of Oxford 1895-1903; Chancellor of the Diocese of Rochester 1903; MP for Warwick and Leamington 1895-1906; and MP for St George's, Hanover Square 1906-13. In 1903 he became a Privy Councillor and was in the Cabinet as Secretary of State for the Colonies 1903-05.

Lyttelton was taken ill at a Foreign Office dinner held to mark his return from a holiday in Africa. It turned out that he had been hit in the stomach by a cricket ball a couple of days earlier during an innings of 89. It was decided to operate and this was carried out by Dr. Watson Cheyne on Sunday 29th June but the operation failed to save his life. Lyttelton was found to have an internal abcess, probably brought on by the blow from the cricket ball but the doctors also found a bad state of things internally and declared that he could not have gone on much longer in any case. His funeral took place during the Oxford v Cambridge cricket match at Lord's and play was suspended for two minutes' silence. At the time of his death his London home was at 16 Great College Street, Westminster while his country home was Wittersham House, Kent.

He was the eighth son of the 4th Lord Lyttelton.

He earned himself a place in cricket legends during the England-Australia Test at The Oval in 1884 when the tourists totalled 551, an almost unheard of score at that time. When Australia had more than 500 runs on the board and only six wickets down, England captain W.G. Grace asked Lyttelton, the wicketkeeper, to bowl. Grace kept wicket while Lyttelton tried his underarm lobs and captured the final four wickets for only 19 runs off 12 overs! It was his final Test match.

LYTTELTON, Rev. Hon. Edward:

b. Westminster, London, 23 July 1855;
d. The Old Palace, Lincoln, 26 January 1942 (£2,734).
Education: Eton College; Trinity College, Cambridge (matric. 1874; BA 1878; MA 1881).
FA Cup runner-up (1): Old Etonians 1876 (both matches).
Career: Eton; Cambridge University (no Blue); Old Etonians. Full internationals (1): England v Scotland 1878.

Half-back and full-back praised as 'a very good back; hard to pass, and a magnificent kick.' He and his brother, the Hon. Alfred Lyttelton, were in the same Old Etonians side in the 1875-76 drawn final and replay. For such an outstanding player it may appear strange that he did not win a football Blue but he preferred to play for the Old Etonians in the Cup and at that time it was policy not to award Blues to those who declined to appear for Cambridge in the F.A. Cup. Like his brother, Edward was also a famous cricketer who was captain of Cambridge University in 1878 when they beat the first Australian tourists by an innings, the Cambridge side that season being among the best ever to represent the university. Lyttelton's century in that match was the first ever scored against the Australians in England. He won his Cambridge cricket Blue in the four years 1875-78, played for Middlesex 1878-82 and was a member of MCC. His first-class record was 2,013 runs, average 22,36 with one century. In 1878 he was second in the national first-class batting averages with 779 runs at 29.96. Earlier he had been 15th in both 1875 and 1876. He was in the Eton XI 1872-74 and also played for Worcestershire (not first-class) and Hertfordshire. In later years he gave his recreations as scenery and music.

Edward Lyttelton, who was the seventh son of the 4th Lord Lyttelton, was a Foundation Scholar and gained a 2nd class Classical Tripos (1878) at Cambridge before becoming a clergyman and schoolmaster. He was assistant master at Wellington College 1880-82; then at Eton College 1882-89; and was headmaster at Haileybury 1890-1905. He was chairman of the Council of Teacher's Guild 1891-1903 before returning to Eton as headmaster 1905-16. He had also been a member of the Commission on Secondary Education 1894 and a member of the Consultative Committee to the Board of Education 1900. On the clerical side of his career, Lyttelton became a BD in 1907 and DD in 1912. He was Chaplain to the Bishop of St Albans 1892, an honorary canon of St Albans 1895-1905 and Rector of Sidestrand, Norfolk 1918-20. He was also an honorary canon of Norwich from 1931 and Dean of Whitelands College, Chelsea. His wife was the daughter of the Dean of St Patrick's, Dublin. At the time of his death his home was at Grangegorman, Overstrand, Norfolk, but he was buried at the Old Palace, Lincoln, where he had died.

He was the author of many publications, mostly on religion or education but including *Cricket* (1890). That he was not afraid of tackling controversial issues is shown by two of his books, *Training for the Young in the Laws of Sex* (1900) and *The Christian and Birth Control* (1929).

MACAULAY, Reginald Heber:

b. Hodnet, Shropshire, 24 August 1858;
d. Ravenswood, 11 Eton Avenue, Hampstead, London, 15 December 1937 (£238,255).
Education: Eton College; King's College, Cambridge (matric. 1878; BA, Classical Tripos 1st Class, 1882; Hon. MA 1914).
FA Cup winner (1): Old Etonians 1882; runner-up (2): Old Etonians 1881, 1883.
Career: Eton (XI 1878); Cambridge University (Blue 1881, 1882); Old Etonians; Clapham Rovers; An England XI. Full internationals (1): England v Scotland 1881.

Centre-forward described as 'fast on the side, and works hard. Heavy centre-forward. Can make a good run, has plenty of pace but over-runs the ball and is not clever in close quarters' while another summary noted that he was a 'good shot at goal.' He scored a hat-trick for an England XI in an international trial game in 1880-81 when they beat Birmingham and District 5-4. At Eton Macaulay played in the Wall Game for three years and was captain of the Field Game in 1877.

Macaulay was also an outstanding athlete who won his athletics Blue in 1879, 1880 and 1881. He won the high jump in 1879 and 1880 as well as the 440 yards in 1880, 1881 and 1882, entering the latter event only because Cambridge were short of a good quarter-miler but he went on to set up a time record for the event. Macaulay helped to found the Amateur Athletic Association and in 1879 was AAA high jump champion.

From 1884 to 1901 Macaulay was a merchant in India with Wallace & Co of Bombay and chairman of the Bombay Burmah Trading Corporation. On his return to England he was an East India merchant with Wallace & Co in the City of London. Macaulay was buried at Hampstead Church. His father was the Rector of Hodnet and a cousin of Lord Macaulay, the historian.

In retirement Macaulay lived partly in Argyll where he was reputed a good shot and cultivated a famous rock garden at Kirnan in which, according to *The Times*, he bred 'one of the most notable additions to gardens of modern times – *Gentiana Macaulayi*'.

MACKARNESS, Ven. Archdeacon Charles Coleridge:
b. Tardebigge, Worcs., 22 July 1850;
d. 1 Polstead Road, Oxford, 1 March 1918 (£2,634).
Education: Winchester College; Exeter College, Oxford (matric. 1869; BA 1873; MA 1876).
FA Cup winner (1): Oxford University 1874; runner-up (1): Oxford University 1873.
Career: Winchester; Oxford University (no Blue).

Full-back or half-back who was described as 'a brilliant back, never misses his kick' and it was also said that 'as a back knows but few superiors.' He was a founder member of the Oxford University Association Football Club when it was formed on 9th November 1871. He played cricket for Devon in 1869 after being in the Winchester XI in 1868. Also captain of the Exeter College cricket XI 1873. Later in life his major recreation was cycling.

Mackarness, whose father was the Bishop of Oxford, was ordained deacon in 1874 and priest in 1875. He was curate of St Mary's, Reading, 1874-79; chaplain to the Bishop of Oxford 1875-78; chaplain and theological lecturer at King's College, London, 1879-1882; vicar of Aylesbury 1882-89; Rural Dean of Aylesbury 1887-89; vicar of St Martin's, Scarborough, 1889-1916; Prebendary of York 1896-1916; and Archdeacon of East Riding 1898-1916. In addition he was a canon of York from 1896, a Fellow of Denstone College from 1901 and became DD in 1914. He published a number of books on religious subjects.

MADDISON, Frederick Brunning (formerly Frederick Patey Chappell; he changed his name in February 1873):
b. 25 Golden Square, Westminster, London, 22 July 1849;
d. Moabit Hospital, Berlin, Germany, 25 September 1907 (£4,221).
Education: Marlborough Grammar School; Brasenose College, Oxford (matric. 1869; BA 1874).
FA Cup winner (2): Oxford University 1874; Wanderers 1876 (both matches); runner-up (1): Oxford University 1873.
Career: Marlborough GS; Oxford University (no Blue); Crystal Palace; Wanderers; Civil Service; London; The South. Full internationals (1): England v Scotland 1873 (1st match). Selected for England v Scotland 1875-76 but unavailable. Pre-official internationals (2): Scotland v England 1871 (both matches).

All-rounder who was said to be 'a very powerful forward, and one that knows not fear. Is always to be found in the vicinity of the leather' also 'a strong and fearless forward, has both weight and pace', then later 'a hard worker and very useful either forward or back.' Maddison's willingness to play anywhere saw him as a forward in his two Cup finals with Oxford but at half-back for the Wanderers. Contemporaries noted not only his work rate but also his enthusiastic charging. Maddison won an athletics Blue in 1871 when he came third in the 120 yards hurdle race.

Originally, Maddison was a barrister who was called to the bar at Lincoln's Inn on 28th June 1876 but he was disbarred at his own request in October 1884 so that he could practise as a solicitor and he was admitted as such in December 1884. Perhaps he made the change because he wished to take over the practice of his father who was also a solicitor.

The metamorphosis of his name is worth a comment. He is shown as simply Frederick Chappell on his birth certificate where his father's names are given as Frederick Patey Chappell. At some stage in his youth he also acquired 'Patey' as his second Christian name. The change to Brunning Maddison no doubt had a family motive as his mother's maiden name was Maddison.

MARINDIN, Colonel Sir Francis Arthur:

b. Melcombe Regis, near Weymouth, Dorset, 1 May 1838;
d. 3 Hans Crescent, Kensington, London SW, 21 April 1900 (£7,075).
Education: Eton College (1851-53); RMA, Woolwich.
FA Cup runner-up (2): Royal Engineers 1872†, 1874†.
FA Cup final referee (8): 1880, 1884-1890.
Career: Eton; RMA, Woolwich; Royal Engineers; Harwich; Old Etonians.

Full-back and goalkeeper. He was valued as a sound player in his two main positions but it was as a football legislator and administrator as well as a referee, that he made his most valuable contribution to the game. He missed out on two F.A. Cup winner's medals; firstly when the Royal Engineers won in 1875 he had been posted away from Chatham and was unavailable; then when the Old Etonians won in 1878-79 he had to miss the semi-final and final because of injury after playing as goalkeeper in all the earlier rounds. There is no truth in the legend that Marindin did not appear in the 1875 final because, as both a Royal Engineer and an Old Etonian, he felt it would be unsporting to oppose one or the other of his clubs. The fact is that he had already left Chatham in 1874 for a new posting and because of this did not appear in any matches in the 1874-75 F.A. Cup. Marindin was instrumental in reviving the Old Etonians in October 1878 after the club had scratched from the 1876-77 competition and not entered in 1877-78. He joined the F.A. committee in 1871 and became President in 1874, a post he held until 1890 when he resigned because of his lack of sympathy with the growing professional club representation on the F.A. He had a high reputation as a strict but fair referee who officiated in eight finals between 1880 and 1890, the last seven in succession.

Marindin was an all-round sportsman who also participated in cricket (he played for the Royal Engineers and was an MCC member), rowing, riding, shooting and lawn tennis. His father was the vicar of Chesterton, Shropshire, and his mother the daughter of a Scottish landowner. He joined the Royal Engineers as an ensign on 28th December 1854 and was promoted to lieutenant on 13th January 1855, serving in the Crimean War 1855-56 when he was based in Turkey. He became ADC and Private Secretary to the Governor of Mauritius 1860-63, which included special service in Madagascar in 1861. He then became adjutant at the School of Military Engineering, Chatham, 1866-68 and Brigade-Major 1869-74. He was promoted to captain on 22nd January 1868 and major on 5th July 1872.

In 1877 Marindin became an Investigating Officer of Railways at the Board of Trade, later being appointed Senior Investigating Officer. He retired from the Army on 29th October 1879 but continued in his railways post where it was his duty to examine the permanent way, bridges, stations and signals of many new railways and branch lines. It also fell to him to hold inquiries into a number of rail accidents. In 1891 one of these revealed a 'slave-labour' system of over-working employees when a goods guard was crushed to death between the buffers of two wagons while in a state of physical collapse after being on duty for over 22 hours at a stretch. Marindin's strongly-worded report led to the appointment of a Select Committee of the House of Commons and to a huge improvement in the working conditions of railway employees. Again, a terrible accident at Thirsk in November 1892 in which ten people died when an express caught fire in a collision with a goods train after a signalman fell asleep through exhaustion brought Marindin to declare forcibly that it was the duty of all railway companies to adopt some combination of mechanical and electrical appliance which would make such an accident impossible unless the driver deliberately ran past red signals. He also urged the engagement of relief signalmen and the importance of housing the men near their work. With repeated plain-speaking of this nature Marindin originated several important railway reforms.

During this stage of his career he renewed his links with the army from 26th January 1897 as an honorary colonel in the Engineer and Railway Volunteer Staff Corps which was entirely composed of high officials connected with railway affairs and administration.

Marindin had married a daughter of the Governor of Mauritius in 1860. In 1887 he was made a CMG after rendering important services to the Egyptian State Railways and was knighted on 22nd June 1897 during the Diamond Jubilee. His funeral took place at the family Scottish property at Craigflower, Torryburn, Dunfermline, and at the same time a memorial service was held in London at Holy Trinity Church, Sloane Street, attended by his old colleague C.W. Alcock and by C.E. Hart representing the F.A.

MAYNE, Colonel Charles Blair:
b. Vellore, India, 15 October 1855;
d. 3 Southwell Park Road, Camberley, Surrey, 17 October 1914 (£5,307).
Education: RMA, Woolwich.
FA Cup runner-up (1): Royal Engineers 1878.
Career: RMA, Woolwich; Royal Engineers.

Half-back who had the remarkable experience of being on active service in Afghanistan in the same year in which he played in the F.A. Cup final. As a result, his football career came to an abrupt end. He was summed up as 'a little uncertain early in the season, but improved towards the end, and was a very useful half-back.'

Mayne joined the Royal Engineers as a lieutenant on 28th January 1875, was promoted to honorary captain on 14th November 1881, captain on 28th January 1886, major on 10th December 1894 and lieut.-colonel on 31st December 1901. After his service in the Afghan War 1878-80 (medal), he became Assistant Instructor in Surveying at the School of Military Engineering, Chatham, from 18th July 1882 to 15th September 1886; Professor at Royal Military College, Canada, 16th September 1886-31st July 1893; and Secretary Royal Engineers Institute 1st July 1894-30th September 1897. Later Mayne was Assistant Inspector-General of Fortifications and then Assistant Director of Fortifications and Works.

MEIN, Colonel Alexander Lechmere:

b. York, 15 July 1854;
d. Gang Bridge, St Mary Bourne, Andover, Hants., 30 November 1927 (£318).
Education: Wellington College; RMA, Woolwich.
FA Cup winner (1): Royal Engineers 1875 (both matches).
Career: Wellington; RMA, Woolwich; Richmond (rugby); Royal Engineers.

Inside-left said to be 'brilliant' and who 'worked untiringly', making many good runs. Mein was another R.E. Cup finalist who saw action in Afghanistan. He also played rugby for Richmond in 1874.

Mein joined the Royal Engineers as a lieutenant on 29th April 1873, was promoted to captain on 8th January 1885, major on 1st October 1892, lieut.-colonel on 24th January

1900 and colonel in 1904. He saw active service in the Afghan War 1878-80 where he was involved in operations during the Wazir Khugianis, Hisarak and Lughman Valley Expeditions (medal and mentioned in despatches). He retired in 1905. His father was an army officer who had been stationed at York at the time of Mein's birth in 1854.

MERRIMAN, Colonel William:

b. 13 Young Street, Kensington, London, 2 April 1838;
d. Creffield House, Gray Road, Colchester, Essex, 11 March 1917 (£427).
Education: Kensington School; Addiscombe College.
FA Cup winner (1): Royal Engineers 1875† (both matches); runner-up (2): Royal Engineers 1872, 1874.
Career: Addiscombe; Royal Engineers.

Goalkeeper who earned many plaudits for his skill, his display in the 1871-72 final being described as 'perfect', while another contemporary summing up was 'the most popular of all football chiefs, and as a goalkeeper is never found wanting', then again 'one of the very best goalkeepers of the day, plucky, cool, and difficult to pass' and also 'always doing the right thing at the right time.' He was on the F.A. committee 1874-77. Merriman was a keen all-round sportsman who also took part in athletics, cricket (he played for the Royal Engineers), golf, rowing, hunting and shooting. While stationed in India he was vice-commodore of the Royal Bombay Yacht Club and a steward of the Bombay Turf Club.

He joined the East India Company's Royal Engineers (Bombay) on 12th December 1856 as an ensign and became lieutenant on 27th August 1858, serving in India 1858-66 where he was adjutant at Poona. Merriman returned to England as a fieldwork instructor at Chatham. He was promoted captain on 31st December 1868 and major on 13th March 1874, becoming District Officer at Colchester 1875-81. Merriman saw active service in South Africa in 1881 in command of the 7th Field Company, then spent many years in India. From 1882 he was involved in the coast defence of Western India, was promoted to colonel 1st July 1885, then in 1892 became Chief Engineer on the staff of CiC, Bombay. Merriman retired in 1893. He was created a Companion of the Indian Empire in 1890 for services involving the coast defences in India and Aden. He was also a Fellow of Bombay University. Merriman's father was a doctor who had been Queen Victoria's physician and he himself married the daughter of an officer in the Royal Engineers.

A memoir in the *The Sapper* for September 1896 three years after Merriman had retired brings him vividly to life: 'Who does not remember the Major Merriman of twenty years ago who was never more delighted than when organizing sports – football, cricket and other matches – for the sapper's pleasure? I can see him now, in winter time, coming out on the Barrack Square with a football under his arm and giving a mighty kick, shouting out for the men to come and join him, and in less time than I can write it the barracks would be swarming, and there would be rare fun.'

MEYSEY-THOMPSON, Albert Childers:
see THOMPSON, Albert Childers.

MEYSEY-THOMPSON, Rev. Charles Maude:
see THOMPSON, Rev. Charles Maude.

MITCHELL, Captain Hugh:

b. 29 Cavendish Road West, Marylebone, London, 3 December 1849;
d. Brakpan, South Africa, 16 August 1937. (£2,008 in England).
Education: Harrow School (1864-67); RMA, Woolwich.
FA Cup runner-up (1): Royal Engineers 1872.
Career: Harrow; RMA, Woolwich; Royal Engineers. Pre-official internationals (2): Scotland v England 1872 (both matches).

Forward who was a typical Harrow product of the dribbling era, Mitchell was described as 'a good charger and useful forward, sticks to the ball well.' He qualified for Scotland in 1872 on the basis of his father's Scottish origins. He was also a good cricketer who appeared for the Royal Engineers and at school had been a member of the Harrow shooting team.

Mitchell joined the Royal Engineers as a lieutenant on 8th January 1870 and was promoted to captain on 8th January 1882. He was posted to Bermuda 1873-75 and Gibraltar 1875-78 before returning home for a spell at the War Office 1881-82. However, unlike most of his R.E. teammates he did not make a career of the army but retired on 11th March 1882 and studied for the law. He was called to the bar at the Inner Temple on 7th May 1884, was a barrister on the South Wales and Chester circuit and Glamorgan Sessions and practised in Gibraltar from 1894. He retired in 1926 and moved to South Africa. Mitchell married a sister of teammate E.W. Creswell in 1878. His father had been a lieut.-colonel in the army.

MORRIS, Colonel Sir William George:

b. Malagaum, India, 12 February 1847;
d. Islwyn, Betws-y-Coed, Caernarvonshire, North Wales, 26 February 1935 (£7,327).
Education: Cheltenham College; RMA, Woolwich.
FA Cup runner-up (1): Royal Engineers 1878.
Career: Cheltenham; RMA, Woolwich; Royal Engineers.

Full-back whose 'excellent' and 'well-directed' throw-in led to the only goal by the R.E. when they lost the 1878 Cup final. By this date he was already approaching the veteran stage in comparison with many of his teammates.

Morris joined the Royal Engineers as a lieutenant in 1867, was promoted to captain in 1879, major in 1886, lieut. colonel in 1893, brevet colonel in 1897 and colonel in 1898. He passed the Staff College with honours 1876, was assistant-instructor in surveying at the School of Military Engineering at Chatham 1877-82; in command of the Training Battalion there 1894-95; and then Assistant-Commandant at Chatham 1895-98. He served in the Boer War 1899-1902 (made CB 1900 and mentioned in despatches twice) and was Colonel on the Staff of the R.E. South Africa 1898-1902.

Morris' speciality was geodetics (to do with the curvature and figure of the earth) and 'gained a reputation in scientific circles outside the Army' (*The Times* in his obituary). He was in charge of the Transit of Venus expedition to Brisbane, Queensland, in 1882 which observed the passage of Venus across the face of the sun and so obtained fresh data for the calculation of the distance between the earth and the sun (the next transit did not occur until 2004). He was then in charge of the survey of South Africa 1883-93 and Superintendant of the Ordnance Survey of Transvaal and Orange River Colony 1902-07. He retired from the army in 1904 but continued in his then current post as a civil appointment. He was created KCMG in 1907. His father had been a lieut.-colonel in the Bombay Army.

MUIRHEAD, Lieut.-Col. Herbert Hugh:

b. 3 Oriental Place, Brighton, 10 December 1850;
d. 32 Seymour Street, Marylebone, London, 4 March 1904 (£16,913).
Education: Eton College; Wellington College; RMA, Woolwich.
FA Cup runner-up (1): Royal Engineers 1872.
Career: Eton; Wellington; RMA, Woolwich; Royal Engineers.

Forward who was noticed for his 'excellent' and 'fine' runs but whose career with the Royal Engineers was not a lengthy one as he was soon posted away from the team's Chatham base.

Muirhead joined the Royal Engineers as a lieutenant on 2nd August 1871, was promoted to captain on 2nd August 1883, major on 17th December 1889, lieut.-colonel on 4th April 1897 and colonel on 4th April 1901. He retired on 4th April 1902 without having seen active service. He held a prominent position at the Royal Arsenal 1883-93 and his postings included Ireland 1873-75, Bermuda 1876-78, Gibraltar 1878-81, Ireland again 1881-83 and Canada 1893-98 (involved in West Coast defence works). Muirhead's death was caused by pleuro-pneumonia. His father achieved fame as the biographer of James Watt (to whom the Muirheads were related), the inventor of the steam engine.

NEPEAN, Rev. Charles Edward Burroughs:

b. Mayfair, London, 5 February 1851;
d. Lenham Vicarage, near Maidstone, Kent, 26 March 1903 (£1,255).
Education: Charterhouse School; University College, Oxford (matric. 1870; BA 1873 from St Alban Hall; MA 1880 from University College).
FA Cup winner (1): Oxford University 1874.
Career: Charterhouse (XI 1865-66 to 1869-70; 1867-68 to 1869-70†); Oxford University (Blue 1874); Middlesex. Pre-official internationals (4): Scotland v England 1871 (both matches); 1872 (both matches).

Goalkeeper in his Cup final but more often played as a forward where he was eulogised as 'may be fairly classed as the best player of the day, works the ball with surprising skill, and never misses a shot at goal; can take any position with credit to himself.' He was also said to be 'energetic, hard-working and conspicuous'. He was selected for Oxford in the 1873 Cup final but was unable to play. He had Scottish family links which qualified him for Scotland in the pre-official internationals. Nepean was a founder member of the Oxford

University Association Football Club when it was formed on 9th November 1871.

At cricket he was a good wicket-keeper, appearing for Oxford 1870-73 (Blue 1873), Middlesex 1873-74 and Dorset, while in 1873 he was selected for the Gentlemen v Players. In his ten first-class matches he caught seven and stumped six. In 1873 he was ninth in the national first-class batting averages. At Charterhouse he was in the XI 1866-69 (captain 1868-69) and later he served on the Kent CCC committee.

Nepean, who was the son of a clergyman, was ordained deacon in 1874 and priest in 1875. He was curate of Hartley Wintney, Hants., 1874-76 and vicar of Lenham, Kent, 1876-1903. He was the brother of the Middlesex cricketer, A.A.St.J.M. Nepean and the uncle of E.A. Nepean, also of Middlesex.

NORRIS, Walter Harry:

b. Ashley House, Epsom, Surrey, 8 April 1863;
d. Steane Park, Brackley, Northants., 14 May 1931 (£33,315).
Education: Charterhouse School (1877-80).
FA Cup winner (1): Old Carthusians 1881.
Career: Charterhouse (XI 1880); Old Carthusians; Surrey.

Full-back who had a meteoric rise, going from the school XI in 1880 to F.A. Cup winner the following year but thereafter his career at the top proved a short one. He was described as a 'capital back; cool, strong kick.'

Norris was a brewer by profession, being a director of the Brackley and Banbury Brewery.

NOVELLI, Philip Charles:

b. Marylebone, London, 17 September 1857;
d. 11 Idol Lane, City of London, 4 December 1905 (£4,240).
Education: Eton College; Trinity College, Cambridge (matric. 1876; BA 1880).
FA Cup winner (1): Old Etonians 1882; runner-up (1): Old Etonians 1881.
Career: Eton (XI 1876); Cambridge University (no Blue); Old Etonians; London.

Outside-left who was described as 'a good side, works hard on and sticks to the ball.' He was also a proficient oarsman who stroked the Eton eight in 1876.

Novelli practised as a solicitor in London 1884-94, then became a merchant banker who specialised in foreign exchanges. At the time of his death his home was at Morden Holt, Datchet, Bucks.

OGILVIE, Robert Andrew Muter Macindoe:

b. 7 Doughty Street, Mecklenburgh Square, London, 20 October 1852;
d. Golf Cottage, St John's, Woking, Surrey, 5 March 1938 (£100,311).
Education: Brentwood School.
FA Cup winner (1): Clapham Rovers 1880†;
runner-up (1): Clapham Rovers 1879†.
FA Cup final umpire (1): 1876.
Career: Brentwood; Upton Park (1871-73); Clapham Rovers; London. Full internationals (1): England v Scotland 1874.

Full-back and half-back, said to be a 'fair back' and 'of great service, though not always certain; works hard throughout and could play forward if wanted'. He was one of the Clapham Rovers stalwarts who helped to run the club for many years. Ogilivie served on the F.A. committee 1874-81 and again 1884-86.

By profession Ogilvie was an insurance underwriter with the Alliance Assurance Co to 1914 then with the War Risks Department 1914-19. He was a Member of Lloyd's and in 1910-11 was chairman of the Institute of London Underwriters. At the time of his death Ogilivie also had a London home at 18 Sheffield Terrace, Campden Hill, Kensington.

OLIVIER, Colonel Henry Dacres:

b. Court Hill, Potterne, Wiltshire, 22 October 1850;
d. Shapley Hill, Winchfield, Basingstoke, Hampshire, 30 March 1935 (£28,054).
Education: Haileybury College; RMA, Woolwich.
FA Cup runner-up (1): Royal Engineers 1874.
Career: Haileybury (rugby); RMA, Woolwich; Royal Engineers.

Centre-forward whose rugby skills which he developed at Haileybury slotted in well with the robust tactics of the Royal Engineers. He was said to be 'a very useful centre-forward' who was often picked out for special praise. Olivier switched from rugby to football at a comparatively late age and then had a very short career indeed as by 1875 he was serving in India where he spent the bulk of his career.

Olivier joined the Royal Engineers as a lieutenant on 15th December 1871 then qualified as AMICE. He served with the Bombay Public Works Department from 1st June 1875 including a spell in Baluchistan 1878-80. He was appointed Executive Engineer and Consulting Engineer for Bombay Railways in March 1884, then joined Sudan Railways in 1885. From 1889-91 Olivier was under-secretary to the Bombay Public Works Department, agent to the Bombay, Baroda & Central India Railway Co. from August 1894 and Superintendent Engineer from September 1900, retiring in April 1904. Olivier, whose father was a clergyman, was buried at Winchfield.

ONSLOW, Colonel Gerald Charles Penrice:

b. Deyrah, India (possibly now Dehra Dun, India), 7 February 1853;
d. Camperdown, Crowborough, Sussex, 16 April 1909 (£11,408).
Education: Cheltenham College; RMA, Woolwich.
FA Cup winner (1): Royal Engineers 1875 (both matches); runner-up (1): Royal Engineers 1874.
Career: Cheltenham (rugby XX 1870); RMA, Woolwich; Royal Engineers.

Half-back who was a key defender for the Engineers during their peak years, being described as 'one of the most brilliant half-backs of the day, very quiet, and a sure kick in any position.'

Onslow joined the Royal Engineers as a lieutenant on 29th April 1873, was promoted to captain on 8th January 1885, major on 21st October 1892, lieut.-colonel on 9th April 1900 and retired with the rank of colonel in 1905. He fought in the Afghan war 1879-80 where he saw action at Charasiah and took part in operations around Kabul in December 1879 (medal with two clasps and mentioned in despatches). Further active service came in the Burmese Expedition 1885-87 (medal with clasp).

OTTAWAY, Cuthbert John:

b. Dover, Kent, 20 July 1850;
d. 34 Westbourne Place, Eaton Square, Westminster, London, 2 April 1878 (under £800).
Education: Eton College; Brasenose College, Oxford (matric. 1869; BA 1874).
FA Cup winner (1): Oxford University 1874†; runner-up (2): Oxford University 1873; Old Etonians 1875 (first match).
Career: Eton; Oxford University (Blue 1874†); Marlow; Crystal Palace; Old Etonians. Full internationals (2): England v Scotland 1873† (1st match); 1874†.

Centre-forward who was described as 'an excellent forward, being fast and very skilful in piloting the ball', then 'as a forward he certainly can hold his own against all rivals' and 'an elegant dribbler and plays well.' In a period noted for vigorous and robust play he was considered to have a graceful style as shown in a report which said that his 'beautiful science exhibited how a ball ought to be taken through a host of foes.' During the first season of the Cup, 1871-72, Ottaway managed to play for two different clubs, representing Marlow in the first round, where they lost to Maidenhead, and Crystal Palace in later rounds, including the semi-final! A bad injury in the drawn Cup final of 1874-75 kept Ottaway out of much cricket during the following summer. He was on the F.A. committee 1872-73.

Ottaway was a multi-talented sportsman who was one of the leading cricketers of the day during his short career. He was in the Eton XI 1867-69, scoring 108 v Harrow in 1869, played for Kent 1869-70, was an Oxford Blue 1870-73 (captain 1873), appeared for Middlesex 1874-76 and also for the Gentlemen v the Players (1870, 1872, 1876), the most important game of the season in the pre-Test match era. In first-class cricket he totalled 1,691 runs, average 27.27 with 2 centuries. He finished seventh in the national first-class batting averages in 1870 and fifth in 1873.

His other sporting feats included an athletics Blue in 1873 when he was third in the 100 yards; rackets Blue in 1870, 1871, 1872 and 1873, being a singles winner in all four years; real tennis Blue in 1870, 1871 and 1872, winning the doubles in 1870 but losing in 1871-72; and Public Schools doubles rackets champion 1868-69. He was no slouch academically either, leaving Oxford with a First in Moderations and a Third in Classics.

Ottaway retired from regular sport in 1876 when he became a barrister, being called to the bar at the Inner Temple. His tragic early death followed a 'rapid decline brought on by a cold' and he was buried at Kensal Green Cemetery in London.

OTTER, Henry Shirecliffe:

b. Westminster, London, 4 February 1856;
d. 3 Half Moon Street, Piccadilly, London, 29 December 1879 (below £100).
Education: Westminster School (1866-74); Christ Church, Oxford (matric. 1874; BA 1878).
FA Cup runner-up (1): Oxford University 1877.

Career: Westminster (XI 1871-74, captain in 1873-74); Oxford University (Blue 1875-76-77-78); Wanderers; Middlesex; London.

Forward who was another famous dribbler, he was especially prominent in his four university matches against Cambridge. He was said to be 'a brilliant forward, being a very skilful dribbler, and a dead shot at goal; dribbles a little too much at times.' Otter also won an athletics Blue in 1878 when he was runner-up in throwing the hammer.

He joined the Indian Civil Service in 1879 where he was based at Tinnevelly, Madras Presidency. He was taken ill that same year and returned to England where he died aged 23 from peritonitis caused by an abscess of the liver.

PAGE, William Robert:

b. 11 Queen Street, Mayfair, Westminster, London, 12 December 1858;
d. 27 Westbourne Park, Paddington, London, 30 June 1884.
Education: Charterhouse School (1869-77); Queen's College, Oxford (matric. 1877).
FA Cup winner (1): Old Carthusians 1881.
Career: Charterhouse (XI 1874-76; captain 1876); Oxford University (Blue 1878; 1879); Old Carthusians; Berkshire; The Rest (v England); London; The South.

Centre-forward renowned for his dribbling. Tributes included: 'A most brilliant dribbler, having considerable pace and sticking to the ball in a wonderful manner'; 'Is small, but has done great service by his "dodgy" dribbling'; 'One of the finest dribblers of the day, but should play more for his side', and this last criticism was expanded elsewhere: 'is rather accustomed to be played for.'

He joined the Royal Irish Constabulary as a sub-inspector in 1884 but tragically died soon afterwards at the age of 25 from meningitis and rheumatic fever. His father was a doctor.

PARES, Rev. Canon Norman:
b. 12 Devonshire Street, Portland Place, London, 16 June 1857;
d. Horsell Vicarage, Surrey, 23 June 1936 (£5,347).
Education: Eton College; Trinity College, Cambridge (matric. 1876; BA, Classical Tripos 3rd Class, 1880; MA 1883).
FA Cup winner (1): Old Etonians 1879.
Career: Eton; Cambridge University (no Blue); Old Etonians; Portsmouth Sunflowers.

Inside-left and yet another honed on the dashing and individualistic skills of the Eton Field Game. He played for Portsmouth Sunflowers in the Hampshire Cup final of 1887-88. He was a member of MCC and, apart from cricket, also played golf and cycled.

He was ordained deacon in 1885 and priest in 1886 while from 1881-97 he was a master at Portsmouth Grammar School (second master 1892-97). Pares was curate at St Jude's, Southsea, 1885-87; curate at Portsmouth Parish Church 1894-97; and finally vicar of Horsell 1897-1935. He was also Rural Dean of Woking 1913-28; Hon. Canon of Winchester 1925-27; and Hon. Canon of Guildford 1928-36.

PARR, Percival Chase:
b. Bickley, Kent, 2 December 1859;
d. Molescroft, Widmore, Bromley, Kent, 3 September 1912 (£2,426).
Education: Winchester College; New College, Oxford (matric. 1878; BA 1883).
FA Cup runner-up (1): Oxford University 1880.
Career: Winchester (XI 1877); Oxford University (Blue 1880, 1881, 1882†); Swifts; West Kent; Old Wykehamists; Kent. Full internationals (1): England v Wales 1882.

Goalkeeper who was the recipient of high praise as 'a splendid goalkeeper, very cool and full of pluck', though he was versatile enough to figure at centre-forward in his England international appearance in which he scored a goal. In this role he was described as 'a hard-working, energetic centre-forward.' Parr also kept goal in his first two University matches but switched to centre-forward in his captaincy year of 1882 so that it seems as if he concentrated on the latter position after 1881, a point perhaps proved by his hat-trick for the Swifts against Upton Park when they won a second round Cup replay 3-2 in 1882-83. He was on the F.A. committee in 1881. Parr was also a good cricketer who was in the Winchester XI 1877-78 and played once in first-class cricket, for the Gentlemen of Kent in 1880.

Although Parr was a barrister by profession who was called to the bar at the Inner Temple in 1885 he branched out into publishing, becoming a partner in the firm of W. H. Allen & Co., the publishers, as well as editing the magazines *National Observer* from 1894 and *Ladies' Field*. His father was a general.

PARRY, Edward Hagarty:

b. Toronto, Canada, 24 April 1855;
d. 12 Dovedale Road, West Bridgford, Nottingham, 19 July 1931 (£3,311).
Education: Charterhouse School (1868-74); Exeter College, Oxford (matric. 1874; BA 1878; MA 1882).
FA Cup winner (1): Old Carthusians 1881†; runner-up (1): Oxford University 1877†.
Career: Charterhouse (XI 1870-73; captain 1872, 1873); Swifts; Oxford University (Blue 1875, 1876, 1877†); Remnants; Old Carthusians; London; Bucks; The Rest (v England); The South; Stoke Poges; Windsor; Berks & Bucks. Full internationals (3): England v Wales 1879; 1882; v Scotland 1882.

Inside-left described as 'a fast dribbler, and useful as a wing, but is rather light and does not stand a charge.' A consistent goalscorer over many years, Parry was still playing at the end of the 1880s; he was in the Old Carthusians team who beat the South of England 3-1 at The Oval in the F.A. Charity Festival on 16th March 1889, scoring one of the goals. His best feats as a goalgetter include five for Old Carthusians in their 10-1 first round Cup win against Reading Minster in 1883-84, four for the Carthusians as they beat Saffron Walden 7-0 in the Cup first round in 1880-81, a hat-trick as the OCs beat Pilgrims 6-0 in the 1882-83 Cup first round, a repeat performance in that season's fourth round as the Royal Engineers succumbed 6-2, and his first hat-trick of all back in 1874-75 when Oxford University beat Brondesbury 6-0 in the first round of the Cup. He was on the F.A. committee in 1881. Parry was also a decent cricketer who was in the Charterhouse XI 1872-74 and later a member of MCC. In 1874 he was joint winner of the Athletic Challenge Cup at Charterhouse.

Parry became a schoolmaster and was at Felsted 1879-80 before settling in at Stoke House Private School, Stoke Poges, near Slough, 1881-1918. He was headmaster from 1892 and retired in 1918. In 1907 he was chairman of the Private Schools Association 1907 and sat on its council for many years. After retirement he helped to run the Officers' Family Fund for the sons of officers who died in the Great War.

Parry suffered much ill-health in his later years, including slowly progressive blindness and great physical weakness. He was buried at Plumtree Church, near West Bridgford, Nottingham. His father was a clergyman who had been serving in Canada at the time of Parry's birth.

In 1881 the Cup went on display at Charterhouse School. Parry wrote to the headmaster's wife on 12th May that year: 'Dear Mrs Haig Brown; I send by my brother the Association Challenge Cup, which I hope you will allow us to put into your charge for the year, as Charterhouse is now its natural resting place. It is fully insured, which perhaps will save you some anxiety. I don't know whether it could placed in the Library; if it were possible after a time, many old Carthusians would be pleased. We were all very glad that you were able to come up and see the final match, especially as you had not to witness a defeat. With kind regard to yourself and Dr Haig Brown; Believe me, yours very truly, E.H. Parry.' His letter is preserved in a scrapbook kept by Mrs Haig Brown which is now in the Charterhouse archives.

Parry's grave, Plumtree, Notts

PATON, Walter Boldero:
b. 13 Hanover Terrace, Regent's Park, Westminster, London, 19 April 1853;
d. 10 Stanhope Gardens, Kensington, London, 11 February 1937 (£28,500).
Education: Harrow School; University College, Oxford (matric. 1872; BA 1876; MA 1879).
FA Cup runner-up (1): Oxford University 1873.
Career: Harrow (captain); Oxford University; Harrow Chequers; Old Harrovians. Pre-official internationals (1): England v Scotland 1871.

Forward who had made his mark already during his years at Harrow. He was not yet 18 and still at school when selected for his pre-official international, turning out at the age of 17 years 214 days. He was summed up as 'a strong and persevering forward, and keeps side well.' By 1878, and illustrating how the passing game was taking over from pure dribbling, it was 'a very pretty dribbler but disinclined to pass the ball; can play extremely well when he likes.'

Paton was the son of a barrister who was himself called to the bar at the Inner Temple on 25th June 1879. Thereafter, he practised on the Western Circuit until he retired in 1916.

PATTON, Frederick Joseph:
b. Malabar Hill, Bombay, India, 21 January 1851;
d. 13 Gildridge Road, Eastbourne, 5 February 1922 (£2,148).
Education: Eton College; Balliol College, Oxford (matric. 1870; BA 1875).
FA Cup winner (1): Oxford University 1874; runner-up (1): Old Etonians 1875 (both matches).
Career: Eton; Oxford University; Surrey; Old Etonians.

Centre-forward who sealed Oxford's Cup final victory with his side's second goal, Patton was summed up concisely as 'very fast, and a sure goal getter.' In the 1875-76 competition he scored a hat-trick in the second round as the University beat Maidenhead 8-0. Later he became a keen golfer and was a founder of the Royal Ascot Golf Club. In fact, at the time of his death his home was The Links, Ascot, Berks., and he was buried at All Saints Church, Ascot Heath.

Patton was in practice as a barrister, having been called to the bar at the Inner Temple on 26th January 1876. When living at Ascot, he became a member of Berkshire County Council and a local JP.

PHILLIPS, Francis Angelo Theodore:
b. Bayswater, London, 3 August 1857;
d. Hyde Gardens Nursing Home, Eastbourne, 15 February 1936 (£3,857).
Education: Winchester College; Balliol College, Oxford (matric. 1878).
FA Cup runner-up (1): Oxford University 1880.
Career: Winchester; Oxford University (Blue 1880).

Half-back who was complimented because he 'played very well for Oxford in the Cup ties; works hard throughout.' After 1880 he was lost to English football as he spent the next 30 years in India. He also played golf and lawn tennis as well as being keen on riding and shooting.

Phillips joined the Indian Civil Service in 1878 and moved out there as Assistant Commissioner of the Central Provinces in 1880. In 1883 he was promoted to personal assistant to the Chief Commissioner, became deputy in 1884 and Commissioner in 1898. Finally he reached the rank of Chief Commissioner 1907-09 and was on the Governor-General's Council in 1910 before retiring back to England. At the time of his death his home was at Avondale, 5 Moat Croft Road, Eastbourne. His father was a major-general in the Indian Army.

PRINSEP, James Frederick McLeod:

b. India, 27 July 1861;
d. Nairn, Scotland, 22 November 1895 (£1,204).
Education: Charterhouse School (1874-78); Royal Military College, Sandhurst (from 1878).
FA Cup winner (1): Old Carthusians 1881; runner-up (1): Clapham Rovers 1879.
Career: Charterhouse (XI 1876, 1877); RMC, Sandhurst; Clapham Rovers; Surrey; Old Carthusians; London; The South; The Rest (v England). Full internationals (1): England v Scotland 1879. He was selected for England v Scotland in 1881-82 but was unavailable.

Half-back whose ability called forth much admiring comment: 'A fine half-back, always cool, very strong on his legs, and combining plenty of strength with great accuracy; kicks splendidly and with judgment; seldom makes a mistake' also 'can kick the ball in any position, and passes it admirably to his forwards.' He became the youngest player to appear in an F.A. Cup final at the age of 17 years and 245 days on 29th March 1879, a record that stood until 2004. He was also the youngest England international player at 17 years 252 days but this record lasted only until March 2003! He was an above-average club cricketer, being especially effective as a bowler, was a member of Free Foresters as well as the Grey Friars, a club for old Carthusians, and featured in the Charterhouse XI in 1877.

Prinsep was a professional soldier as a lieutenant with the Essex Regiment 1882-85, and was involved in the march to Khartoum in a vain effort to save the besieged General Gordon. Prinsep stayed in Egypt and transferred to the Egyptian Army 1885-90 as a major (then, of course, under British control with British officers). Finally he joined the Egyptian Coastguard Service from 1890 until his death, reaching the rank of Sub-Inspector General.

He died while on holiday at Nairn in Scotland where he had many relations. Prinsep played a game of golf one wet day while suffering from a cold and this turned to pneumonia. After seven weeks of illness he died of blood poisoning and kidney failure. At the time of his death Prinsep's home in Britain was at 46 Thurloe Square, Middlesex, and he also had his own residence in Alexandria, Egypt.

He received **TWO** Royal Humane Society awards for rescuing men from the Nile. Firstly, the Bronze Medal for saving a fellow-soldier from drowning at Shaban Rapids on the river near Kanneck on 23rd December 1884. *The Times* described how Lieut. Prinsep, fully-clothed, plunged into the water and swam to the spot 30 yards lower down where the drowning man, Private G. Wheeler, had risen to the surface. Prinsep seized hold and supported Wheeler, who could not swim, until other help arrived. A year later he received the Bronze Clasp for his second Nile rescue. This time his act of bravery took place on 19th December 1885 near El Sabon and the man he saved was a Sudanese sailor. Prinsep was the first of two members of the Old Carthusians Cup-winning side to receive such awards. See under E.G. Wynyard for details of his Royal Humane Society Medal.

RAM, Edward Albert:

b. Hammersmith, between July 1858 and January 1859 (see note);
d. 45 Pembroke Square, Kensington, London, 27 January 1946 (£4,502).
Education: Private in Upper Norwood; Royal Academy Schools.
FA Cup winner (1): Clapham Rovers 1880.
Career: South Norwood; Hawks; Clapham Rovers; Surrey; London.

Outside-left, a nippy, small, dapper player who was the prototype for many wingers to come. He was one of those wingers who could cut in to get on the scoresheet which he did regularly, to such effect in the Cup second round in 1882-83 that he ended up with a hat-trick as Clapham Rovers demolished Hanover United 7-1. Ram was educated at home by his father who was a professional tutor for candidates for the army, the church and the other major professions, but, with an enlightened attitude, Ram senior arranged for his son to visit a local private school for football and cricket only. He proved to be a good all-round sportsman and apart from achieving special distinction as a footballer, was also a keen cricketer who later represented Hong Kong.

Ram became an architect of distinction. He was an articled pupil of a leading Victorian architect, George Somers Clarke (1825-82) between 1877-82. Meanwhile he had attended the Royal Academy Schools for architectural studies from 6th July 1880. After the death of his mentor he continued as an assistant in Clarke's old firm until 1885 during which time he travelled to study architecture in Belgium and Holland, then set up his own practice in Westminster.

Later he moved to Hong Kong where he was based on the Queen's Road and from where, in June 1897, he became a Fellow of the Royal Institute of British Architects. While in Hong Kong he was involved in a number of major architectural projects including the Public Library around 1900 and the Hong Kong racecourse grandstand.

After the Great War he returned to England and resumed practice in Kensington until 1928 when he retired. His death was caused by bronchitis and emphysema. Ram's sister, Jane, ran an art school in London near Victoria, and it was one of her pupils whom he married while on home leave in 1902. Apart from his skill as an architect Ram was also a very talented water-colourist and painter of miniature portraits.

His grandson, John Miskin, writing in 2003, recalled Ram politely lifting his straw boater hat as he greeted his nanny as they met while walking in Kensington Gardens in 1933, adding: 'I was only five at the time yet I have a distinct image of an extremely dapper little man, immaculately dressed and carrying a cane or a tightly rolled umbrella. I've been told that he was no more than about 5ft. 5in. tall. He was debonair, reminding me in postwar days of a smaller Maurice Chevalier. His sporting prowess is entirely consistent with my impressions of a very athletic grandpa joining me, my brother and cousins in a game of catch in the garden at Dymchurch in 1936. He outran all of us and, leaping over a low gate, tripped and fell, breaking his nose!'

NOTE: A search of both local and national birth registers has failed to locate an entry for Ram, while the family archives also lack this information. From his age as given when he registered for the Royal Academy Schools in July 1880, from his entry in the census of April 1881 and the age on his death certificate it has been possible to establish a six-month period during which his birth must have taken place.

RAWLINSON, Rt. Hon. John Frederick Peel:

b. New Alresford, Hants, 21 December 1860;
d. 5 Crown Office Row, Temple, London, 14 January 1926 (£86,102).
Education: Eton College; Trinity College, Cambridge (matric. 1879; Law Tripos 1st Class 1882; LL.B. 1883; LL.M. 1887; Hon. LL.D. 1920).
FA Cup winner (1): Old Etonians 1882; runner-up (2): Old Etonians 1881, 1883.
Career: Eton; Cambridge University (Blue 1882, 1883); Old Etonians; Corinthians. Full internationals (1): England v Ireland 1882.

Goalkeeper who was described as an 'excellent goalkeeper, cool and sure' though he was said to be too almost too casual at times. He served on the F.A. committee 1885-86 and was also on the original committee of the Corinthians in 1882.

At university Rawlinson was a Prizeman in Common Law and by profession a barrister who was called to the bar at the Inner Temple on 25th June 1884, becoming a QC in 1897 on the South-East Circuit, then later KC. Rawlinson was Recorder of Cambridge 1898-1926 and MP for Cambridge University 1906-26 in the days when the universities sent members to Parliament. In 1923 he became a Privy Councillor and had been a member (eventually vice-chairman) of the General Council of the Bar since its formation. He was also a member of the governing bodies of Eton, Malvern and Brighton colleges.

He had many other posts and honours, being a Cambridgeshire JP from 1901, Deputy High Steward of Cambridge University from 1918, Fellow of Eton College, Hon. Fellow of Pembroke College and a temporary chairman of Committees in the House of Commons from 1916. Rawlinson represented the Treasury in the official inquiry into the Jameson Raid of 1895. His *Rawlinson's Municipal Corporations' Acts* went into ten editions, becoming the standard work on the subject. He died in his chambers where he had been confined for ten days with pleurisy. His father had been Chief Justice of Madras.

RAWSON, Frederick Lawrence:
b. Westminster, London, 27 July 1859;
d. Hotel Astor, Times Square, New York, United States, 10 November 1923 (£1,230).
Education: Westminster School (1873-76).
FA Cup runner-up (1): Clapham Rovers 1879.
Career: Westminster (XI 1875-76); Clapham Rovers.

Outside-right of whom it was said: 'A useful wing player; middles well' and 'at times brilliant, though rather lacking in weight.' Rawson was also a useful cricketer who featured in the Westminster XI in 1874.

He was related to H.E. Rawson and W.S. Rawson, who were also Cup finalists, and went into business as an electrical engineer with Woodhouse & Rawson Ltd. Rawson was the founder of the Society for Spreading the Knowledge of True Prayer. He devoted much time to and spent much money on this project, including publications on the subject. In fact he died while on a lecture tour of the United States to promote his beliefs. At the time of his death his home was at Barwell Court, Chessington, Surrey.

RAWSON, Colonel Herbert Edward:

b. Port Louis, Mauritius, 3 September 1852;
d. 46 St George's Road, Westminster, London, 18 October 1924 (£2,536).
Education: Wallace's School, Cheltenham; Westminster School (1865-71); RMA, Woolwich.
FA Cup winner (1): Royal Engineers 1875 (both matches); runner-up (1): Royal Engineers 1874.
Career: Westminster (XI 1869-71; captain 1870-71); RMA, Woolwich; Royal Engineers; Kent. Full internationals (1): England v Scotland 1875.

Centre-forward of all-round ability who was praised highly: 'As a centre can hardly be surpassed; dribbles closely and cleverly, and is a dead shot at goal; always works hard.' Rawson became the second player on record to clock up five goals in a Cup-tie which he did in the first round of the 1875-76 competition when Royal Engineers beat High Wycombe 15-0. He and his brother, W.S. Rawson, were on opposing sides in the 1873-74 Cup final. A good cricketer as wicketkeeper with the Royal Engineers XI, Rawson played one first-class match for Kent in 1873 but scored two noughts though behind the stumps he caught one and stumped three. He was in the Westminster XI in 1869 and 1870, was also a member of MCC and Free Foresters and in later life president of the Old Westminsters CC.

Rawson joined the Royal Engineers as a lieutenant in 1872, specialised in submarine mining in 1874, was involved with Bermuda defence in 1877 and was seconded to the Treasury 1880-84. He was in Malta in 1885 then spent 1885-89 in Canada raising submarine mining militia. He was secretary of the R.E. committee and War Office Ordnance committee 1890-94. He saw much active service in the Boer War 1899-1902 where he was involved in the engagements at Tugela Heights, the Relief of Ladysmith and Laing's Nek. Rawson commanded the district Natal and Zululand Frontier during operations in 1901, taking part in the battle of Itala (medals and four clasps, mentioned in despatches eight times and created CB).

After the war he was a member of the Natal Defences Commission 1902 and the Natal Native Affairs Commission 1906-07. Finally he was Chief Engineer and Commanding R.E. in South Africa 1905-07 then Chief Engineer Northern Command 1907-09 before he retired in 1909.

He was interested in aeronautics and meteorology, being author of a number of publications on these subjects. He became vice-president of the Meteorological Society and was on the council of the African Royal Aeronautical Society, also a Fellow of the Royal Geographical Society and involved with the Hertfordshire Natural History Society. At the time of his death his home was at Home Close, Heronsgate, Herts.

RAWSON, William Stepney:

b. Cape Town, South Africa, 14 October 1854; d. Yew Tree Cottage, Whitchurch, Oxon., 4 November 1932 (£260).
Education: Westminster School (1867-73); Christ Church, Oxford (matric. 1873; BA 1877; MA 1880).
FA Cup winner (1): Oxford University 1874; runner-up (1): Oxford University 1877.
FA Cup final referee (1): 1876.
Career: Westminster (XI 1871-73, captain in 1872-83); Oxford University (Blue 1874, 1875, 1876†, 1877); Old Westminsters; Swifts; Wanderers; London. Full internationals (2): England v Scotland 1875; 1877†.

In the forward line in his first Cup final, Rawson later became an excellent defender who was described as 'a safe player, back or half-back, getting very fast to the ball, and, being short and strong, can stand any amount of charging'. At the close of the 1874-75 season he was said to be 'the best half-back, perhaps, of the year, always cool and to be relied upon in his kicks; a brilliant player at all times, and singularly effective in the International Match.' He and his brother, H.E. Rawson, were on opposing sides in the 1873-74 Cup final. He was on the F.A. committee 1876-77 and again in 1879. Rawson was also a fine lacrosse player who represented the South v the North in both 1889 and 1899. He was a useful cricketer, too, who was in the Westminster XI 1869-73, played for Herefordshire in 1878 and was a member of MCC.

Rawson went into the family business of electrical engineering, eventually becoming managing director of Mabor Ltd. by 1903.

RENNY-TAILYOUR, Colonel Henry Waugh:

b. Mussoorie, North-West Province, India, 9 October 1849;
d. Newmanswalls, Montrose, Forfarshire, 15 June 1920.
Education: Cheltenham College (August 1859-December 1867); RMA, Woolwich (1868-70).
FA Cup winner (1): Royal Engineers 1875 (both matches); runner-up (2): Royal Engineers 1872, 1874.
Career: Cheltenham (rugby); RMA, Woolwich (XI 1868-69); Royal Engineers. Full internationals (1): Scotland v England 1873 (2nd match). Pre-official internationals (1): Scotland v England 1872.

Centre-forward who was a goal poacher before that term had been invented; he scored the equalising goal against the Old Etonians in the 1874-75 final and both goals in the 2-0 replay victory. In addition he twice scored a brace of goals in Cup semi-finals to put the Engineers through to the final: in a 3-0 win against Crystal Place in 1871-72; and in a 2-0 win over Swifts in 1873-74. He was summed up as 'one of the very best forwards of the day, being very quick on his legs, and difficult to stop when on the ball; dribbles very well and is a sure shot at goal.'

Renny, as he was known to his colleagues, was probably the finest all-round sportsman ever produced by the Royal Engineers. He was a double international for Scotland, adding to his football honour a rugby appearance against England in 1872. He played for the RMA, Woolwich, rugby XV in 1868 and 1869. In the RMA, Woolwich, sports of 1870 he won the mile and half-mile races and v Sandhurst won the half-mile and throwing the cricket ball.

In addition he was an outstanding cricketer who played three times for the Gentlemen against the Players which was the most important accolade available in those pre-Test cricket days. He turned out for Kent 1873-83 and had a first-class career batting record of 818 runs, average 19.02 with one century. Renny-Tailyour was in the Cheltenham cricket XI in 1867, then in the RMA, Woolwich, XI 1868-70 (captain 1870). He also played for Aberdeenshire and was a regular member of the Royal Engineers XI for whom he scored 331 not out against the Civil Service in 1880. Between 1871-75 his R.E. batting average each season was never below 40, in 1875 it was 50 and in 1880 66. In 1873 he took 62 wickets at below 13 each for R.E. From 1870 to 1888 he had 307 innings for the Engineers, scored 12,291 runs at an average of 44 and hit 52 centuries. He was also a member of MCC. In later years his main sporting interests were fishing, shooting and golf.

Renny-Tailyour joined the Royal Engineers as a lieutenant on 23rd August 1870, was promoted to captain on 23rd July 1882, major on 1st December 1888, lieut.-colonel on 12th August 1895 and colonel on 12th August 1899. He was ADC to the Lord Lieutenant of Ireland in 1876, then was in Gibraltar 1877-78. He returned to England as assistant instructor in telegraphy at Chatham 1878-80; instructor in fortifications at RMA, Woolwich 1881-84; and assistant instructor in field fortification at Chatham 1884-88. He returned to Gibraltar 1888-91 and then became Commanding R.E. Defences New South Wales, Australia, 1891-94. Finally he was Commanding R.E. Training Battalion at Chatham 1894-99 before retiring in October 1899 to take a post as assistant managing director at the Arthur Guinness & Co. Brewery, Dublin, as well as personal assistant in Ireland to the Guinness proprietor, the 1st Earl of Iveagh. Renny-Tailyour became managing director in 1913 and retired in 1919.

His father was a colonel in the Bengal Royal Engineers. Renny-Tailyour married a sister of Royal Engineers teammate Cecil Vernon Wingfield-Stratford on 9th September 1875.

RICH, Captain Henry Bayard:

b. Berbice, British Guiana, 14 June 1849;
d. Rawalapindi, India, 17 November 1884 (£5,162).
Education: Marlborough College; RMA, Woolwich (1867-70).
FA Cup runner-up (1): Royal Engineers 1872.
Career: Marlborough; RMA, Woolwich; Royal Engineers.

Forward who was ranked as 'one of the best football players of his day' who strove hard 'to pass the backs.' As a cadet he was also noted as one of the fastest runners on the athletics track. Later he was widely known as one of the best horsemen in the R.E.

Rich joined the Royal Engineers as a lieutenant on 8th January 1870 and was promoted to captain in 1882. He was posted to Hong Kong 1874-76 and saw active service in three campaigns, the Perak expedition of 1875-76 (medal with clasp, mentioned in despatches), the Zulu war of 1879 where he was in signalling and telegraph (medal with clasp) and the Egyptian expedition of 1882 (medal and bronze star). His father was a colonel in the Royal Engineers.

He was posted to India in 1882 and died in an accident while playing an afternoon game of polo at Rawalpindi. He and another officer came into violent collision and Rich was flung to the ground, suffering a fractured skull. He never spoke again after the accident.

RICHARDS, Lewis Matthew:

b. Swansea, 14 September 1861;
d. 16 Sloane Gardens, London, 30 November 1918 (£56,510).
Education: Charterhouse School; Trinity College, Cambridge (matric. 1880; LL.B. 1884).
FA Cup winner (1): Old Carthusians 1881.
Career: Charterhouse (XI 1879, 1880); Cambridge University (Blue 1882); Old Carthusians.

Inside-right who earned praise as 'a most useful forward, always playing up hard, a splendid dribbler and sticks well to the ball.' He was also a useful cricketer at good club level, being a member of Free Foresters. At Charterhouse he was in the XI in 1879 and 1880.

Richards was a barrister who was called to the bar at the Inner Temple on 17th November 1884. He practised as a Special Pleader and was on the South Wales circuit. He also had property in Swansea at Westcross House and became a Glamorgan JP. His wife was the daughter of a judge.

ROGERS, Bertram Mitford Heron:
b. 4 Wellington Place, Oxford, 25 August 1860;
d. 14 Northmoor Road, Oxford, 10 February 1953 (£27,804).
Education: Westminster School (1873-77); Exeter College, Oxford (matric. 1880; BA 1883; later B.Ch.); medical studies at University College, London.
FA Cup runner-up (1): Oxford University 1880.
Career: Westminster (not in the XI); Oxford University (Blue 1880, 1881).

Half-back who received the less than enthusiastic verdict of 'very cool, but not difficult to pass'. In 1882 Rogers was on the F.A. committee. At Westminster he was in the cricket XI in 1876.

Rogers was a physician who was a MRCS and LRCP. He was in practice in Clifton where he became consulting physician to the Royal Hospital for Sick Children, Bristol; president of the Bristol Medico-Chirurgical Society; and the Regional Medical Officer, Ministry of Health. He published numerous articles in medical journals.

He was a lieut.-colonel in the Territorial Army (RAMC) and in retirement in Oxford he discovered in 1937 two previously unknown letters by Lewis Carroll. His father was Professor of Political Economy at Oxford and King's College, London, while his mother was the daughter of the Solicitor to the Treasury.

RUCK, Colonel Oliver Edwal:
b. Pennal, Merionethshire, Wales, 27 June 1856;
d. Brynderw, Aberdovey, Merionethshire, 24 July 1934 (£555).
Education: Private school; RMA, Woolwich.
FA Cup runner-up (1): Royal Engineers 1878.
Career: RMA, Woolwich; Royal Engineers.

Outside-left who was noted as promising in this comment: 'Plays forward, and needs only to "know" the game better to be a capital player.' He was the younger brother of R.M. Ruck who was on the winning R.E. side in the 1875 Cup final.

Oliver Ruck joined the Royal Engineers as a lieutenant on 28th January 1875, was promoted to captain on 28th January 1886, major on 3rd November 1894 and lieut.-colonel on 7th October 1901. He saw action in the South African war 1881 in the Transvaal campaign. Later he became a noted Welsh archaeologist who wrote treatises and articles on the subject. He was the uncle of a well-known novelist of the 1930s, Miss Berta Ruck.

RUCK, Maj.-Gen. Sir Richard Mathews:

b. Pennal, Merionethshire, Wales, 27 May 1851;
d. 47 St John's Wood Park, London, 17 March 1935 (£269).
Education: Private school; RMA, Woolwich.
FA Cup winner (1): Royal Engineers 1875 (both matches).
Career: RMA, Woolwich; Royal Engineers; Kent.

Half-back who was described as 'good half-back, being a sure kick, and using his weight well.' His brother, O.E. Ruck, played for R.E. in the 1877-78 Cup final. Ruck also represented the Royal Engineers at cricket, billiards and golf. He later became vice-president of the Welsh Golfing Union, being a member of both the Aberdovey and Woking clubs. He was the author of a valuable article in the Royal Engineers 1928 Journal on 'R.E. Football in the Early 'Seventies'.

Richard Ruck joined the Royal Engineers as a lieutenant in 1871, was promoted to captain in 1883, major in 1889, lieut.-colonel in 1896, colonel in 1904 and major-general in 1908. He was assistant-inspector of submarine defences 1886-91, inspector submarine mining defences, Army HQ, 1891-96, deputy inspector-general of fortifications 1902-04, director of fortifications and works 1904-08, major-general i/c administration Eastern Command 1908-12 when he retired. On the outbreak of the Great War he was recalled to active service in October 1914 as chief engineer Central Force, then GoC London Defences 1915 and major-general i/c administration Central Force and Eastern Command October 1915-June 1916.

At this period he was also involved in aeronautics as chairman of the council of the Royal Aeronautical Society of Great Britain 1912-19, vice-president of the same body 1920, vice-chairman of the Air Inventions Committee 1917-19 and a member of the Civil Aerial Transport Committee 1917-18. He was also a member of the Institute of Electrical Engineers. At the time of his death his home was at 11 Charles Street, St James', Westminster, London.

SAVORY, Rev. James Henry:

b. Binfield, Bracknell, Berks, 20 March 1855; d. Bayham Old Abbey, Sussex, near Lamberhurst, Kent, 5 August 1903 (£200).

Education: Winchester College; Trinity College, Oxford (matric. 1874; BA 1879; MA 1885).

FA Cup runner-up (1): Oxford University 1877.

Career: Winchester; Oxford University (Blue 1877, 1878†); Remnants; Swifts; Berkshire; Berks. & Bucks.

Described as 'a very useful half-back, kicking well and with judgment', Savory was also a useful cricketer who was in the Winchester XI 1873-74 and gained his Blue at the sport in 1877 and 1878. He was an attacking right-hand batsman who was a member of MCC and Free Foresters, playing many club matches for the latter. His final first-class cricket match was for MCC in 1887. He was also in Winchester's rifle shooting XI at the Wimbledon championships from 1872 to 1874 and helped to win the Ashburton Shield in 1872.

Savory, whose father was also a clergyman, was ordained deacon in 1883 and priest in 1885. He was curate at Buckingham 1883-85, then Vicar of Little Dalby, near Melton Mowbray, Leicestershire 1886-96 and finally chaplain to the Marquis of Camden at the latter's country home, Bayham Old Abbey, until his death there.

One Free Forester colleague, Edward Rutter, recalled a cricket match in 1894 when the Foresters were heading for certain defeat: 'As last man I joined J.H. Savory. Always a hard hitter, he quite excelled himself on this occasion, and as I stuck in, he smacked away till he was stumped with 125 to his credit, while I was not out 41, thereby converting probable defeat into a certain win.'

SCOTT, Stanley Winckworth:

b. Bombay, India, 24 March 1854;
d. 68 King's Hall Road, Beckenham, Kent, 8 December 1933 (£377).
Education: Streatham School (1863); Epsom School; Brentwood School (Feb.1868-Dec.1870).
FA Cup runner-up (1): Clapham Rovers 1879.
Career: Brentwood; Brondesbury; Clapham Rovers; Pilgrims.

Outside-left who played both rugby and football at school where he developed into a useful winger. Scott was an outstanding cricketer who was chosen as one of the 'Cricketers of the Year' in the 1893 edition of *Wisden's Cricketers' Almanack*. He played for Middlesex 1878-93, finishing with a first-class career record of 4,432 runs, average 25.61 with 4 centuries. These included 224 for Middlesex v Gloucestershire in 1892 which was his great year when he finished third in the national batting averages with 1,015 runs, averages 39.03. He also finished ninth in 1885 and seventh in 1886.

Scott was a member of MCC, also played for Herefordshire for whom he scored 138 not out on debut in 1874 and had a long career with leading southern clubs such as Southgate, Incogniti, Kensington Park, Upper Clapton, Leatherhead, Devonshire Park, Hendon and the Stock Exchange XI. In his last year at Brentwood School, 1870, he topped both the batting and bowling averages though he was only 16. Professionally, he began in 1871 as a marine insurance underwriter, moved to the London Joint Stock Bank later that year and became a member of the Stock Exchange in 1877. Scott's father was an army officer. His 'Reminiscences of Cricket 1863-1904' were serialised in *The Cricketer* magazine in 1930, starting in the Spring Annual.

There, he recalled that in August 1899 at the age of 45, he opened the innings in a club match for Southgate with his 17-year-old son. Scott scored 113 retired and his son 119 not out, thus both father and son made centuries as opening partners!

SEALY, Rev. Predendary Robert Walpole:
see VIDAL, Rev. Prebendary Robert Walpole Sealy.

SIM, Colonel George Hamilton:

b. Paddington, London, 19 November 1852;
d. The Barracks, Pontefract, Yorks, 27 December 1929 (£8,981).
Education: Rugby; RMA, Woolwich.
FA Cup winner (1): Royal Engineers 1875 (both matches).
Career: Rugby; RMA, Woolwich; Royal Engineers.

Full-back who was a key defender in the great years of the Royal Engineers, Sim was described as 'a very useful back' and especially acknowledged as the southern pioneer of the practice of heading the ball.

He joined the Royal Engineers as a lieutenant in 1872, was promoted to captain in 1884, major in 1898, lieut.-colonel in 1899 and colonel in 1903. He saw active service in the Afghan War 1879-80 (medal); Sudan 1885 (medal with clasp, Khedive's Star) and the Boer War 1899-1902 (Queen's medal with six clasps, King's medal with two clasps, mentioned in despatches and created CB). He was officer i/c records 1905-09 when he retired.

Sim was recalled in the Great War 1914-18 and in 1917 was made a CMG. At the time of his death his home was at The Junior United Service Club, Charles Street, Haymarket, London.

SMITH, Rev. Arnold Kirke:
b. Ecclesfield, Sheffield, 23 April 1850;
d. The Rectory, Boxworth, near Cambridge, 8 October 1927 (£30,969).
Education: Cheltenham; University College, Oxford (matric. 1869; BA 1873; MA 1876).
FA Cup runner-up (1): Oxford University 1873†.
Career: Cheltenham; Oxford University (1872† and 1873†: pre-university match); Sheffield Club; Sheffield F.A. Full internationals (1): England v Scotland 1873 (1st match). Pre-official internationals (3): Scotland v England 1871 (both matches); 1872.

Forward who was described as 'a very active and useful man, usually plays forward and takes a great deal of punishment' but also criticised as follows: 'A strong and useful forward, but is often too much inclined to usurp the functions of the half-backs.' He sometimes appears in match reports as Kirke-Smith. His qualification for Scotland in the pre-official internationals was based on family property there. Smith was a founder member of the Oxford University Association Football Club when it was formed on 9th November 1871.

Smith was ordained in 1875 and had successive curacies at Biggleswade 1875-77, East Socon, Beds. 1877-81 and Somersham, Cambs. 1881-82. He was then vicar of Somersham 1883-89 and finally of Boxworth from 1889 to his death in 1927. It is said that in his later years he would arrive at his church after a Sunday morning in the hunting field and mount the pulpit to deliver his sermon still wearing his riding outfit under his clerical gown.

SPARKS, Francis John:

b. North Benfleet, Essex, 4 July 1855;
d. 1 Oldchurch Road, Romford, Essex, 13 February 1934 (£64.12s.10d).
Education: King's School, Rochester 1870-74.
FA Cup winner (1): Clapham Rovers 1880.
Career: King's School (XI 1872-73-74); Old Roffensians; Brondesbury; Hertfordshire Rangers; Clapham Rovers; Essex; London. Full internationals (3): England v Scotland 1879; 1880; v Wales 1880†

Centre-forward who played a captain's part when he led England to a 3-2 win over Wales in 1879-80 as he scored two of the goals. He went one better that same season with a hat-trick in the third round of the Cup when Clapham Rovers beat Pilgrims 7-0. Away from the Cup, he scored six goals when Herts Rangers beat Hendon 9-0 in 1876-77. Sparks was said to be 'a strong, fast centre and splendid shot at goal; is apt to get slack if the game is against him.' Earlier it had been stated: 'A useful forward, plays hard and is never away from the ball, but is a little slow', though a season later in 1876-77 this last phrase is amended to 'has improved in pace.' He was on the F.A. Committee 1878-80. Sparks was also a useful cricketer who was in the King's School XI 1872-73 and later played for the Gentlemen of Hertfordshire.

He was the son of a commission agent and entered a City merchant's office as a clerk after leaving school in 1874 but by 1901 he was a coal traveller based at 141 Clarendon Place, Dover. Sparks was an associate member of the Voluntary Recruiting League. At the time of his death his home was at 6 Pembroke Road, Seven Kings, Essex.

STAFFORD, Brig.-Gen. William Francis Howard:

b. Hansi, Punjab, India, 19 December 1854;
d. Thornbury, Crowthorne, Berks, 8 August 1942 (£13,349).
Education: Wellington College (1867-71); RMA, Woolwich (1872-73).
FA Cup winner (1): Royal Engineers 1875 (both matches).
Career: Wellington; RMA, Woolwich; Richmond (rugby); Royal Engineers.

Centre-forward who was said to be 'a resolute forward, working to the very last; is a little too fond of a charge.' Stafford played for England v Scotland at rugby in 1874 though he failed to match that achievement at football international level. He was also a good cricketer who played for Norfolk in 1889.

Stafford joined the Royal Engineers as a lieutenant in 1873. He was promoted to captain in 1885, major in 1892 and lieut.-colonel in 1900. He saw action in the Afghan War 1878-80 (medal) and the Mahsood Wuzeeree Expedition (North-West Frontier) 1881. He was involved in the Boer War 1899-1902 (Queen's medal with three clasps, King's medal with two clasps, mentioned in despatches and created CB 1902). He retired in 1911 with the rank of brigadier but was recalled in 1914, serving in France 1917-18 (mentioned in despatches).

STANLEY, Arthur John:
b. Paddington, London, 26 June 1853;
d. 53 Lancaster Gate, Hyde Park, London, 16 July 1935 (£18,491).
Education: Repton School; Trinity College, Cambridge (matric. 1872).
FA Cup winner (1): Clapham Rovers 1880; runner-up (1): Clapham Rovers 1879.
Career: Repton (XI 1871); Cambridge University (no Blue); Old Reptonians; Clapham Rovers; Upton Park; London.

Inside-right who was praised as 'a fair forward, works hard, and is generally on the ball.' Stanley had a spell as secretary of Clapham Rovers at the time of their first Cup final appearance. He was a fair cricketer who was in the Repton XI in 1871 and later a member of MCC, but he was a finer lawn tennis player. In both 1885 and 1886 he reached the final of the Wimbledon men's doubles in partnership with C.E. Farrar.

By profession Stanley was a member of the Stock Exchange. In his will he displays the not uncommon contemporary fear of being buried alive and goes to extreme lengths to prevent this, saying: 'I direct that before burial my death shall be certified and confirmed ... by a qualified medical practitioner and that he shall also sever my jugular vein'!

STEWART, Rev. Henry Holmes:
b. Cairnsmore, Newton Stewart, Kirkcudbrightshire, 8 November 1847;
d. Strathella, Highwalls Road, Dinas Powys, Glamorgan, Wales, 20 March 1937 (£8,560).
Education: Repton School; Loretto College; Trinity College, Cambridge (matric. 1867; BA 1871; MA 1874).
FA Cup winner (1): Wanderers 1873.
Career: Repton (XI 1865-67); Loretto; Cambridge University (pre-university match); Wanderers. Pre-official internationals (2): Scotland v England 1872 (both matches).

Forward who was praised as follows: 'Sticks close to the ball and follows up hard; a very useful forward' and 'keeps well on the ball and never flags.' Stewart was an ordained clergyman by the time of his Cup final appearance. He was an outstanding schoolboy cricketer at Repton, being in the XI 1865-67 and the side's best batsman in his final season. He also played cricket for Cambridge University in 1869 in matches ruled not first-class and continued with success in local Glamorgan village cricket well into the 20th century.

Stewart was ordained deacon in 1872 and priest in 1873. He became curate of St John,

Holborn, London, 1872-74; vicar of East Witton, north Yorkshire, 1874-78; rector of Brington, Northants., 1878-98; rector of Porth Kerry with Barry, Glam., 1898-1914; vicar of St Lythans, Glam., 1914-25; and rector of Michaelston-le-Pit, Glam., 1925-34 when he retired. He was buried at Michaelston-le-Pit. Stewart married a daughter of the 9th Earl of Southesk.

STIRLING-HOME-DRUMMOND, Lieut.-Colonel Henry Edward:
   see DRUMMOND MORAY, Lieut.-Colonel Henry Edward.

STRATFORD, Alfred Hugh:
b. Kensington, London, 5 September 1853;
d. Newark, New Jersey, United States, 2 May 1914.
Education: Malvern College.
FA Cup winner (3): Wanderers 1876 (both matches), 1877, 1878.
Career: Malvern (XI 1871-72-73-74†); Wanderers; London; Middlesex; Probables (v The Rest); The Rest (v England). Full internationals (1): England v Scotland 1874. He was selected for England v Scotland in 1875-76 but was unavailable.

Full-back whose talent was recognised early in his career when it was said: 'A first-rate back with an extraordinary power of kicking off. With a little more "head" will make a most useful player'. Later, it was stated: 'Can play forward and back; plays well as full back, being a good and strong tackler', while another account refers to his being 'a strong kicker and charger.'

Stratford was a fine cricketer who was in the Malvern XI 1871-73 and played 18 matches for Middlesex 1877-80. Altogether he scored 577 first-class runs, average 12.82, took 83 wickets, average 16.32 with best figures of 6-44 and was 14th in the national first-class batting averages in 1878. He also played for Herefordshire, Incogniti and later New York, Winnipeg, Pittsburgh and Newark NJ.

Around 1890 Stratford emigrated to the United States where he died. He played much cricket there as well as in Canada and appears to have been one of those Victorian gentlemen who were able to live off their income. No census returns, other archive records or obituaries mention any profession.

STRONGE, Rt. Hon. Sir James Henry (5th Baronet):

b. Laurel Lodge, Kingstown (now Dun Laoghaire), Co. Dublin, Ireland, 8 December 1849;
d. Tynan Abbey, Co. Armagh, Northern Ireland, 20 May 1928.
Education: Eton College; Brasenose College, Oxford (matric. 1868; BA 1872; MA 1875).
FA Cup runner-up (2): Old Etonians 1875 (both matches), 1876 (replay).
Career: Eton; Oxford University (pre-university match); Old Etonians; Gitanos.

Outside-left who was vigorous, energetic 'always conspicuous' and backed up well in addition to being 'hard-working', Stronge retired at the age of 30 to concentrate on his legal and political career.

He was a barrister who was called to the bar at Lincoln's Inn on 30th April 1874 but spent many years involved in Ulster politics where he became a Privy Councillor Northern Ireland in 1924. Stronge had been High Sheriff of Tyrone in 1880; High Sheriff of Armagh in 1885; secretary to the Ulster Defence Union in 1894; chairman of Armagh District Council 1899-1900; and Grand Master of the Orange Order. In addition he wrote many articles on Irish affairs including 'A Plea for Charity in Irish History'. Stronge was in the Royal Inniskilling Fusiliers 1870-85 when he retired with the honorary rank of major.

More than half a century after Stronge's death, modern Irish politics intruded violently into Tynan Abbey. The then baronet, Sir Norman Stronge, who was aged 86, and his heir James, were murdered in a terrorist attack on 21st January 1981 and the abbey partially destroyed by fire. It was demolished finally in 1989.

STURGIS, Julian Russell:
b. Boston, Mass., United States, 21 October 1848;
d. 16 Hans Road, Chelsea, London SW, 13 April 1904 (£79,435).
Education: Eton College; Balliol College, Oxford (matric. 1868; BA 1875; MA also 1875).
FA Cup winner (1): Wanderers 1873; runner-up (1): Old Etonians 1876 (both matches).
Career: Eton; Oxford University (1868-72: pre-university match); Wanderers; Old Etonians; Gitanos; Middlesex.

Forward who was the first foreign-born player to appear in a Cup final (the other overseas finalists at that time had all been born in the British Empire to British parents). He was a sharp-shooting performer who notched a hat-trick for the Etonians in a 5-2 Cup third round victory over Minerva in 1878-79. Sturgis was praised for the fact that he 'worked hard from first to last' and was 'most conspicuous.' Apart from football, Sturgis also took part in most other outdoor sports. He was a member of MCC and rowed for three years in the Balliol College eight. At Eton he was Keeper of the Field (captain of the football XI) and Chairman of Pop (the famous college debating society).

Sturgis was a barrister by profession who was called to the bar at the Inner Temple on 26th January 1876 but he earned a reputation and made his living as an author. He wrote many once-popular novels as well as plays and libretti. These latter included that for *Ivanhoe*, the only grand opera by Sir Arthur Sullivan (of Gilbert and Sullivan fame), and *Much Ado About Nothing* by Sir Charles Villiers Stanford, whose most famous piece is probably the song 'Drake's Drum'.

An Eton schoolmate of Sturgis was the composer Sir Hubert Parry, best-known for his setting of Blake's 'Jerusalem'. Parry, like Sturgis, was a keen sportsman and Keeper of the Field, and the two remained lifelong friends. In six of his eleven groups of English Lyrics published between 1895 and 1920, Parry included alongside Shakespeare, Milton, Keats, Shelley and other great names, nine poems by Sturgis: 'Through the ivory gate' (Set III, No.5); 'A stray nymph of Dian (Set V, No.1); 'A girl to her glass' (Set V, No.6); 'Sleep' (Set VII, No.6); 'Whence' (Set VIII, No.1); 'Looking backward' (Set VIII, No.5); 'Grapes' (Set VIII, No.6); 'A moment of farewell' (Set X, No.3); and 'If I might ride on puissant wing' (Set XI, No.6).

Although Sturgis was born in the United States he was brought to England when only seven months old and eventually became a British subject. His father was an anglophile who settled in England as a banker and was one of those on whom Henry James drew for the character of old Mr Touchett in his great novel *The Portrait of a Lady*. A couple of years after his last Cup final appearance Sturgis travelled through the Levant in 1878 where he visited the Turkish and Russian armies before Constantinople. He returned to America for nine months in 1880 when he visited the then new city of Leadville in the Rocky Mountains. In England he had a country home at Wancote, Wanborough, near Guildford, Surrey.

SUMNER, John Robert Edwards:
b. Southchurch, Essex, 14 November 1850;
d. Scripps Memorial Hospital, La Jolla, San Diego, California, United States, 15 October 1933 (£4,027 in England).
Education: Harrow School; Trinity College, Oxford (matric. 1869; BA 1875).
FA Cup runner-up (1): Oxford University 1873.
Career: Harrow; Oxford University (no Blue); High Wycombe; Buckinghamshire.

Forward who earned praise for his 'fine runs', 'vigour', being 'most effective' as well as doing his utmost and playing up well.

After leaving university Sumner spent some time as a schoolmaster and in 1881 he held a post at The Lodge Prep School, Dunchurch, near Rugby, Warwickshire. However by 1900 he was listed in the Harrow Register as a rancher at Yampa, Routt County, Colorado, United States, and was still there in 1911. At the time of his death his home was at 1241 Cave Street, La Jolla. His father was the Rector of Ellesborough, near Tring.

THOMPSON, Albert Childers (from 19th February 1874 A. C. Meysey-Thompson):
b. Kirby Hall, Yorks, 13 July 1848;
d. 12 Montague Square, Marylebone, London, 20 March 1894 (£14,618).
Education: Eton College (1862-65); Trinity College, Cambridge (matric. 1867; BA 1871).
FA Cup winner (1): Wanderers 1872; runner-up (2): Old Etonians 1875 (first match), 1876 (first match).
Career: Eton; Eton Cambridge Club; Cambridge University (pre-university match); Wanderers; Old Etonians; Surrey; Middlesex; London. Pre-official internationals (2): England v Scotland 1872 (both matches).

Half-back or full-back who was rated one of the most dependable defenders of his day for a period of some ten years. He was described as *'facile princeps*, the king of backs. The ease with which he kicks the ball in the most difficult positions suggests the belief that at one time in his life he must have gone into training with a view to an acrobatic career.' He was also praised as 'the best half-back out, an unerring kick and the most reliable back against any team' while in 1876 it was said: 'Still holds his own as a half-back; one of the most brilliant kickers of the day.' He and his brother Charles appeared together for the Old Etonians in the drawn final of 1875-76 though the fact that he played as Meysey-Thompson and Charles as simply Meysey has caused confusion to football historians. Thompson was a useful cricketer who was a member of MCC.

By profession Thompson was a barrister who was called to the bar at the Inner Temple on 6th June 1872. He became a noted QC on the North-Eastern Circuit. He was a younger brother of the 1st Baron Knaresborough and married a granddaughter of the 3rd Earl of Harewood. Thompson died only three days after returning home from the West Coast of America where he had been compelled to spend the winters because of failing health over the previous three years.

THOMPSON, Rev. Charles Maude (from 19 February 1874 C. M. Meysey-Thompson):

b. York, 5 December 1849;
d. Pesa, Utah, United States, 11 September 1881 (£14,885).
Education: Eton College; Trinity College, Cambridge (matric. 1868; BA 1872; MA 1876).
FA Cup winner (1): Wanderers 1873; runner-up (1): Old Etonians 1876 (first match).
Career: Eton; Cambridge University (pre-university match); Wanderers; Old Etonians. Pre-official internationals (2): Scotland v England 1872 (both matches).

Forward in the dribbling Etonian style of the day. He was the brother of A.C. Thompson and they played together for the Old Etonians against the Wanderers in the drawn first game of the 1875-76 Cup final. He appeared as 'Meysey' in this match. His qualification for Scotland in the pre-official internationals was a very loose one, being based on family property north of the border. He won an athletics Blue for Cambridge in 1872 but was unplaced in throwing the hammer.

C.M. Thompson was a clergyman who became curate at Whitby 1873-75; curate at St Pancras 1875-76; and rector of Middle Claydon, Bucks, 1876-79. He died in Utah while he was visiting the state in the hope of improving his declining health. At the time his English home was Kirby Hall, Yorks.

TOD, Alexander Hay:

b. at sea, 25 March 1857;
d. 2 Prince's Buildings, Clifton, Bristol, 22 January 1942 (£16,124).
Education: Charterhouse School (entered as Prize Scholar 1869-76); Trinity College, Oxford (matric. 1876; BA 1880; MA 1883).
FA Cup winner (1): Old Carthusians 1881.
Career: Charterhouse (XI 1875, 1876); Oxford University (no Blue); Old Carthusians; London.

Outside-left who also had scoring skills as mentioned in this contemporary summing up: 'An energetic forward; of great use in the proximity of goal.'

Apart from his period at university, Tod's life was bound up with Charterhouse. He entered the school at the age of 12 and returned there as a master in 1880. He was captain of the Charterhouse Cadet Corps 1881-1905 and became housemaster of Verites from 1906. Tod was joint editor of the *Charterhouse Register* and author of *Charterhouse* (a history, 1900, revised edition 1919) in Bell's series of 'Handbooks to the Great Public Schools'. He retired in 1920 but kept his connection with the school as treasurer of the Charterhouse War Memorial Fund from 1920.

Care must be taken not to confuse him with another Oxford footballer and Cup finalist, Arthur Horatio Todd, who appears here in the next entry.

TODD, Arthur Horatio:
b. 51 Wimpole Street, Marylebone, London, 7 July 1854;
d. Combined Military Hospital, Kasauli, Punjab, India, 21 May 1945 (£434 in England).
Education: Eton College; University College, Oxford (matric. 1873; BA 1878).
FA Cup runner-up (1): Oxford University 1877.
Career: Eton; Oxford University (Blue 1877).

Forward who was noted for his 'brilliant runs' which he combined with hard work throughout. He did not continue the game at an important level after leaving university.

By profession Todd was a barrister who was called to the bar at the Inner Temple on 17th November 1880. His son, Arthur Henry Ashworth Todd (1884-1938), was a magistrate in the Indian Civil Service and it is presumed that on retirement, the father joined him in India. At the time of Todd's death his home was at Sunnyside, Kasauli.

VIDAL, Rev. Prebendary Robert Walpole Sealy (from 1892 R. W. Sealy)**:**
b. Cornborough House, Abbotsham, near Bideford, Devon, 3 September 1853;
d. Abbotsham Vicarage, 5 November 1914 (£5,702).
Education: Westminster School (1867-72, Captain of School 1872); Christ Church, Oxford (matric. 1872; BA 1876; MA 1879).
FA Cup winner (2): Wanderers 1872; Oxford University 1874; runner-up (1): Oxford University 1873.
Career: Westminster (XI 1869-72, captain 1871-72); Wanderers; Oxford University (Blue 1874, 1875†); Remnants; Old Westminsters; London; The South. Full internationals (1): England v Scotland 1873 (2nd match). Pre-official internationals (5): England v Scotland 1870; 1871 (both matches); 1872 (both matches).

Centre-forward and a brilliant dribbler, Vidal was the original 'prince of dribblers', a title afterwards awarded often enough to become hackneyed. He was described as 'one of the fastest and best dribblers of the day, and well known for his marvellous side shots at goal.' His reputation was so high when he was at Westminster that he was selected for England in the pre-official international of 1870 while still a schoolboy and played at the age of 16 years, 183 days. He was also the only player to gain an F.A. Cup-winner's medal while still at school. In 1872 and 1874 he was on the F.A. committee.

Vidal was good at many sports and also earned a rugby Blue for Oxford in 1873. He played county cricket for Devon in 1874, club cricket for North Devon CC and was in the Westminster XI 1869-72, the final year as captain. Furthermore, he was a good oarsman at Oxford; was founder and first president of the Oxford University Golf Club; a member of the Royal North Devon Golf Club (a past president); and a fine golfer on the Westward Ho! course near Bideford.

He studied at Cuddesdon Theological College, near Oxford, and was ordained in 1877. Vidal became curate of St Edmunds, Salisbury, 1877-79; Vice-Principal of Ely Theological College, 1879-81; curate of Holy Trinity, Ely, 1880-81; and finally Vicar of Abbotsham, Devon, 1881-1914. In addition he was Rural Dean of Hartland and not long before his death was made a Prebendary of Exeter Cathedral.

Vidal, who changed his name back to the original family one of Sealy on 26th May 1892 after his father had assumed that of Vidal on succeeding to the Cornborough estate, threw himself into parish and Devon affairs. He was on Bideford Rural District Council; was vice-chairman of the Bideford Board of Guardians; chairman of Abbotsham Parish Council; Commissioner for Income Tax; a member of the Devon County Education Committee; and a committee member of North Devon Choral Union from 1893. He suffered a breakdown of health some months before his death, then appeared to recover but had another attack which left him unconscious until the end. He was buried at Abbotsham where his funeral produced a huge turnout. One of his sons also became a clergyman.

VINTCENT, Sir Joseph:

b. Mossel Bay, Cape Colony, South Africa, 12 November 1861;
d. Bulawayo, Southern Rhodesia, 14 August 1914 (£242 in England).
Education: Diocesan College, Rondebosch; Charterhouse School (1877-1880); Trinity Hall, Cambridge (matric. 1880; BA 1884; LL.B. also 1884).
FA Cup winner (1): Old Carthusians 1881.
Career: Charterhouse (XI 1879); Cambridge University (Blue 1883); Old Carthusians; Barnes; Corinthians; London.

Half-back whose heading skills were noticed in this contemporary comment: 'A very safe half-back, plays well to the forwards, can place the ball almost where he likes; nearly as good with his head as his legs.' Another notice which was full of praise said 'one of the best half-backs in England; kicks well to his forwards and rarely makes a mistake.' He was soon lost to English football as he returned to South Africa in 1885, the year in which he made two appearances for the Corinthians. Vintcent was a fair cricketer who was in the Charterhouse XI in 1879. His brother was the South African Test cricketer, Charles Henry Vintcent.

Joseph Vintcent was a barrister who was called to the bar at the Middle Temple on 26th January 1885, then returned home as an advocate in Cape Colony later that same year. He began a climb to the top ranks of his profession as Crown Prosecutor in British Bechuanaland 1886-94, then Judge of the High Court of Matebeleland 1894-98 and finally Senior Judge of the High Court of Southern Rhodesia 1898-1914 as well as of North West Rhodesia from 1906. He was knighted in 1910.

Vintcent should not be confused with James Edmund Vincent, Winchester and Christ Church, Oxford, an 1879 Oxford football Blue, also a half-back, who played for Barnes and Clapham Rovers as well as London representative sides in the same seasons that Joseph Vintcent was with Old Carthusians. The two were on opposing sides in the fifth round F.A. Cup tie between Old Carthusians and Clapham Rovers in 1882-83.

VON DONOP, Lieut.-Col. Pelham George:

b. Southsea, Hants, 28 April 1851;
d. 11 Montpelier Square, South Kensington, London, 7 November 1921 (£4,522).
Education: Somerset College, Bath; RMA, Woolwich.
FA Cup winner (1): Royal Engineers 1875 (both matches); runner-up (1): Royal Engineers 1874.
Career: Somerset College; RMA, Woolwich; Royal Engineers; London. Full internationals (2): England v Scotland 1873 (2nd match); 1875.

Outside-right, he was another player given the title of 'prince of dribblers', being the best right-winger of his day who could produce tremendous speed as mentioned in this comment: 'One of the fastest wing players, always playing on the right side; is a very fine dribbler, possessed of great speed.' It was also reported: 'A most efficient dribbler and is always up with the ball.' Von Donop was also a prominent batsman for the Royal Engineers after being in the RMA, Woolwich XI 1870-71. Perhaps his most memorable cricketing achievement was to score a century in a R.E. total of 726 for 8 wickets against I Zingari at Chatham in 1875. He was a member of MCC from 1886 and also Free Foresters. In addition he was a proficient lawn tennis player who won the open doubles championship along with Cup finalist C.K. Wood while stationed in Bermuda and was West of England champion at Bath in 1884. He was also a keen golfer and often, after a hard day's work, he would finish up on the local golf course, wherever he might be.

Von Donop joined the Royal Engineers as a lieutenant in December 1871, being promoted to captain in 1883 and major 1890. After a posting to Bermuda 1879-80, he was in charge of the Postal Telegraph service south of the Thames 1880-84. He was called into active service on the Egyptian expedition 1884-86 when he was traffic manager of railways supplying the field forces. A spell followed as inspector of submarine defences in India 1889-94 then he returned to England as c/o 2nd Division Telegraph Battalion, supervising the whole of the postal telegraphs south of the Thames 1894-98. He was promoted to lieut.-colonel in 1897 and was Commanding R.E. at Dover 1898-99 when he retired.

He followed his old friend and colleague Francis Marindin as an Inspecting Officer of Railways at the Board of Trade 1899-1913, then Chief Inspecting Officer to 1916 when he retired. Von Donop's father was a vice-admiral and his younger brother was a major-general. After his retirement he lived mainly at Camberley, his chief interests being gardening and golf. At his funeral at East Sheen, among his old R.E. colleagues around the grave were Cup final players G.W. Addison, J.E. Blackburn and H.D. Olivier.

WACE, Henry:
b. Shrewsbury, 21 September 1853;
d. 1 Lansdowne Place West, Bath, 5 November 1947 (£56,859).
Education: Shrewsbury School; St John's College, Cambridge (matric. 1872; BA, Senior Classic, 1876; MA 1879).
FA Cup winner (2): Wanderers 1877, 1878.
Career: Shrewsbury; Cambridge University (no Blue); Shropshire Wanderers; Clapham Rovers; London; The South; England (v The Rest). Full internationals (3); England v Scotland 1878; 1879; v Wales 1879†.

Centre-forward described as 'a very good and dangerous centre; plays pluckily and sticks to the ball; a thoroughly hard worker' though also that he 'at times gets a little too forward.' He was in the Shrewsbury side who won the Birmingham Senior Cup in 1877-78. Wace was also a good rugby player who gained Blues in 1873-74 and 1874-75 though sources which describe him as a double Blue at football and rugby are incorrect as he never won a football Blue.

He had a notable academic record at university, winning the Porson Prize in 1873, 1874 and 1875; the Powis Medal in 1873 and 1874; and the 1st Chancellor's Medal in 1876. From 1876-86 he was a Fellow of St John's College. Wace was the son of a Shrewsbury solicitor and by profession was a barrister who was called to the bar at the Inner Temple on 17th November 1879. He became an acknowledged expert in bankruptcy law, being the joint author of Yate Lee's *Law of Bankruptcy*.

Wace's participation in the 1877-78 Birmingham Senior Cup final mentioned above produced one of the more far-fetched protests of that period. Although Wace was Shrewsbury-born and had been a member of the town club for seven years, the fact that he was away in London for much of that year studying law encouraged losing finalists Wednesbury Strollers to protest against his qualifications and ask for a replay. The Birmingham and District F.A. committee voted by 8-4 to turn down the protest.

WADDINGTON, Evelyn:

b. Llanllowel, Monmouth, Wales, 5 July 1857;
d. Beech Hill, Usk, Mon., 25 August 1928 (£5,192 gross; £2,292 net).
Education: Westminster School (1871-76); Oriel College, Oxford (matric. 1876).
FA Cup runner-up (1): Oxford University 1877.
Career: Westminster (XI 1874-76); Oxford University (Blue 1877, 1878); England (v The Rest).

Half-back who came close to England international selection with his appearance in the England v The Rest trial match and was praised as 'a most brilliant half-back at times; never misses his kick, and plays well for his forwards.' He was also a useful cricketer who was in the Westminster XI 1873-75, being captain in his final season.

Waddington was admitted a solicitor in July 1885 and spent the rest of his life in practice in his home town of Usk, where his father had also been in business.

WELCH, Reginald (de) Courtenay:

b. 6 Westbourne Place, Paddington, London, 17 October 1851;
d. Army College, Heath End, Farnham, Surrey, 4 June 1939 (£19,478).
Education: Harrow School (1864-1871).
FA Cup winner (2): Wanderers 1872, 1873.
Career: Harrow (XI 1871); Harrow Chequers; Wanderers; Old Harrovians; Remnants; London; Middlesex; Berks & Bucks. Full internationals (2): England v Scotland 1873 (1st match); 1874.

Goalkeeper mainly but also featured in defence, appearing at full-back on his England debut. He had a reputation for reliability in either position, being described as 'a good and safe goalkeeper', and there was reference to his 'working hard and kicking accurately.' Welch served on the F.A. committee 1873-75 and 1879-80. He was a useful cricketer who was in the Harrow XI in 1871 and later a member of MCC. He was also a pioneer English skier in Switzerland.

He was joint editor of *The Harrovian* 1869-71 and the *Harrow Register 1801-93*. By profession Welch was an Army tutor 1883-95, then became Principal of the Army College at Heath End, Farnham, Surrey, until his death. Although many match reports show him as R. de C. Welch, both the Harrow School Register and the Probate Records list him without the 'de'.

WELLDON, The Right. Rev. James Edward Cowell:

b. Tonbridge School, Kent, 25 April 1854;
d. The Dell, Granville Road, Sevenoaks, Kent, 17 June 1937 (£70,765).
Education: Eton College; King's College, Cambridge (matric. 1873; BA, Senior Classic, 1877; MA 1880).
FA Cup runner-up (1): Old Etonians 1876 (first match).
Career: Eton; Old Etonians; Hertfordshire Rangers; Upton Park; Essex; London.

Full-back and a rugged defender as one might expect from one who earned a brilliant reputation at Eton in both the Wall Game and the Field Game.

Welldon became Eton school captain and his academic achievements were also impressive. He won many awards including the Carus Prize in 1873; the Browne Medal in 1875 and 1876; the Senior Chancellor's Medal in 1877; while he was Bell Scholar in 1874 and president of the Cambridge Union in 1876. Welldon was a highly respected classicist and his 1892 translation of Aristotle's *Politics*, *Rhetoric* and *Ethics* gained great critical esteem.

He was born at Tonbridge School where his father, a clergyman, was Second Master and his uncle Headmaster. After leaving university he lived abroad for a short time before he became a Fellow of King's College, Cambridge, 1878-83; Master of Dulwich College 1883-85; then Headmaster of Harrow School (an Old Etonian!) 1885-98.

Welldon was ordained deacon in 1883, priest in 1885 and became DD in 1899. He was Chaplain in Ordinary to Queen Victoria 1892-98, several times Select Preacher at Oxford and Cambridge, and speaker at various church congresses. In 1898 he was appointed Bishop of Calcutta but in 1902 returned to England, ostensibly on grounds of health though in reality a move engineered by the Viceroy who was appalled at a sermon preached by Welldon in which he announced that the British task in India would not be complete until the whole country had been converted to Christianity! He continued to hold important church posts: Canon of Westminster 1902-06; Dean of Manchester 1906-18; and Dean of Durham 1918-33 when he retired. He published many books and pamphlets on religion and in his later years gave his recreations as riding and travelling.

Welldon managed to cause controversy in the football world as late as 1922 when, in his role as Dean of Durham, he wrote to *The Times* to complain that the game was now only secondary to financial profit, be it from the buying and selling of players or from betting on results. He said: 'Where the love of money comes in, the love of sport for its own sake dies out.' Stanley Harris, former Corinthian and England captain, supported him but the *Athletic News*, a newspaper strongly on the side of the Football League, scornfully suggested that it was doubtful whether the Dean had actually seen any betting at a League match. It pointed out that Test matches, the Boat Race and even General Elections were subject to betting among the highest in the land. Finally it summed up Welldon's indignation in verse:

O shame, where is the blush? Religion weep!
If such the shepherds, what must be the sheep?

WESTON, Vincent Edward:
b. Hulme House, Hampton Wick, Surrey, 14 November 1855;
d. Douglas Villa, Florence Road, Shanklin, Isle of Wight, 12 December 1937 (£422).
Education: not found.
FA Cup winner (1): Clapham Rovers 1880.
Career: Barnes; Clapham Rovers; London; The South; The Rest (v England).

Half-back who was praised as an effective and efficient performer: 'A very useful and plucky half-back; has a wonderful aptitude for kicking the ball in the most difficult position.' Weston slowly rose to the top through the second half of the 1870s and came close to an England call-up after appearing for The Rest in an international trial match.

Weston came from a footballing family which had a close connection with the Barnes club, a number of them playing for it in the late 1860s and early 1870s. Vincent himself, three days before his 16th birthday, appeared alongside two other Westons for Barnes against the Civil Service on the very first day of any F.A. Cup ties, 11th November 1871. At 15 years 362 days he immediately set a record for the youngest player in a Cup match.

Weston did not have a long playing career following on from his Cup final success, instead concentrating on his professional life where, as with many of the Clapham Rovers players, he was involved with the City as a member of the Stock Exchange.

WHITFELD, Herbert:

b. Hamsey House, Lewes, Sussex, 25 November 1858;
d. Warrenwood, Newick, near Chailey, Sussex, 6 May 1909 (£34,419).
Education: Eton College; Trinity College, Cambridge (matric. 1877; BA 1881).
FA Cup winner (1): Old Etonians 1879; runner-up (1): Old Etonians 1881.

Career: Eton (XI 1877); Cambridge University (Blue 1879, 1880, 1881); Old Etonians; London; England (v The Rest). Full internationals (1): England v Wales 1879.

Outside-left of whom it was said: 'A very good wing player; dribbles well and works unceasingly; much improved in pace'. Whitfeld was a cricketer of note who played for Sussex 1878-85 and was county captain in 1883-84. He was in the Eton XI 1875-77, the last as captain, then a Cambridge Blue for the four seasons 1878-81 and his final first-class match was for I Zingari in 1889. Altogether he scored 2,400 first-class runs at an average 20.16 with 1 century. In 1883 he was sixth in the national first-class batting averages. Whitfeld was also a member of MCC. In 1879 he won an athletics Blue but was unplaced in the mile race. He was a real tennis Blue in 1880 when he won his doubles match.

By profession Whitfeld was a local director of Barclay's Bank in Sussex. His brother and a nephew were also Sussex cricketers. It should be pointed out that his name sometimes appears as Whitfield but Whitfeld is the correct version.

WILSON, Claude William:
b. Banbury, Oxfordshire, 9 September 1858;
d. Reigate, Surrey, 7 June 1881.
Education: Brighton College; Exeter College, Oxford (matric. 1878).
FA Cup runner-up (1): Oxford University 1880.
Career: Brighton College (XI 1875-76; 1876-77†); Oxford University (Blue 1879, 1880, 1881); Old Brightonians; Sussex; London; The South; England XI. Full internationals (2): England v Wales 1879; v Scotland 1881.

Full-back who looked to have a great future, receiving praise as 'a splendid back; strong kick; very fast and active', and 'a fine back, kicks accurately and strongly.' Wilson was also a good cricketer who played for Oxford University in 1881 and would probably have been awarded his Blue but for his tragic early death. He also made a single appearance for Surrey in the 1881 season in which he scored 51 in one of his first-class innings.

It was cricket which led to Wilson's early death as he caught sunstroke while playing in a club match at Reigate and died from its effects. The temperature in Surrey at that time was measured at 146 F in the direct sun! He was still a student at the time of his death. His father was a clergyman.

WILSON, Francis Heathcote:
b. Ampfield, near Hursley, Hants., 9 April 1848;
d. Munster House, Fulham Road, Fulham, London, 11 September 1886 (£1,908).
Education: Eton College; University College, Oxford (matric. 1866; BA 1871).
FA Cup runner-up (2): Old Etonians 1875 (both matches), 1876 (replay).
Career: Eton; Oxford University; Gitanos; Old Etonians.

Versatile defender who filled the role of full-back, half-back and goalkeeper in his three Cup final appearances. He replaced the unavailable Quintin Hogg as goalkeeper in the 1875-76 replay as established in contemporary accounts of the game, though modern record books erroneously credit Hogg with the appearance. He was usually stated to have 'played well', whatever his position.

By profession Wilson was a barrister who was called to the bar at Lincoln's Inn on 7th June 1873. He then practised on the Western Circuit, concentrating on the Hampshire, Southampton and Portsmouth Sessions. He had considerable legal reporting experience as he was for a short time on the staff of the *Law Journal Reports* and then for several years on the staff of another legal publication, *The Weekly Reporter*.

His death was a tragic one. It was put down to the effects of a severe fall on the ice followed by immersion in the bitterly cold water early in 1886. Severe seizures caused him to be placed in Munster House, a lunatic asylum specialising in treatment for epileptic cases among the gentry. At that time the treatment of epileptics differed little from that of lunatics. Wilson suffered general paralysis of the insane for seven months, then died after 14 days of epileptiform convulsions. These are epileptic-like in effect but do not mean that the sufferer has epilepsy.

At the time of his death Wilson's home was at 36 Belgrave Road, Eccleston Bridge, Pimlico, London, and he had chambers in The Temple. His father was the Rev. Robert Francis Wilson, Vicar of Ampfield.

WINGFIELD-STRATFORD, Brig.-Gen. Cecil Vernon:
b. West Malling, Kent, 7 October 1853;
d. Fartherwell, West Malling, 5 February 1939 (£2,764).
Education: RMA, Woolwich.
FA Cup winner (1): Royal Engineers 1875 (both matches).
Career: RMA, Woolwich; Royal Engineers; Kent. Full internationals (1): England v Scotland 1877.

Outside-left who was said to be 'very fast and useful as a wing; wants a little more "last".' Presumably, staying-power is what is meant here. He was also a useful cricketer who was a member of MCC. One of his sisters was married to his Cup final colleague H.W. Renny-Tailyour in 1875.

He joined the Royal Engineers as a lieutenant on 29th October 1873, eventually becoming Chief Engineer in Ireland, 1906-10, when he retired without having seen any active service. However when he was recalled in the Great War he served throughout on the Western Front 1914-18 (mentioned in despatches four times; CMG 1916; CB 1918). He was involved in the Battle of Loos 1915, Gommecourt on the first day of the Somme 1916 and was Commanding R.E. of the 46th Division when it broke the Hindenburg Line in the advance to victory in 1918.

WOLLASTON, Charles Henry Reynolds:
b. Felpham Vicarage, Sussex, 31 July 1849;
d. 46 Belgrave Road, Victoria, London SW1, 22 June 1926 (£22,726).
Education: Lancing College (Aug. 1862-Sept.1868); Trinity College, Oxford (matric. 1868; BA 1871).
FA Cup winner (5): Wanderers 1872, 1873, 1876 (both matches), 1877, 1878.
FA Cup final umpire (5): 1874, 1881, 1882, 1884, 1885.
Career: Lancing (XI 1864-68, captain 1867-68); Oxford University (pre-university match); Wanderers; Clapham Rovers; Lancing Old Boys; London; Middlesex; The South. Full internationals (4): England v Scotland 1874; 1875; 1877; 1880†. Pre-official internationals (2): England v Scotland 1872 (both matches).

Inside-right whose dribbling and shooting skills were of the highest order; 'a very pretty and effective player; usually acting as a wing; especially good as a dribbler, and always about goal when the ball is in the way' was the contemporary verdict, while earlier it had been 'an extremely skilful dribbler and sure kick at goal, wants more weight but plays well against the best men' and 'guides the leather with the most consummate skill, and is unerring in his shots at goal.' To prove this last claim, when the Wanderers beat Farningham 16-0 in the first round of the Cup in 1874-75, Wollaston scored four goals though he saw his teammate, R.K. Kingsford, set the then Cup record with five! He also clocked up four for London in a representative match in 1877-78 when they beat Birmingham and district 11-0. His tally of five Cup winning medals is the record, shared with the Hon. A.F. (later Lord) Kinnaird and J.H. Forrest of Blackburn Rovers. Wollaston was a founder member of the Oxford University Association Football Club when it was formed on 9th November 1871, he served on the F.A. committee 1879-85 and had a spell as secretary of the Wanderers late in the 1870s.

Wollaston was a solicitor by profession, being admitted in 1875, then he was employed successively as assistant secretary and secretary of the Union Bank of London 1878-98. He was the son of a clergyman and became brother-in-law to A.C. Bartholomew who played first-class cricket for Oxford University as well as Minor County matches for Devonshire. Wollaston was cremated at Golders Green.

WOOD, Colonel Charles Knight:

b. Ledbury, Herefordshire, 1 July 1851;
d. The Moor, Bodenham, Herefordshire, 12 February 1923 (£4,834).
Education: Cheltenham College (1868-December 1869); RMA, Woolwich (1870-72).
FA Cup winner (1): Royal Engineers 1875 (both matches); runner-up (1): Royal Engineers 1874.
Career: Cheltenham College (rugby XX 1869); RMA, Woolwich; Royal Engineers.

Inside-right, Wood was said to have 'worked untiringly' and formed a redoubtable wing partnership with P.G. von Donop who carried all before them in the early 70s. An all-round sportsman, he was an outstanding athlete as a runner and long jumper (his best was 21ft 7in.), who also excelled at cricket for the Royal Engineers and lawn tennis (winning the Bermuda open doubles title with P.G. von Donop), besides being a good horseman, an expert canoeist and fine cyclist. It is reported that at the age of 52 he cycled 162 miles across England by a route he had never travelled before.

He also had artistic tastes and pursuits, being a fine and versatile actor who took part in a charity performance at the Kemble Theatre, Hereford, a few days before his death.

Wood joined the Royal Engineers as a lieutenant on 6th January 1872. He was promoted to captain on 6th January 1884, major on 6th May 1891, lieut.-colonel on 1st September 1898 and colonel on 29th November 1900. He served in Bermuda and Malta, then saw active service in the Sudan war 1884-85 in the Telegraph Department (medal with clasp & bronze star). He was adjutant of the R.E. volunteers 15th May 1889 to 16th September 1894.

Wood took part in the Boer War 1899-1901 including the Relief of Ladysmith plus action at Colenso, Spion Kop, Vaal Kranz, Tugela Heights, Pieters Hill, Laings Nek, Belfast and Lydenberg; (mentioned in despatches by Sir Redvers Buller; Queen's Medal with six clasps). From 25th April 1900 to 9th January 1901 he was Chief Engineer on the Staff in Natal. Wood retired in December 1904 and was later secretary of the Herefordshire Territorial Association from its initiation, only giving up the work when he was over 70. He died from broncho-pneumonia and was buried at Humber Church.

During his spell in the 1884-85 Sudan war Wood had charge of about 1,200 miles of telegraph line. The day after his arrival in the country he had to settle an urgent and disputed point between the military and civilian telegraph authorities so he immediately started up the Nile on a donkey to inspect the wires and offices. He stayed with sheiks overnight, covering 42 miles in one day on his donkey to establish conclusively the military point of view which was later confirmed by the experience of the war.

WYLIE, John George:
b. Coton Hill, St Mary's, Shrewsbury, 5 October 1854;
d. Wandsworth, London, 30 July 1924.
Education: Shrewsbury School.
FA Cup winner (1): Wanderers 1878.
Career: Shrewsbury; Shropshire Wanderers; Sheffield Club; Doncaster; Wanderers; London; Sheffield F.A.; North Wales F.A. Full internationals (1): England v Scotland 1878. Selected for England v Scotland 1873-74 but unavailable. He played for Sheffield v Glasgow in 1874-75 and 1875-76.

Centre-forward who was praised as 'a good centre, with pace and strength; should play for his side more.' His marksmanship was also noted but the criticism of his concentration on individual effort at the cost of teamwork was an indication of the changing attitude to the game during his heyday.

By profession Wylie was a solicitor who was admitted in 1878 and practised in London after spending the mid-1870s in Yorkshire.

WYNYARD, Major Edward George:

b. Saharanpur (now in Uttar Pradesh), India, 1 April 1861;
d. The Red House, Knotty Green, Beaconsfield, Bucks, 30 October 1936 (£1,651).
Education: Woodcote House, Windlesham; Charterhouse School (1874-77); St Edward's School, Oxford (1877-79).
FA Cup winner (1): Old Carthusians 1881.
Career: Charterhouse (XI 1876); Old Carthusians; London; Corinthians; St Edward's School (rugby XV).

Centre-forward who scored one of the goals in the F.A. Cup final victory. He was described as 'a heavy forward, charging and dribbling well; always middles splendidly' and again 'good forward, plenty of dash; makes himself obnoxious to the opposing backs.' He kept up his form into his thirties, playing twice for the Corinthians in 1893 and scoring five goals. Wynyard was president of the Old Carthusians Cricket and Football Club 1913-19. During his time at St Edward's School, Oxford, he also took up rugby, developing into a splendid player of whom it was said: 'He was a glorious three-quarter, fast and strong, and could turn on a sixpence when in full cry. Had he not gone into the army, he would have reached the top in the rugger world.' He was in the college rugby XV and the cricket XI.

Despite his Cup final success, Wynyard's footballing feats were overshadowed by his prowess as a cricketer. He played in three Test matches for England (one v Australia 1896; two v South Africa 1905-06) and was invited to captain England on the Test tour to Australia in 1907-08 but had to decline for family reasons. He also had to decline a place on the Test tour to Australia in 1897-98 because of army duties. However, he did captain MCC in New Zealand 1906-07 (no Test matches). Others tours included: West Indies 1904-05 when he topped the batting with 562 runs at 40.14; MCC in North America 1907; Egypt 1909; South Africa 1909-10; United States 1920; and Canada 1923. On this last tour, at the age of 62, he headed the bowling averages with his underarm lobs!

He played for Hampshire 1878-1908 (they were not first-class 1886-94), being captain 1896-99. His final first-class match was for MCC in 1912 and in all he scored 8,318 first-class runs, average 33.00 with 13 centuries including 268 for Hampshire v Yorkshire in 1896. He made 1,038 runs, average 49.42 in 1896 when he finished second in the national first-class batting averages, and 1,281 at 41.32 in 1899 when he was 15th. Wynyard was a member of MCC and Free Foresters who served on the MCC committee 1920-24 and also represented the South African Cricket Association in England in 1908.

He was active in other sports too and won the European international toboggan championship at Davos in 1894. He played county hockey for Hampshire and later took up golf, forming his own club, the Jokers, of which he was Chief Joker, mostly composed of cricketers of some fame. Other golf clubs with which he was connected were Beaconsfield, Royal Wimbledon (hon. life member 1930) and Oxford Graduates' Golfing Society (hon. life member 1931).

Wynyard joined the army and in 1881 was a lieutenant with the 1st Regiment Warwick Militia. From 1883 to 1890 he was with the King's Liverpool Regiment with which he saw active service on the Burma Expedition 1885-87 (medal with clasp, DSO 1887, mentioned in despatches twice). He was promoted to captain and joined the Welch Regiment 1890. He was adjutant of the Oxford University Volunteers 1899-1900, then instructor in military engineering at the Royal Military College, Sandhurst, 1900-03 when he retired. Wynyard was recalled for the Great War in September 1914 as a major back with the King's Liverpool Regiment, then was attached for duty to the Army Ordnance Corps May 1915. He was appointed to the Middlesex Regiment in November 1916 and became Commandant at Thornhill Labour Camp, 1916-19. He finally retired in April 1919 when he received the OBE. Wynyard, who was the son of William Wynyard, a magistrate in the Bengal Civil Service, was buried at Penn Church, Bucks.

In 1895 Wynyard was awarded the Royal Humane Society medal for his bravery on 9th December 1893 when 'at great personal risk, he attempted to rescue a Swiss peasant from drowning in the lake at Davos, Switzerland.' He was the second member of the Old Carthusians Cup-winning side to receive such an award. See also under J.F.M. Prinsep for details of his two Royal Humane Society awards.

As will be realised from the title of his own golfing society, 'The Jokers', Wynyard had a great sense of humour as illustrated in an anecdote from his former c/o at Sandhurst. In 1901 when Wynyard was in charge of cricket at the college he arranged a match against W.G. Grace's XI. Two days before the game Grace wrote to say he himself could not play. Wynyard was much annoyed and in talking over the coming match with the cadets it came to light that not one of them had seen Grace play. Whereupon Wynyard decided that he himself would make him appear and so on the day of the match, after a session with a make-up expert, 'Dr W.G. Grace' was ready. He batted, made several runs and then got purposely hit on the hand to retire hurt. At lunch, when both teams were assembled, Wynyard appeared, still in disguise except for his cap and false beard, and said: 'I think I have spoofed you all this time.' The make-up and Wynyard's imitation of Grace's batting style were so good that no one had spotted the deception.

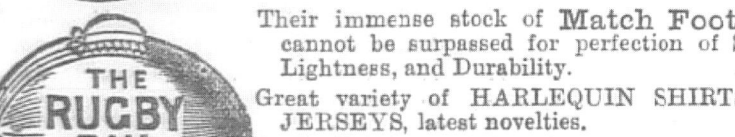

BIBLIOGRAPHY

Books
Alcock, Charles William (editor). The Football Annual (London, 1871-1885).
Alcock, Charles William (editor). James Lillywhite's Cricketers' Annual (London, 1872-1900).
Ashley-Cooper, F.S. Cricket Scores and Biographies; Volume 15 (London, 1925).
Bailey, John. A Pleasing and Unobjectionable Recreation; An Exploration of the Origins of Association Football in the Thames Valley (Upminster, 2003).
Bailey, Philip, Philip Thorn and Peter Wynne-Thomas. Who's Who of Cricketers (Feltham, 1984).
Barnard, Derek. An Index to Wisden 1864-1984 (London, 1985).
Barton, Bob. History of the F.A. Amateur Cup (Newcastle upon Tyne, 1984).
Booth, Keith. The Father of Modern Sport: The Life and Times of Charles W. Alcock (Manchester, 2002).
Brighton College Register 1847-1922.
Brown, Tony. The F.A. Cup Complete Results (Toton, Nottingham, 1999).
Burke's Landed Gentry (London, various years).
Burke's Peerage (London, various years).
Butler, Bryon. The Official Illustrated History of the F.A. Cup (London, 1996).
Charterhouse Register 1872-1910.
Clifton College Register 1862-1941.
Cochrane, Alfred. Repton Cricket 1865-1905 (Repton, 1908).
Crockford's Clerical Directory (London, various years).
Davies, Gareth M. and Ian Garland. Who's Who of Welsh International Soccer Players (Wrexham, 1991).
Dibble, Jeremy. C. Hubert H. Parry. His Life and Music (Oxford, 1992).
Dictionary of National Biography (London, various years).
Ellis, Bernard (editor). A Complete Record of Scores with Bowling Analyses of all Cricket Matches, and full particulars of all Football Matches and Rifle Contests between Charterhouse and other Public Schools from 1850 to 1890 (London, 1891).
Eton School Lists 1853-1892.
Farror, Morley, and Douglas Lamming. A Century of English International Football, 1872-1972 (London, 1972).
Foster, Joseph. Alumni Oxonienses 1715-1886; four volumes (Oxford, 1888).
Foster, Joseph. Men at the Bar 1885 (London, 1885).
Gibson, Alfred, and William Pickford. Association Football and the Men Who Made It; four volumes (London, 1905-06).
Golesworthy, Maurice (compiler). The Encyclopædia of Association Football (12th edition, London, 1976).
Goulstone, John. Football's Secret History (Upminster, 2001).
Green, Geoffrey. The History of the Football Association; general editor, Harvey V. Usill (London, 1953).
Green, Geoffrey. The Official History of the F.A. Cup (new and enlarged edition, London, 1960).
Haileybury Register 1862-1961.
Harrow School Register 1801-1900.
Haygarth, Arthur. Cricket Scores and Biographies; 14 volumes (London, various years).
Highgate School Roll 1833-1922.
Historical Record of the Q.V.O. Madras Sappers and Miners, Volume One (N.D.).
Inglis, Simon. Soccer in the Dock. A History of British Football Scandals 1900 to 1965 (London, 1985).
Lamming, Douglas. An English Football Internationalists' Who's Who, 1872-1988 (Beverley, 1990).
Lamming, Douglas. A Scottish Soccer Internationalists' Who's Who, 1872-1986 (Beverley, 1987).
John Lillywhite's Cricketers' Companion (London, 1865-1885).
Lyon, W.R. (editor). The Elevens of Three Great Schools 1805-1929, being all recorded scores of cricket matches played between Winchester, Eton & Harrow, with memoirs & biographies of the players (Eton, 1930).
Lyttelton, Edith. Alfred Lyttelton: An Account of His Life (abridged edition, London, 1923).

Mackay, Moray. Doune Historical Notes (Stirling, 1953).
Malvern College Register 1865-1949.
Marlborough College Register 1843-1933.
Medical Directory, The. (London, 1933).
Mill Hill School Register 1807-1926.
Powell, William A. Cricket Grounds of Middlesex (Nottingham, 1990).
Powell, William A. Cricket Grounds of Surrey (Nottingham, 2001).
Radley Register 1847-1947.
Records of Old Westminsters to 1927.
Repton School Register 1857-1957.
Roffensian Register 1835-1936, The. (Rochester, 1937).
Roy, David, Ian Bevan, Stuart Hibberd and Michael Gilbert. The Centenary History of the Arthur Dunn Cup (Beckenham, 2003).
Shearman, Montague. Athletics and Football (The Badminton Library; London, 1887).
Sherborne Register 1550-1950.
Smales, Ken. Forest. The First 125 Years (Nottingham, 1991).
Smart, John Blythe. The Wow Factor: A Concise History of Early Soccer and the Men Who Made It (Hailsham, Sussex, 2003).
Spiller, Ray (compiler). The Early Years; four volumes, 1863-78; 1878-83; 1883-86; 1886-88; (Basildon, 1983-84).
Spiller, Ray (compiler). Football Association Cup 1871-81 (Basildon, 1985).
Turner, Arthur J. The Hundred Years Story of the Nottingham Forest Football Club 1865 to 1965 (Nottingham, 1965).
Tyler, Martin. Cup Final Extra! (London, 1981).
Various authors. The Book of Football: a Complete History and Record of the Association and Rugby Games (London, 1906).
Venn, J.A. Alumni Cantabrigienses, Part Two 1752-1900; six volumes. (Cambridge 1940-54).
Weir, Colin. The History of Oxford University Association Football Club 1872-1998 (Harefield, 1999).
Wellington College Register 1859-1948.
Who Was Who Volumes 1-5: 1897-1960 (London, 1967 reprint).
Winchester Scholars 1397-1887.
Wisden's Cricketers' Almanack (London, various years).
Young, Percy M. Football in Sheffield (London, 1962).
Young, Percy M. A History of British Football (London, 1968; paperback edition, 1973).

Journals, magazines and newspapers
Association of Football Statisticians' Reports
Bell's Life in London
Bideford and North Devon Weekly Gazette, The
Carthusian, The (Charterhouse School magazine)
Chard and Ilminster News
Eton College Chronicle
Field, The
Forest School Magazine, The
Harrovian, The (Harrow School magazine)
Law Journal, The
Law Times, The
Morning Post, The
Royal Engineers Journal, The
Sapper, The

Shrewsbury Chronicle, The
Solicitors' Journal and Reporter, The
Sporting Life, The
Sportsman, The
Stirling Journal
Stirling Saturday Observer and Perthshire Herald
Times, The

CD-Rom
1881 British Census and National Index (Birmingham, 1999)

Famous Football Players – an engraving issued with the Boy's Own Paper volume 4 of 1881-82. Standing (from left): C Campbell (Queen's Park), CJ Caborn (Nottingham Forest), T Marshall (Darwen), HA Swepstone (Pilgrims), J Hunter (Sheffield Heeley), SW Widdowson (Nottingham Forest), E Luntley (Nottingham Forest), JFM Prinsep (Old Carthusians), H McNeil (Queen's Park), HEM Lindsay (Royal Engineers), J Sands (Nottingham Forest), T Brindle (Darwen) W Mosforth (Sheffield Wednesday). Sitting: H Whitfeld (Old Etonians), NC Bailey (Clapham Rovers), EC Bambridge (Swifts), FJ Sparks (Clapham Rovers) (on stool), FW Earp (Nottingham Forest) (on ground). Messrs Bailey, Lindsay, Prinsep, Sparks and Whitfeld played in early F.A. Cup finals and feature in this book. Hunter was a member of the victorious Blackburn Olympic team in 1883 and Campbell played in the finals of 1884 and 1885.

Acknowledgments

Mrs Audrey Allfree (for help with her ancestor, Edward Albert Ram); John Bailey; Mervyn Baker (for his telephone call which initiated this project); Kit Bartlett; Philippa Bassett, archivist of the University of Birmingham Information Services Special Collections; Nigel Bishop (for research into Henry Edward Drummond Moray); Sir Nicholas Bonsor, Bart.; Tony Brown; David Castle-Smith and Shirley Murdoch of Fife Council Libraries at Cupar; Sophie Chessum, research assistant, Historic Buildings Department of the National Trust South East Region at Polesden Lacey, Dorking, Surrey; John Day (for the photograph of E.H. Parry's grave); Felsted School bursar's office, Essex; Les Franklin of the North Devon Athenaeum at Barnstaple; Philip Gale, archivist and records manager of the Church of England Record Centre at South Bermondsey, London SE; Karen Garvey, archivist to St Edward's School, Oxford; Rita M. Gibbs, archivist to Harrow School; Mike Grimshaw of the Amateur Football Alliance; Hallward Library at Nottingham University; Hammersmith and Fulham Archives and Local History Centre; John Harding (for help with some of the portraits); Guy Holborn, librarian of Lincoln's Inn Library; Mike Holgate of Torquay Local Studies Library; Irish and Local Studies Library at Armagh; Peter Holme, research assistant at the National Football Museum, Preston; Mr T. Jones-Parry, Head Master of Westminster School; Jean Lear of Medway Archives and Local Studies Centre at Strood, Rochester; Mr R.W. Lloyd-Jones; Howard Milton; Ian Nannestad, editor of *Soccer History*; Nottingham Local Studies Library; Nottinghamshire Archives; Reading Central Library Local Studies Collection; Dr Clare Rider, archivist to The Honourable Society of the Inner Temple; Ms Maggie Lindsay Roxbrough and Mrs Ronnie Schnable of the Royal Engineers Library at Brompton Barracks; David A. Roy, secretary of the Arthur Dunn Cup; Royal Academy of Arts Library; Royal Institute of British Architects Library and Information Centre; Dr James Russell (for help over medical descriptions on death certificates); Shropshire Records and Research Centre at Shrewsbury; John Blythe Smart; Somerset Studies Library at Taunton; Southend-on-Sea Local Studies Library; Peter Jefferson Smith (for help over JFM Prinsep); Mike Spurrier (for research into service personnel); Surrey Family History Centre at Woking; Philip Thorn of the Association of Cricket Statisticians and Historians' Biographical Research team; Michael Webb (for research into Clopton Allen Lloyd-Jones); Colin Weir; Mrs Ann Wheeler, archivist to Charterhouse School; John Williams, secretary of the Arthurian League; Gerald Wright, archivist to Forest School; Peter Wynne-Thomas, librarian to Nottinghamshire County Cricket Club.

Photographs of the Royal Engineers are published by kind permission of the Royal Engineers Library, Chatham. Photographs of Old Carthusians are published by kind permission of the Governing Body of Charterhouse. Photographs of Harrow footballers are reproduced by kind permission of Harrow School. The F.A. Cup medals are reproduced by kind permission of Gordon Wallis.

Defending in depth ... 1874 style.

Printed in Dunstable, United Kingdom

Tips for Adapting Recipes for Large-Scale Baking

1. Scaling Up: Increase ingredients proportionally, but consider testing in smaller increments first to ensure the recipe scales well.

2. Ingredient Adjustments: Ingredients like baking powder, baking soda, and spices may need to be adjusted differently when scaling recipes

3. Equipment Considerations: Larger mixers and ovens may affect the cooking time and temperature. Reduce oven temperature by ten °C for convection ovens

- Sweet, use half the amount of sweetener called for.
- Substitutions will work in most recipes. They may not work in candies, such as caramel.

NUTRITION

*Calories: **219.2***
*Carbohydrates: **6.1g***
*Protein: **12.1g***
*Fat: **16.4g***
*Saturated Fat: **5.2g***
*Polyunsaturated Fat: **0.5g***
*Monounsaturated Fat: **2.1g***
*Trans Fat: **0.2g***
*Cholesterol: **57mg***
*Sodium: **370.5mg***
*Potassium: **154.6mg***
*Fiber: **1.8g***
*Sugar: **3.6g***
*Vitamin A: **283.1IU***
*Vitamin C: **0.1mg***
*Calcium: **212.4mg***
*Iron: **0.9mg***

NOTES

- **Nutrition:** The nutrition facts are for one serving, which is one-tenth of the cheesecake. There are 4.3 NET carbs per serving.
- **Springform Pan:** The baking time listed is for an 8-inch pan. If you use a larger pan, reduce the time. A standard cheesecake pan usually is 9 inches and may cook in as little as 40 minutes since it will be thinner. This can be made into bars, mini cheesecakes, etc.; adjust the time accordingly.
- **To Store:** The cheesecake can be stored in the fridge for up to 5 days. You could also keep it in a covered container.
- **To Freeze:** Either slice the cheesecake into pieces and store it in small containers or freeze the entire thing —Thaw in the fridge before serving.

Notes on Sweeteners:

- My recipes use my blend of xylitol, erythritol, and stevia. This is twice as sweet as sugar and comparable to Trim Healthy Mama Gentle Sweet and Truvia.
- To substitute Swerve or Lakanto Monk Fruit, use 1.5 times the amount of sweetener called for.
- To sub in Pyure or Trim Healthy Mama Super

⟶ *½ cup Joy Filled Eats Sweetener (or see alternatives in recipe notes)*
⟶ *Two eggs*
⟶ *One teaspoon vanilla*

INSTRUCTIONS

- Preheat oven to 350.
- Combine the crust ingredients in a food processor and process until well combined. Press into the bottom and up the sides of an 8-inch springform pan. Bake the crust for 10 minutes until slightly golden browned.
- Meanwhile, process the cream cheese in the food processor until smooth. Add the sour cream, eggs, vanilla, and sweetener. Process until well combined, scraping down the sides and needed.
- After the crust has been partially baked, add the filling.
- Bake for 50-60 minutes or until the center no longer jiggles. Let cool to room temperature.
- Chill the cheesecake for 3-4 hours before serving.

Keto Cheesecake

Prep time: 15 mins

Cook time: 50 Minutes

Servings: 10

Total time: 1 hour 5minutes

COURSE: Dessert
CUISINE: American
CALORIES: 219.2

EQUIPMENT
8-inch springform pan

INGREDIENTS

⟶ *Crust*
⟶ *1.5 cups almond flour*
⟶ *Four tablespoon butter*
⟶ *Filling*
⟶ *16 oz cream cheese*
⟶ *½ cup sour cream*

METHOD

- Preheat oven to 180 degrees Celsius.
- Grease a loaf pan with some coconut oil and line with baking paper.
- Put all dry ingredients except walnuts into your food processor and whizz for a few seconds to combine.
- Add wet ingredients and whizz together, making a batter.
- Roughly chop the walnuts and fold them through the batter.
- Pour into loaf pan, spreading it evenly.
- Bake for 40-45 minutes until the skewer comes out clean.

Recipe Tip

If you have over-ripe bananas but don't have time to make the bread today, freeze the bananas in a sandwich bag. They will work fine when you want to make this.

→ *Two tablespoons coconut oil, plus a little extra for greasing tin*

→ *Two tablespoons of maple syrup*

→ *Two eggs, lightly beaten*

→ *One teaspoon of baking powder*

→ *One teaspoon of baking soda*

→ *One teaspoon cinnamon*

→ *One teaspoon of vanilla extract*

→ *Pinch sea salt*

4. Specialty Diet Recipes
Paleo Banana Bread

The Antipodean version is less sweet and cakey than others, so it's suitable for a snack and perfect for toasting. It makes use of over-ripe bananas that you would normally toss out. I used hazelnut meal in this recipe; it adds a lovely flavor to the bread, but all almond meal will work fine. I make my hazelnut meal by roasting a load of hazelnuts for about 12 minutes at 160 degrees Celsius, then roughing them around in a clean tea towel while they are hot to remove all the brown skin. Whizz the skinless hazelnuts in your food processor, and voila, it's done.

INGREDIENTS

⟶ *1 cup hazelnut meal*

⟶ *1 cup almond powder*

⟶ *1/2 cup desiccated coconut*

⟶ *Heaped 1/2 cup of walnuts, roughly chopped*

⟶ *Two very ripe bananas*

Enjoy warm, or allow to cool until room temperature and store in an airtight container for later.

INSTRUCTIONS

- Preheat the oven to 375 degrees F—line 2 cookie sheets with parchment paper.
- In a large mixing bowl, beat the almond butter, eggs, coconut oil, and vanilla until smooth. Add the sugar and mix until well incorporated.
- Stir in the almond flour, baking soda, cinnamon (if using), and sea salt until combined.
- Fold in the oats, raisins, chocolate, and chopped nuts (if using).
- Transfer the bowl to the refrigerator for at least 10 minutes or cover overnight. (Note: If baking your cookies later, once cool, the dough can be portioned into balls and stored in the fridge for up to a week.)
- When ready to bake, scoop the batter using a medium cookie scoop or rounded tablespoon onto the sheet pans, spacing the cookies 2 inches apart. There should be six cookies on each sheet.
- Bake the cookies in the middle of the oven (top rack, if you have to choose) for about 8 minutes, until the edges are turning golden brown and the top is just set —they will still look a little gooey and raw.
- Allow the cookies to cool on the pan for at least 10 minutes.

[65]

Course Dessert

Cuisine American
Diet Gluten Free, Low Lactose,
Vegetarian

Prep time: 7 minutes

Cook time: 8 minutes

Servings 12 Cookies

INGREDIENTS

→ *¼ cup applesauce equals 1 egg.*
→ *3 tablespoons water with 1 tablespoon of ground flaxseed equals one egg.*
→ *1 egg equals ¼ cup pureed silken tofu.*
→ *1/4 cup yogurt equals 1 egg.*
→ *1/4 cup buttermilk equals 1 egg.*
→ *1/4 cup sweetened condensed milk equals one egg.*
→ *½ mashed banana equals 1 egg*

Low-Sugar Oatmeal Cookies

Low Sugar Oatmeal Cookies with Almond Flour

These healthy almond flour and oatmeal cookies are soft and baked to perfection, thanks to almond butter, which gives them a lovely chew, and whole rolled oats. They have less sugar and more fiber than regular gluten-free oatmeal cookies and can be made with raisins or chocolate—for more fiber; you can even add some chopped walnuts or pecans! They are loosely adapted from my friend Liz Moody's Healthier Together recipe for The Best Healthy

Chocolate Chip Cookie

Since the cookies are dairy-free, a safe low-FODMAP serving is one cookie. Raisins are a medium-FODMAP food, so chocolate is a safer bet if you want to eat more than that. But you will be fine having one cookie with either mix-in in these quantities.

The almond flour oatmeal cookies taste best on day one, so feel free to keep the dough pre-rolled into balls and bake to order! They are swift in the oven.

- Scoop out rounded 1 tbsp balls of dough and transfer to a prepared baking sheet
- Bake for 10 - 12 minutes, being careful not to overbake, then transfer to a wire rack to cool
- It is best when served fresh but will keep for a few days in an airtight container

⚔ **Prep time: 10 minutes**

🥗 **Cook time: 10minutes**

⏱ **Total time: 20 minutes**

🍽 **Servings 12**

These easy-to-make vegan spiced spelled flour cookies are soft, chewy, and perfectly sweet.

Recipe type: Dessert

Cuisine: Vegan

INSTRUCTIONS

- In a small bowl, combine flax and water and let sit for a few minutes
- Preheat oven to 325F, line a baking sheet with parchment paper, and set aside
- Add the softened coconut oil to a large bowl and beat until light and fluffy
- Beat in the flax egg, coconut sugar, and molasses until well combined
- In a medium bowl, whisk together the spelled flour, baking soda, spices, and salt
- Add the dry ingredients to the wet ingredients and mix until just incorporated

3. Cookies
Spelt Flour Cookies (Vegetarian)

VEGAN SPICED SPELT FLOUR
COOKIES

Ingredients

- ½ tbsp ground flax + 1½ tbsp water
- ¼ cup + 2 tbsp (6 tbsp) coconut oil, softened but not liquid
- ½ cup coconut sugar
- 2 tsp molasses

Optional: ½ tsp white rum
- 1⅓ cup spelt flour
- 1 tsp baking soda
- 1 tsp cinnamon
- ½ tsp allspice
- ¼ tsp clove
- ¼ tsp nutmeg
- ¼ tsp salt

NOTES

This un-iced cake can be kept at room temperature and wrapped to prevent drying for up to 4 days.

If you are icing and filling your cake, the type of icing & filling will determine if it needs refrigeration.

- Combine the cocoa powder with the hot coffee in another mixing bowl and whisk smooth.
- Add the Vegetable oil, vanilla extract, and vinegar, then add all the liquids to the dry ingredients in the large mixing bowl.
- Whisk vigorously to combine well; the batter will seem thick at first, but be sure to keep whisking smooth
- Pour all the batter into your prepared pan(s)
- bake immediately in a preheated 350°F oven for approximately 40 minutes for the 9" x 13" pan or until a toothpick inserted into the center comes out clean.
- Cool the cake in the pan(s) until you can easily touch it without burning yourself.
- Then flip the cake(s) out onto a cooling rack to cool to cold.
- While the cakes are baking, prepare the fudge icing:
- In a small pot on the stove, combine the first three ingredients and bring to a boil.

- Pour the sugar syrup into the cocoa powder and whisk smooth
- In the bowl of your Kitchen Aid mixer fitted with a paddle attachment or in a large mixing bowl with a hand beater, add the cocoa powder and the vanilla extract
- Next, add the Vegetable oil or Melted Coconut Oil and the additional measure of corn syrup
- Next, add the softened vegan ButterButter and mix well.
- Add the sifted confectioner's sugar and mix until smooth.

FOR THE FUDGE RECIPE

- Granulated Sugar 5 Tablespoons (63g)
- Water 5 Tablespoons (75ml)
- Corn Syrup 2 Tablespoons (40g) (30ml)
- Unsweetened Cocoa Powder 1 cup (90g)
- Coconut or Vegetable Oil 2 Tablespoons (27g) (30ml)
- Corn Syrup 4 Tablespoons (80g) (60ml)
- * you can sub glucose, agave or golden syrup here
- Vegan Butter softened 8 ounces (2 Sticks) (226g)
- Vanilla Extract 2 teaspoons
- Confectioner's Sugar or Icing Sugar 3 cups (320g)

INSTRUCTIONS

- Prepare your cake pans with professional bakery pan grease and a parchment paper liner.
- Preheat the oven to 350°F
- Combine the flour, baking soda, salt, and sugar in a large mixing bowl and whisk to combine well.

[56]

Equipment

- Measuring Utensils
- Food Processor
- 9 Inch Springform Pan

Instructions

- Wash the oranges and boil them whole (peel and all) for 1½ hours, or until soft
- Place whole oranges (peel and all) in a food processor and blend until smooth
- Pulse in eggs, honey, almond flour, salt, and baking soda until well combined
- Pour batter into a greased 9 Inch Springform Pan
- Bake at 375°F for 35-45 minutes, until a toothpick stuck in the center comes out clean
- Cool in the pan for 2 hours
- Serve

Vegan Chocolate Cake

ONE HOUR CHOCOLATE CAKE RECIPE

Prep time: 25 minutes

Cook time: 35 minutes

Total time: 1 hours

INGREDIENTS

*FOR THE CAKE
RECIPE*

- All Purpose Flour 3 cups (375g)
- Natural Cocoa Powder 8 Tablespoons
- Granulated Sugar 1¾ cups (350g)
- Salt 1 teaspoon (6g)
- Baking Soda 2 teaspoons
- Apple Cider Vinegar 2 teaspoons
- Vanilla Extract 2 teaspoons
- Vegetable Oil ¾ cup (177ml)
- Strong Brewed Coffee 2 cups *see note above

2. Cakes
Almond Flour Cake (Gluten-Free)

Gluten Free Orange Almond Flour
Cake

Ingredients

- o 2 small oranges, 6.5 ounces each
- o 4 large eggs
- o ¾ cup honey.
- o 2 cups blanched almond flour (not almond meal).
- o ½ teaspoon Celtic sea salt
- o 1 teaspoon baking soda

Prep time: 1hour 45minutes

Cook time: 45minutes

Total time: 2hours 30minutes

Servings 8

Cook Mode Prevent your screen from going dark

EQUIPMENT

·Bread Machine

INGREDIENTS

·1 1/2 cups water
·1/3 cup plant milk
·1 1/2 tsp. salt
·3 tbsp. packed brown sugar
·3 tbsp. canola oil
·3 3/4 cups whole wheat flour
·1 3/4 tsp. bread machine yeast

INSTRUCTIONS

1.Add your ingredients to your breadmaker in the order specified by the manufacturer. My bread maker (and most) say to add the liquids first, followed by the dry ingredients.

2.Select the loaf size. The above allotments will make a 2 pound loaf.

3.Select the Whole Wheat cycle on your bread maker.

Whole Wheat Vegan Bread

Ingredients?

1. Whole Wheat flour. If you have bread flour that is better. If you go with an all purpose whole wheat flour that's ok too-you're loaf may not rise as much. It's still going to taste delicious and have a light texture.
2. Plant milk. I like using Silk Soy Original milk. Any plant milk will work. I would avoid using any flavored milk such as vanilla.
3. Brown Sugar.
4. Salt.
5. Water.
6. Oil. I use canola oil, but any neutral tasting oil will work-do NOT use olive oil. This is way too flavored for this loaf.
7. Bread Machine yeast. You cannot use traditional yeast in a bread maker. It will not break down properly and your loaf will not rise.

Prep time: 5 mins

Cook time: 3 hrs

Servings: 2 loaves

[51]

☑ Brown rice flour: You can use millet flour instead.

☑ Buckwheat flour: You can use white teff flour, sorghum flour or oat flour instead.

A note on measurements (if possible, use a scale)

Although the recipe card below provides the volume measurements (in cups and spoons), I can't stress this enough: USE METRIC GRAM MEASUREMENTS IF YOU CAN.

They are much more accurate and consistently provide beautiful results. A kitchen scale will always give better results when baking than cups and tablespoons. This is true for almost all baking applications.

Recommended products for gluten free bread baking

The resources listed below will give you the most successful gluten-free bread experience. Keep in mind that not all of them are required. For example, a bowl lined with a fresh tea towel may serve as a proofing basket; a sharp knife can score the bread, and a robust baking pan that retains heat well can replace a cast iron skillet.

But since that's what they were designed and optimized for, this equipment will produce the most fantastic bread. For example, the cast iron pan and Dutch oven are excellent at retaining heat, which contributes to the bread's deliciously crispy crust.

☑ 7 inch round proofing basket

☑ Bread lame set with 5 razor blades

☑ 10 inch cast iron skillet

☑ 5 quart cast iron Dutch oven

☑ 5 quart cast iron combo cooker

Cooling the loaf

Here is where I'm meant to tell you how crucial it is for gluten-free bread to cool fully before cutting into it. Indeed, it is. Cooling sets the crumb and keeps it from becoming sticky or unpleasantly gummy.

However, I'm a really impatient person, and I lose patience quickly when anything becomes mediocre. It's still acceptable.

This means that if the loaf feels just slightly lukewarm to the touch and you really want to go for it, then slice away. However, avoid cutting into the loaf when it is really hot or heated.
Who could resist this, after all?

Possible substitutions

Even though all of the components in this recipe should be readily found online or at your neighborhood grocery shop, I am providing you with a list of possible alternatives. (NOTE: Instead of substituting by volume, please use weight for all replacements.)

- ☑ Active dried yeast: You can use instant yeast, in which case you don't need to activate it, but just add it straight to the dry ingredients along with the sugar. Add the water that would be used in activating the active dried yeast to the dry ingredients along with the psyllium gel and apple cider vinegar.

- ☑ Apple cider vinegar: You can use other types of vinegar, although I recommend sticking to apple cider vinegar if at all possible.

- ☑ Psyllium husk: YOU CAN'T SUBSTITUTE IT WITH A DIFFERENT INGREDIENT. But if you use psyllium husk powder as opposed to the rough husk form, use only 75% of the weight listed in the recipe.

- ☑ Potato starch: You can use corn starch, tapioca starch or arrowroot starch instead.

[49]

first 20 minutes of baking. (Note that using a Dutch oven or combination cooker, which retains the steam produced by the bread itself, eliminates the need for this.)

Preheating the skillet, Dutch oven, combination cooker, and baking pan in the oven is crucial to ensure that everything is blazing hot and prepared for the flawlessly proofed bread.

during the first 20 minutes of baking. (Note that using a Dutch oven or combination cooker, which retains the steam produced by the bread itself, eliminates the need for this.)

Preheating the skillet, Dutch oven, combination cooker, and baking pan in the oven is crucial to ensure that everything is blazing hot and prepared for the flawlessly proofed bread. Preheating the skillet, Dutch oven, combination cooker, and baking pan in the oven is crucial to ensure that everything is blazing hot and prepared for the flawlessly proofed bread.

Baking the gluten-free bread
Once proofed and doubled in volume:
turn the bread out onto a piece of baking/greaseproof paper (I like to use a baking sheet to help with this step),
score the dough with a sharp knife or a bread lame,
transfer the dough to the hot skillet,
place the skillet/Dutch oven/combo cooker in the oven,
pour hot water into the bottom baking tray,
add 3 – 4 ice cubes around the bread (between the baking/greaseproof paper and the skillet) and
close the oven door.

After 20 minutes of steam baking at 480 oF (250 C), remove the water tray, lower the oven temperature to 450 oF (230 C), and continue baking for 40 to 50 minutes. (If the top begins to brown too soon, you may cover the loaf with aluminum foil, shiny side up.)

[48]

Place the dough onto a lightly floured surface. Fold sections of the dough back upon themselves as you go, and use the heel of your hand to knead the dough into form. After the initial 360-degree spin, the dough won't be perfectly smooth. Just keep kneading it until you're satisfied with its appearance.
To seal the seams, turn the dough seam-side down onto a portion of the work area that isn't dusted with flour and spin it in place.

2nd rise: final proof

Place the formed dough, seam side up, into a 7-inch circular proofing basket that has been lightly floured. If needed, seal and close the seams by pinching them together.

location a moist tea towel over the top and let it proof in a warm area for about an hour or until the volume has about doubled.

Oven set-up

Preheat the oven to 480 ºF (250 ºC) for thirty to forty-five minutes before baking the bread.

This is how I set up my oven:
Although I own a Dutch oven/combo cooker, I prefer a cast iron skillet. Using a skillet produces somewhat greater oven spring, resulting in higher-cooked loaves when making gluten-free bread.

That being said, use a Dutch oven/combo cooker if that's all you have available. The bread will still come out beautifully and taste fantastic. Although the article covers how to use a skillet, there is a recipe at the bottom with instructions for using both a skillet and a Dutch oven/combo cooker.

To maintain the bread's crust sufficiently pliable for the last expansion (also known as the oven spring) to occur before the crust begins to set, hot water will be placed in the baking tray on the bottom shelf of the oven during the

THEN

1. Add the potato starch, brown rice flour, buckwheat flour, and salt to a bowl

mix thoroughly to combine

Make a well in the middle and add the yeast mixture, the psyllium gel, and the apple cider vinegar

1st rise: bulk fermentation

To initiate bulk fermentation, transfer the dough into a bowl that has been gently oiled, cover it with a moist tea towel, and let it rise in a warm location for one hour. In volume, it will about double.

The main goal of the bulk fermentation process is to create the bread's flavor, which is what gives your loaf the deliciously nuanced flavor that comes from freshly baked bread.

Shaping the dough

The dough may be formed when it has doubled in bulk. Except for working on a surface that has been gently dusted with flour (I like to use brown rice flour to dust the work surface and proofing basket), the procedure is similar to the shaping done before the bulk fermentation.

What is psyllium husk and what is its role in gluten free bread?

This is the only strange item on the above list, but making good gluten-free bread is essential.

Psyllium husk comes in two different forms: fine powder and rough husk. The rough husk, which is used in this recipe, looks like this:

Pseudo-saccharide husks gel when combined with water, replacing gluten in the dough and cooked bread.

Unlike bread "batter," which must be spooned or poured into a loaf pan, psyllium gel helps to generate a dough that can be kneaded and shaped before baking.

Additionally, it provides the dough with the right amount of flexibility to let it expand throughout the bulk fermentation and final proof while retaining the gas generated by the yeast's activity.

Psyllium gives the finished baked loaf its distinct elasticity, flexibility, and wonderful chewy texture with an open crumb.

ORIGINAL RECIPES

1. Breads
(Gluten-Free Bread)

Ingredients

- ☑ Sugar (to kick-start the yeast action)
- ☑ Warm water
- ☑ Psyllium husk
- ☑ Potato starch (not to be confused with potato flour – these are two completely different things!)
- ☑ Brown rice flour (needs to be very finely milled, also called "superfine")
- ☑ Buckwheat flour
- ☑ Salt (adds flavor)
- ☑ Apple cider vinegar (gives the yeast an extra boost of activity by creating a slightly acidic environment)

Conclusion

Adapting recipes for large-scale baking requires careful consideration of ingredient proportions, equipment capabilities, and cooking techniques. Following these guidelines and making necessary adjustments can achieve consistent and high-quality results in your large-scale baking endeavors. Remember to record any changes and monitor the cooking process closely to ensure each batch meets your standards.

When creating a comprehensive recipe book that addresses diverse dietary needs, it's essential to include a variety of recipes that span different categories, such as breads, cakes, cookies, and more. These recipes should cater to various dietary restrictions and preferences, including gluten-free, vegetarian, vegan, and low-sugar. This approach not only ensures inclusivity but also broadens the appeal of the cookbook. Below is a detailed exploration of diverse recipes tailored to specific dietary needs.

5. Lemon Meringue Pie

Original Recipe (Makes one 9-inch pie)	Adapted Recipe (Makes ten 9-inch pies)
- 1 pre-baked 9-inch pie crust	- 10 pre-baked 9-inch pie crusts
- 1 ½ cups granulated sugar	- 15 cups granulated sugar
- ¼ cup cornstarch	- 2 ½ cups cornstarch
- 1 ½ cups water	- 15 cups water
- 3 large egg yolks, beaten	- 30 large egg yolks, beaten
- 2 tablespoons unsalted butter	- 20 tablespoons unsalted butter
- ⅓ cup lemon juice	- 3 ⅓ cups lemon juice
- 1 tablespoon lemon zest	- 10 tablespoons lemon zest
- 3 large egg whites	- 30 large egg whites
- 6 tablespoons granulated sugar	- 60 tablespoons granulated sugar

Adjustments

1. Lemon Filling: Prepare the filling in large pots, ensuring even heating and mixing.

2. Meringue: Use large mixers to whip egg whites and sugar to stiff peaks.

3. Baking: Bake multiple pies at once, adjusting oven racks and temperatures as needed. Cool pies rapidly to maintain texture and prevent overcooking.

4. Whole Wheat Bread

Original Recipe (Makes 2 loaves)

- *3 ½ cups whole wheat flour*
- *1 ½ teaspoons salt*
- *2 teaspoons active dry yeast*
- *1 ¼ cups warm water*
- *2 tablespoons honey*
- *2 tablespoons olive oil*

Adapted Recipe (Makes 20 loaves)

- *35 cups whole wheat flour*
- *15 teaspoons salt*
- *20 teaspoons active dry yeast (increased by 1.5 times when scaling up)*
- *12 ½ cups warm water*
- *20 tablespoons honey*
- *20 tablespoons olive oil*

Adjustments

1. Yeast: Increased to ensure proper fermentation and rise.
2. Mixing: Use large-scale dough mixers to ensure even distribution of ingredients.
3. Proofing: Use commercial proofing cabinets to control temperature and humidity.
4. Baking: Bake in industrial ovens, reducing the temperature slightly if using convection settings.

3. Creamy Cheesecake

Original Recipe (Makes one 9-inch cheesecake)

- *1 ½ cups graham cracker crumbs*
- *¼ cup granulated sugar*
- *½ cup unsalted butter, melted*
- *4 packages (8 oz each) cream cheese, softened*
- *1 cup granulated sugar*
- *1 teaspoon vanilla extract*
- *4 large eggs*

Adapted Recipe (Makes ten 9-inch cheesecakes)

- *15 cups graham cracker crumbs*
- *2 ½ cups granulated sugar*
- *5 cups unsalted butter, melted*
- *40 packages (8 oz each) cream cheese, softened*
- *10 cups granulated sugar*
- *10 teaspoons vanilla extract*
- *40 large eggs*

Adjustments

1. Crust: Mix graham cracker crumbs, sugar, and melted butter in large batches.

2. Filling: Use commercial mixers to blend the cream cheese, sugar, vanilla, and eggs until smooth.

3. Baking: Use large ovens or multiple racks. Cool cheesecakes rapidly using blast chillers to ensure food safety and maintain texture.

2. Classic Vanilla Cake

Original Recipe (Makes one 9-inch cake)	Adapted Recipe (Makes ten 9-inch cakes)
- 2 ½ cups all-purpose flour	- 25 cups all-purpose flour
- 2 ½ teaspoons baking powder	- 25 teaspoons baking powder (increased by 1.5 times when scaling up)
- ½ teaspoon salt	- 5 teaspoons salt
- 1 ¾ cups granulated sugar	- 17 ½ cups granulated sugar
- ¾ cup unsalted butter, softened	- 7 ½ cups unsalted butter, softened
- 1 ¼ cups whole milk	- 12 ½ cups whole milk
- 1 teaspoon vanilla extract	- 10 teaspoons vanilla extract
- 3 large eggs	- 30 large eggs

Adjustments

1. Baking Powder: Increased to ensure proper leavening.
2. Mixing: Use large industrial mixers to blend ingredients uniformly.
3. Baking: Bake in batches, adjusting oven racks and rotating pans to ensure even baking. Reduce the oven temperature by 10°C if using convection ovens.

1. Chocolate Chip Cookies

Original Recipe (Makes 24 cookies)	Adapted Recipe (Makes 240 cookies)
- 2 ¼ cups all-purpose flour	- 2 ¼ cups all-purpose flour
- 1 teaspoon baking soda	- 1 teaspoon baking soda
- 1 teaspoon salt	- 1 teaspoon salt
- 1 cup unsalted butter, softened	- 1 cup unsalted butter, softened
- ¾ cup granulated sugar	- ¾ cup granulated sugar
- ¾ cup packed brown sugar	- ¾ cup packed brown sugar
- 1 teaspoon vanilla extract	- 1 teaspoon vanilla extract
- 2 large eggs	- 2 large eggs
- 2 cups semi-sweet chocolate chips	- 2 cups semi-sweet chocolate chips

Adjustments

1. Baking Soda: Increased to ensure proper rise.
2. Mixing: Use a commercial mixer to handle the large volume of dough.
3. Baking: Bake in batches to ensure even cooking and use multiple oven racks, rotating pans halfway through baking.

- You may need to reduce the added liquids, use more concentrated stocks in smaller amounts, and cook longer to achieve the same results.

2. Baked or Roasted Recipes
 - Ensure the depth of Food in pans is maintained as per the original recipe, regardless of pan size.
 - Larger objects in the oven may need longer cooking times; to avoid burning or drying out the exterior, you may need to lower the oven temperature. Please note the cooking times and check them often for future use.
the original recipe, regardless of pan size.
- Larger objects in the oven may need longer cooking times; to avoid burning or drying out the exterior, you may need to lower the oven temperature. Make a note of the cooking times and check them often for future use.

Cooling Considerations

When in larger quantities, Food may stay in the danger zone (4°C–60°C) for longer, which can be problematic for food safety.
- Ensure that much Food cools quickly to avoid overcooking and preserve food safety.

[37]

- Baking powder, baking soda, yeast
- Spices
- Salt

3. Equipment Considerations
- Consider the equipment used in the original recipe and what you have available.
- Oven temperatures may need to be reduced.
- Large surface areas in brat pans may cause foods to reduce too quickly.
- Batters and doughs behave differently in large mixers compared to domestic mixers.

4. Convection Ovens
- To adapt baking recipes from conventional ovens for cooking in a convection oven:
- Reduce the cooking time by 25%.
- Reduce the oven temperature by 10°C.

Specific Adjustments for Cooking and Baking
1. Pot Cooking
- When scaling up recipes cooked in a pot, remember the surface area to volume ratio is reduced:
- It will take longer to come to the boil.
- It will take longer to reduce and thicken.

- Increase the size of recipes gradually to see how much can be made in a single batch.

2. Trial and Error

- Adapting a recipe involves trial and error and often demands discretion. Make careful to document any modifications you make so that future planning is consistent.

Tips for Successful Recipe Scaling

1. Scaling Factor

- Scaling a recipe more than four times may compromise its quality and accuracy.
- Measure the materials precisely as directed, recording the weights or volumes in milliliters or grams.

2. Ingredient Adjustments

When a recipe is scaled up, even small errors in ingredient quantities may have a significant impact, particularly when substances like baking powder, salt, and spices are used in tiny amounts.

- When doubling a recipe, think about adding twice as much of the following ingredients, then taste or determine if more is required:

RECIPE ADAPTATION GUIDELINES FOR LARGE SCALE BAKING

It's better to start with established and tested recipes before modifying them for large-scale baking. If you have a comparable recipe in your files, you may modify an existing recipe to fit the new one. Large-scale recipes may also be found in food service cookbooks and internet resources. Here are some suggestions to assist you in modifying home recipes for food service operations if you are still looking for a suitable large-scale recipe to utilize or change.

Critical Considerations for Scaling Recipes

1. Equipment and Physical Limitations

Certain recipes are difficult to scale up because of technological constraints or the physical makeup of the dish. Cooking in batches may be necessary to get the required yield.

Alternatives to Eggs

Although I'm still relatively new to egg replacements, I've compiled a list of popular and easily accessible ones. Although the final product of your bake may taste or feel different from the original, it should still turn out to be rather tasty. Don't quit if one replacement doesn't work out as planned; try another. Please share any reliable egg replacements you may think of!

I've heard that combining your preferred boxed cake mix with a can of Sprite is a terrific trick. Follow the baking instructions to make an eggless cake! Did you ever give that one a try?

Here are some other possibilities in addition to commercial egg replacement products:

⟶ *¼ cup applesauce equals 1 egg.*

⟶ *3 tablespoons water with 1 tablespoon of ground flaxseed equals one egg.*

⟶ *1 egg equals ¼ cup pureed silken tofu.*

⟶ *1/4 cup yogurt equals 1 egg.*

⟶ *1/4 cup buttermilk equals 1 egg.*

⟶ *1/4 cup sweetened condensed milk equals one egg.*

⟶ *½ mashed banana equals 1 egg*

Generally speaking, adding oil or shortening won't affect the taste of your bake. To make them resemble real butter, many dairy-free kinds of butter have salts or other "butter flavor" added. This is useful for cooking, although baking recipes are often affected by the use of salt. You'll be set in taste if you locate some unsalted dairy-free butter! Miyoko's Creamery creates a very mild-flavored, unsalted cashew and coconut oil spread especially for baking. I tried a lot of different brands while creating dairy-free buttercream, but Miyoko's was my favorite. The consistency held up wonderfully, even for a southern July wedding, and the mildness of the "butter" gave the cake a more authentic buttercream taste!

The difference in your bake might come from the consistency of your dairy-free choice. For instance, you can frequently replace oil with melted butter in recipes because oil is also liquid. However, oil would not be a suitable alternative for softened butter in a recipe. If so, you must locate something comparable in consistency to softened butter. It would be preferable to use solid coconut oil, vegan butter sticks, or shortening. Thus, take notice of the specifications for the present recipe and use that information to guide your decision.

While they may be purchased at various supermarkets, Whole Foods has regularly stocked them.

Alternatives to Dairy

Butter and milk are often used in baking to create cakes, frostings, pastries, cookies, breads, and a host of other baked goods. One thing is very important to remember while looking for a suitable replacement for the diary in your recipe is that the taste of the dairy-free milk or butter you chose will come through in your baked products.

Dairy-Free Milk

These days, many dairy-free milk choices are available, and each one has a distinct taste. Oat, almond, coconut, soy, rice, cashew, or macadamia are a few of the offered varieties. Just use unflavored and unsweetened ones for the finest baking results. If nut products bother you, remember that certain dairy-free milks are created with them.

Dairy-Free Butter

Coconut oil, shortening, oils, and vegan butter are dairy-free alternatives. Flavor and consistency are the primary factors when selecting a dairy-free choice.

Remember that the recipe may turn out differently than you had hoped when making replacements. Because baking is a science, modifying a recipe's components will change how it bakes. Be patient during the process; know it can take many tries to perfect the recipe. If the recipe you attempt doesn't work out, look for one made just for you and work your way from there.

Alternatives to Gluten

You will need decent gluten-free flour and probably xanthan gum to bake a gluten-free dish from scratch. I've discovered two gluten-free flour options from King Arthur to be very useful. The first kind, GF All-Purpose flour, lacks xanthan gum; thus, it must be added to the bake as directed by the recipe. This flour is better suited for use in recipes that are designed to be gluten-free. Xanthan gum is included in the second kind of flour, GF Measure for Measure flour. If you want to make a conventional dish gluten-free, this flour is perfect for you.

Additionally, gluten-free mixtures are an excellent and dependable tool. Having tried many gluten-free cake mixes, I've discovered that King Arthur makes the best goods. These are my two favorite cake mixes if you must bake a gluten-free cake. The cakes taste unique, and nobody I made them for noticed they were gluten-free!

Baking Substitutions for Gluten, Dairy, and Eggs (Ingredient Substitutions)

Food allergies are the leading cause of substitutions while baking. However, there are other causes as well. Due to the prevalence of food sensitivities, many individuals cannot purchase baked products. Because gluten, dairy, and eggs are staples in many baking recipes, managing allergies to these items may be particularly challenging. Fortunately, many incredible items enable practically anybody to enjoy baked delicacies! Although I don't have these allergies, I'm offering some strategies that have helped me accommodate them. Remember that these are not exhaustive lists; you could be aware of another effective product. If so, do let us know in the comments! Additionally, be sure that all of the components you are using are suitable for you by doing a self-check.

development in the history of animal-free food production. It makes it possible to produce delicious, nutritious, and sustainable food without sacrificing any of these qualities.

Utilizing water, sugar, and certain minerals, the biotech method produces egg protein by using the microbe Trichoderma reesei. The process is similar to making beer in that the microbe is given sugar to make alcohol. Large industrial bioreactors may be built using the production technique, producing the required protein with almost little waste.

eggs' aeration and structural characteristics.

Nevertheless, soy adds another allergy to the mixture. Unwanted interactions might occur with other substances added to extend the usage of genuine eggs.

Finding an item that can fully replace eggs in baked products is incredibly difficult. Depending on the application, most substitutes may provide comparable viscosity and emulsification qualities; structure, taste, and color are more challenging to replicate completely. Reformulation may be necessary due to potential changes in moisture and water activity during egg replacement, which may impact shelf life.

One food biotech business is replacing eggs differently. Using precise fermentation, the business created egg proteins devoid of animal products. These proteins provide the same functionality and nutrition as egg whites without the ethical, environmental, or safety issues associated with eggs from hens since their component is bio-identical to ovalbumin, the main protein in egg whites.

It is the actual thing, not a replacement. It belongs to a newly emerging class of fermented foods devoid of animal products. Precision fermentation is the most recent

When baked, eggs solidify at a specific temperature, forming a gel that gives the final product its structure. The volume decreases when you subtract eggs from a cake or muffin recipe. While functional systems, volume and structure may fill part of the hole make it challenging to sustain the deeper incisions.

No single item can take the place of whole eggs' more than 20 functions. A more complicated ingredient statement is produced by using several components, some of which may be unfamiliar to customers.

Plant-based substitutes exist for all three essential components of an egg: protein, fat, and lecithin. To assist with partial egg replacement, a variety of solutions have been created, such as modified starches that replicate the emulsifying and processing qualities of eggs. These solutions may replace 25% to 50% of liquid whole eggs depending on the purpose. They provide vital structure and texture for recipes like cookies, pancakes, and muffins.

Soy flour is another substance used to extend the egg supply. It mimics fat's properties and aids in moisture retention. Additionally, useful technologies may be utilized to lessen the eggs required in angel food and high-ratio cakes. The key to these applications is to imitate

Bakers usually use egg products because of this unpredictability and the difficulty of shattering shells. Egg products are in bulk in dried, frozen, and liquid versions. They might be cracked into the whites and yolks or be entire eggs. Additionally, improved-performance variants provide the most significant functional advantages for cost management.

For instance, pasteurized egg whites come in regular, high whip, and high gel varieties. Sometimes, the high-whip kind is referred to as angel whites. It creates a beautiful foam that aerates meringue and angel food cake. To keep the substance intact, protein bars often employ high gel.

Pasteurizing egg products ensures food safety. They also have a long shelf life, are simple to use, and provide uniformity from batch to batch.

Replacing eggs might present difficulties. Certain qualities, particularly texture and structure, are lost when the number of eggs in a recipe is lowered. Gumminess is a prevalent issue that may be challenging to manage. While soy flour may be helpful, there are limitations to how much you can minimize eggs in applications that need eggs, such as cakes.

expenses and prevent supply problems.

Approximately once a day, healthy hens lay one egg, each of which has a yolk and a white. When combined, these ingredients comprise a powerful performance ingredient that each serves a specific purpose in baked meals.

Eggs are very useful in many kinds of baking recipes because of their special functionality. They serve more than 20 purposes, ranging from binding and aeration to adhesion and browning. Eggs affect batter quality, texture, general look and taste, moisture/water activity, and overall richness in baked items.

Eggs are used in cakes, pastries, meringues, cookies, custards, and other baked goods to thicken, emulsify, create volume, stabilize, and add taste and color. Eggs' protein helps them brown, and their yolks' carotenoids give them a deep, golden hue. The hen's food affects the color of the yolk, which may range from light yellow to deep orange.

ROLE OF DIARY AND EGGS

Bakers know that croissants need dough laminated with layers of butter, whereas angel food cakes and meringues depend on egg whites for a light, airy structure. For brioche to be light and fluffy, the proper proportions of eggs, butter, and milk or cream must be used.

Bakers nowadays face difficulty in adhering to these guidelines without going over budget. Due to problems with the supply chain and the high cost of numerous raw materials, they are looking for additives to improve the taste, color, and functioning of dairy and eggs. They are aware that the solution is seldom eradicated. Formulation changes to increase profitability may be achieved by comprehending the function and science of dairy and egg constituents.

Customers are attracted to baked goods prepared with well-known ingredients; dairy and eggs undoubtedly align with the clean label movement. These components also give a formula excellent capability.

The cost of eggs, butter, buttermilk, and milk products is rising, and it doesn't seem like this trend will be reversed very soon. Egg replacers and substitutes for milk and buttermilk are becoming more popular as a way to save everyday meals that are often produced with wheat.

Even though this is a lengthy list, many gluten-free meals are still available! You can pick from a wide variety of fresh, healthful foods, including grains free of gluten, quinoa, rice, beans, dairy, and nuts. Most grocery shops also provide gluten-free versions of many items listed above, making it easier to maintain a gluten-free diet. All you need to do is search for them!

Additional Gluten Sources:-

Unexpectedly, gluten may also be found in the following foods:

matzo

malt

modified food starch

broth in soups and

bouillon cubes

breadcrumbs and

croutons

certain sweets

fried meals

imitation fish

some lunch meats and

hot dogs

GLUTEN PROTEIN SOURCES

Gluten protein is present in various cereals, goods, and substances. We utilize each of these items daily. The primary sources of gluten protein are the cereals rye, barley, and wheat. The following is a quick list of sources organized by category:

Food Sources:- Any food prepared with wheat, rye, barley, or any other grain contains gluten. Avoiding wheat might be particularly difficult since it involves avoiding all flours and products that include wheat. These consist of but are not limited to:

Triticale

Kamut

Spelt

Semolina

White Flour

Whole Wheat Flour

Durum Wheat

Graham Flour

Wheat Germ

Wheat Bran

Pasta, couscous, bread, flour tortillas, cookies, cakes, muffins, pastries, cereal, crackers, beer, oats (see the section on oats below), gravy, dressings, and sauces are celiac disease may cause tiredness, anemia, digestive problems, nutritional shortages, and an increased risk of many catastrophic illnesses.

Furthermore, gluten may compromise the function of the intestine's barrier, opening the door for dangerous chemicals to enter the circulation. A gluten-containing diet may make symptoms of irritable bowel syndrome worse in individuals, including discomfort, bloating, irregular stools, and exhaustion. Furthermore, gluten has been linked to the aggravation of several neurological conditions, including epilepsy, autism, and schizophrenia. According to some research, gluten sensitivity may increase the risk of infertility and may have addictive qualities.

In those who are sensitive to gluten, eating gluten may set off an immunological reaction that targets an enzyme in the digestive system as well as gluten proteins, damaging the intestinal wall. Because of this immune response, celiac disease is now considered an autoimmune condition, which has serious consequences for overall health and well-being.

Based on their solubility in aqueous alcohols, gluten proteins may be separated into two primary fractions: soluble gliadins and insoluble glutenins. Most gliadins are monomeric proteins with molecular weights between 28,000 and 55,000. Their main architectures categorize them into alpha/beta, gamma, and omega kinds. They have intrachain crosslinks or don't have disulfide bonds.

Conversely, aggregated proteins connected by interchain disulfide connections make up glutenins. Like gliadins, glutenin subunits show solubility in aqueous alcohols after breaking these disulfide links. High-molecular-weight (HMW) subunits (67,000–88,000 MW) and low-molecular-weight (LMW) subunits (32,000–35,000 MW) are the two subunit categories for glutenin. Two or three distinct structural domains are present in each kind of gluten protein, including special repeated sequences high in proline and glutamine.

People sensitive to gluten may have negative effects from these particular gluten protein complexes. When gluten enters the digestive system, the immune system may misinterpret it as a dangerous material and launch an attack. When a person has celiac disease, their immune system targets not only the gluten proteins but also tissue transglutaminase, an enzyme in the digestive tract that damages the intestinal wall. An autoimmune condition, trapped CO_2 bubbles in the batter expand, giving the cake a light, fluffy texture. $Na+ + H_2O + CO_2 \rightarrow NaHCO_3 + H+$

Egg

The eggs provide the cake with its moisture. Albumen, or egg white, contains 90% water and 10% protein, which includes albumins, which are globular proteins. Water (~52%), vitamins, minerals, proteins (~16%), carbs (~3.5%), cholesterol (~1%), and fats (~26.5%), including lecithin, are all present in egg yolks. Lecithin is a fatty material with parts of the molecule that are lipophilic (loving fat) and hydrophilic (loving water). This indicates that the egg may continue functioning as an emulsifier, keeping the fatty and wet elements together. An egg may retain carbon dioxide bubbles in the mixture after it has been beaten. The egg clings to the components and holds them together.

The function of dairy, eggs, gluten, and other substances

GLUTEN

The gluten proteins that give dough cohesion, viscosity, elasticity, and ability to absorb water are crucial in defining wheat's special baking properties.

golden hue. Sucrose caramelizes at 160°C. The brown color and distinctive caramel flavor result from a multi-step, intricate procedure. Any reducing sugar in the combination with a carbonyl group can undergo the Maillard reaction with amino groups on amino acids, producing a different mixture of molecules that impart flavor and a brown color.

Flour

The cake gets its structure and volume from the flour. Protein and starch, a polymer of sugar molecules, are found in flour. The goal of preparing the components is to capture air bubbles, which will give the combination a light feel. When the flour cooks, the starch within gels, breaking down the connections between starch molecules and causing the starch granules to enlarge and form hydrogen bonds with water.

Baking powder

This may be mixed with self-raising flour or used as a stand-alone ingredient. Baking powder is a combination of weak solid acid (like phosphate, $Ca(H_2PO_4)_2$), which may release H^+ when it dissolves, and sodium hydrogen carbonate (bicarbonate of soda, $NaHCO_3$). The baking powder releases Carbon dioxide gas when it comes into contact with the wet cake batter. As the cake bakes, these

The Science of Baking

Chemistry and baking go hand in hand.

An experimental technique and a recipe are similar in that both need to be planned so that the elements combine in the correct sequence to produce a finished product. When ingredients interact with one another throughout the baking process, each one goes through a chemical transformation and fulfills a certain purpose.

Butter

Butter is an emulsion of water in butterfat. When butter is added, the mixture becomes softer. Butter also improves the cake's flavor and aids in capturing carbon dioxide bubbles.

Sweetener

Caster sugar is often used in cake making because it has tiny sucrose crystals that trap air between them before dissolving readily. In addition to making the cake sweeter, sugar contributes to the baked good's pleasing

With any luck, this book will encourage you to try new things, grow with your cooking, and discover what makes you happy. Remember that the love and attention you put into your baking makes it, whether you're baking for your friends, family, or yourself. Let's make baking a happy, inclusive activity for everybody.

A Private Remark

I have a little letter I would like to leave you. Baking has taught me so much about perseverance, patience, and the value of community. It reminds me that beautiful things can always be created despite obstacles. It has been a pleasure to share my path of discovery and connection to the chemistry of baking with you.

I appreciate your participation in this trip. Let's hope for many more cakes, cookies, and loaves that unite us all. Happy baking!

A Group of Bakers

I've connected with other bakers who understand my enthusiasm and difficulties along this road. We've cheered one another on, shared advice, and encouraged one another when things didn't work out. I've learned from this community that baking is a means of creating, interacting, and spreading joy—not simply a pastime or a career.

The tales from people who have returned to baking because of my efforts have been among the most touching parts of this trip. The grandma who could now prepare bread for her family with varying dietary requirements, the father who made gluten-free cookies with his daughter, and the young lady who created her first vegan birthday cake for her closest friend are just a few examples.

Gazing Forward

Upon reflecting on my experience, I am overwhelmed with thankfulness. Although my dietary limitations presented obstacles, they also deepened my knowledge of baking and solidified my dedication to diversity in the kitchen. "The Chemistry Behind Baking" is more than simply a book; it celebrates perseverance, imagination, and the timeless pleasure of baking.

Notably, one statement jumped out. It came from a woman whose kid was allergic to several different foods.

She told me how my recipes had made it possible for her to create his first safe and tasty birthday cake, even though he had never been able to enjoy one. I felt a fantastic sense of pleasure and accomplishment as she recalled the delight on his face as he took his first taste.

The Choice to Compose

I decided to put my expertise and recipes into a book because of these tales as well as my own experience. The idea of "The Chemistry Behind Baking" was to enable everyone, regardless of dietary constraints, to bake. I wanted to provide people with more than simply recipes; I wanted to explain the science behind the approaches and replacements, enabling anyone to modify any meal to fit their needs.

The book was a labor of passion to write. I read endless scientific articles, tried many experiments in the kitchen, and asked friends, family, and internet followers for their opinions. Every chapter and recipe was meticulously developed to ensure the explanations were understandable and the outcomes trustworthy.

produced thick, crumbly loaves that were everything but delicious. However, something clicked that evening. Based on my most recent study, I changed my ingredient ratios and added a few extras. The dough felt different, more elastic, and hopeful in my hands.

A cozy, familiar fragrance permeated the kitchen as the bread cooked. When I eventually pulled it out of the oven, it was flawless — gorgeously risen and golden brown. I waited for what seemed like an age to cool off before cutting into it. My eyes welled up with tears when I bit into the first piece. It was tasty, soft, and all I had hoped for. It was a success not just in baking but also in conquering seemingly insurmountable challenges.

Spreading the Happiness

That triumph gave rise to an idea. If I could figure out how to do so, I could assist others in making similar adjustments to recipes. I started posting my recipes online and maintained a blog where I spoke about my trials and offered advice on how to bake successfully without allergens. The outpouring of support was tremendous. Globally, people expressed gratitude for the recipes that brought back their love of baking.

baking. This understanding served as the basis for my quest to modify my favorite meals to fit my new dietary requirements.

College and Upcoming Difficulties

I was so fascinated by how things functioned at the molecular level that I decided to major in chemistry in college. Thanks to my education, I now have a better knowledge of the scientific concepts behind baking. I gained knowledge of the chemical processes involved in bread rising, the role that gluten's proteins play in giving bread structure, and how fats affect pastry texture.

Even though I did well academically, college was difficult. My food constraints made me feel alone a lot of the time. I was unable to consume most social gathering meals; therefore, I was deprived of little pleasures like birthday cake and pizza with friends. However, these difficulties only strengthened my resolve. I experimented with and refined recipes for many hours in the kitchen. My goal was to make baked items that were as delicious as conventional recipes but also something I could enjoy.

The Revolution

One winter evening in my final year of college, I had my eureka moment. I worked on a dairy-free, egg-free, and gluten-free bread recipe for weeks. Every effort had

She let me mix a batter or sift flour, making me feel like a vital operation component.

More than simply a place to bake, Grandma's kitchen was a haven of safety and love for me. She used to tell me tales about her early years, including her time spent in a little, cozy kitchen during the winter making bread with her mother. I felt like I was a part of a long line of bakers since those tales were usually warm and funny.

A Shift in Direction

As I grew older, my passion for baking only expanded. I began experimenting with my own recipes, often ending up with a disaster but sometimes discovering something very good. However, when I started high school, my life changed. I had severe food allergies that made consuming some meals unsafe and unpleasant. I have an allergy to eggs, dairy, and gluten, which are the main ingredients in most baking recipes.

I was inconsolable. My haven, the kitchen, suddenly seemed like a minefield. I couldn't indulge in my favorite breads and pastries. I wasn't prepared to give up, however. I started looking at substitute materials and techniques. It helped that I had a background in science, especially chemistry. I began to comprehend the functions of various components and their interactions in

My Journey into the Chemistry of Baking

The scent of freshly baked bread and the reassuring hum of the oven have always brought me comfort in the kitchen. Baking became my haven and a place where I could create and experiment when I was little. However, there's more to my authoring "The Chemistry Behind Baking" than simply a simple fondness for combining wheat, sugar, and eggs. It's a tale of exploration, adjustment, and a sincere want to make baking enjoyable and accessible to everybody.

Initial Steps

My grandmother's kitchen has special memories for me regarding baking. Her technique with dough was almost mystical. Her hands were tired but steady and could turn essential ingredients into the most delicious breads and pastries. I recall observing her every move while perched on a seat and being unable to look over the counter.

and drastically lower the possibility of baking errors. "The Chemistry Behind Baking" seeks to provide you with the scientific understanding and useful advice you need to become an expert in these areas so that your baking is always excellent.

condensing on the dough surface.

A Practical Guide to Baking Optimization

Think about the following elements to produce consistently excellent baked products:

- Design of the Oven: Ensure uniform and effective heat distribution.
- Dough Properties: Modify for oven spacing, weight, and size of the dough.

Improved heat-transfer efficiency will guarantee consistent baking.

Control humidity to influence the texture and production of crust.

Adjust baking time according to dough characteristics and intended outcome.

Producing consistently great baked products while lowering energy usage and flaws will be possible by knowing and managing these factors.

Thorough knowledge of heat-energy input, heat transmission processes, and thermodynamic concepts is necessary to optimize the baking process. Effective management of these factors will help you to obtain reliable, excellent outcomes, increase energy efficiency,

In thermodynamics, the second law: "Without outside assistance, heat cannot naturally go from a colder to a hotter body."

Thermodynamics' Third Law: "Specific heat of a material decreases with temperature as it gets closer to zero."

Application in Baking: In baking, temperature gauges the average kinetic energy of the molecules in the dough. Bakers regulate the interior oven and dough temperature by regulating the heat-energy input. One kilogram loaf typically requires between 500 and 600 kJ of energy. Because this energy is mostly delivered by radiated heat, oven chamber walls must reach 300–400°C. Further heat transport inside the dough occurs via steam condensation, convection, and conduction.

Processes of Heat Transfer

Radiation: Heat transmission to the dough surface from the oven walls.

Direct heat transmission inside the dough is known as conduction.

- Convection Currents: Heat transmission inside the oven by air currents.

Additional heat transmission results from steam

conductivity.

Joules (SI unit) or calories (CGS unit) are units of measurement for the amount of heat generated by thermal contact, often known as "heat". Denoted by s, specific heat is the quantity of heat needed to increase a unit mass of a substance's temperature by one degree Celsius:

$$dQ = smdt$$

in which place:

- dQ = heat absorbed - s = heat specific

Mass equals m

+ dt = temperature change

The heating conditions, either constant pressure or constant volume, determine specific heat; the former is often higher. It makes little difference for solid materials like dough.

Thermodynamic Ideas used in Baking

First Law of Thermodynamics: "The total of the work done dW and the heat absorbed dQ equals the change in internal energy dI of a system":

$$dI \backslash dQ + dW$$

RESEARCH AND PLAN

The Chemistry Behind Baking

Among the trickiest and most energy-intensive culinary processes is baking. Actually, inadequacies in the baking process itself account for thirty to forty percent of all baking problems. Improving the efficiency of your baking process as well as the quality of your baked products depend on optimizing the controllable factors. Considerations for heat-energy intake and temperature, heat transport, humidity, and baking time are the primary ones.

Temperature and Heat-Energy Input Understanding Transfer of Internal Energy and Heat:

In baking, internal energy includes intramolecular energy, potential energy of molecular interactions, and total kinetic energy of molecular motion inside the dough. Energy moves mostly in two directions:

1. Mechanical Interaction: Energy transmission via electromagnetic or mechanical working.

2. Thermal interaction is the energy transfer by molecule motion that produces thermal radiation or heat

- Someone with unique dietary restrictions who refuses to compromise on wonderful baked products.

recipes that call for common allergies or non-vegan components. Find out what alternatives to gluten, dairy, eggs, and more are and how to use them based on scientific evidence.

- Practical Baking Tips: Discover tips and methods to boost your baking talents. From knowing how various flours interact to mastering the art of vegan meringues, these insights can help you become a more confident and varied baker.

- Tested Recipes: A broad selection of reliable recipes that have been extensively tested to guarantee they satisfy the highest standards of flavor and consistency. Each recipe is meant to be customizable, enabling you to accommodate diverse dietary choices and constraints. You'll feel considered and accommodated with our versatile recipes.

Who Is This Book For?

This book is for everyone who likes baking and wants to discover the world of inclusive recipes, whether you're a home baker trying to satisfy family and friends with dietary constraints.
- A professional baker striving to broaden your range and give more inclusive alternatives.

INTRODUCTION

Step right up to the next level of baking! This book provides the information and skills necessary to make mouth-watering baked items suitable for a wide range of dietary restrictions. In this tutorial, you will find practical baking methods and ingredient replacements that are perfect for those who are gluten-free, dairy-free, egg-free, vegan, or a mix of the above. Get ready to experience the joy of baking and the satisfaction of creating delicious treats, no matter what your dietary restrictions may be.

For What Reasons Is This Book Recommended?

Whatever your dietary limitations, baking should still be something you enjoy. However, finding trustworthy recipes and comprehending ingredient swaps' logic can be challenging. That's why I've compiled this all-inclusive guide—a product of my love of baking and investigating its science.

Contents Included

The ingredient substitutions section provides in-depth descriptions and how-to instructions for veganizing

Table Of Contents

- Introduction

- Research and Plan

- My Journey into the Chemistry of Baking

- The Science of Baking

- Gluten Protein Sources

- Baking Substitutions for Gluten, Dairy, and Eggs (Ingredient Substitutions)

- Recipe Adaptation Guidelines For Large Scale Baking

- Original Recipes

ALL RIGHTS RESERVED. NO PART OF THIS PUBLICATION MAY BE REPRODUCED, DISTRIBUTED, OR TRANSMITTED IN ANY FORM OR BY ANY MEANS, INCLUDING PHOTOCOPYING, RECORDING, OR OTHER ELECTRONIC OR MECHANICAL METHODS, WITHOUT THE PRIOR WRITTEN PERMISSION OF THE PUBLISHER, EXCEPT IN THE CASE OF BRIEF QUOTATIONS EMBODIED IN CRITICAL REVIEWS AND CERTAIN OTHER NONCOMMERCIAL USES PERMITTED BY COPYRIGHT LAW.

© AMORETTE PIEDALUE, 2024.

FOR ANY CONCERN OR QUESTIONS REGARDING THE CONTENT OF THIS BOOK, OR SUGGESTIONS, OR PERMISSION REQUEST, PLEASE CONTACT THE AUTHOR VIA **AUTHOR CENTRAL PAGE**"

The Gluten-Free Alchemist Cookbook

From Beginner Blunders to Baking Bae – Essential Techniques, Troubleshooting Tips, Delicious Recipes for Gluten-Free Fun & Baking Hacks for Everyone

Amorette Piedalue